Database Security

Protecting Against Internal and External Threats

Database Security
Protecting Against Internal and External Threats

Jocelyn O. Padallan

ARCLER
PRESS

www.arclerpress.com

Database Security: Protecting Against Internal and External Threats

Jocelyn O. Padallan

Arcler Press
4164 Lakeshore Road
Burlington, ON L7L 1A4
Canada
www.arclerpress.com
Email: orders@arclereducation.com

ISBN: 978-1-77956-418-4 (Hardcover)

ABOUT THE AUTHOR

Jocelyn O. Padallan is Associate Professor I from Laguna State Polytechnic University, Philippines and she is currently pursuing her Doctor in Information Technology has Master in Information Technology and Master of Arts in Education from the same University. She has passion for teaching been Instruction and College of Computer Studies - Student Council Adviser at Laguna State Polytechnic University.

TABLE OF CONTENTS

LIST OF FIGURES

LIST OF TABLES

PREFACE

Database security has become increasingly important as industry, military, and government organizations have adopted Internet-based technologies on a broad scale due to their convenience, ease of use, and potential to capitalize on quick improvements in the commercial market. In addition to ensuring data integrity and availability, there is a growing focus on data privacy research and development. The rapid advancement of technology and the increasing reliance on data-driven decision-making have made database security a critical concern for organizations of all sizes. As databases store valuable and sensitive information, they are prime targets for both internal and external threats.

This book, aims to provide a comprehensive guide to securing databases against a wide range of threats. It covers the fundamentals of database security, investigates into common vulnerabilities, and presents best practices for safeguarding data.

This book comprises of eight chapters; the first chapter discusses the fundamental concepts of database security with overview of security models, risks and issues in databases. The second chapter confers the practical aspects of implementing security features within databases. From access control mechanisms to user permission control and cloud audit services,

Chapter 3 confronts the potential security threats faced by modern databases. By examining both internal and external threats, and detailing preventive measures against structured query language (SQL) injection, privilege abuse, robust security policies governing access control, administration, identification, authentication, and auditing. Fourth chapter covers database security policies, focusing on access control, administration, identification, authentication, and auditing. It details authorization mechanisms, role-based access control, and distributed access strategies.

Chapter 5 explores innovative strategies for revamping database security. From insider misuse detection to security reconfiguration and gradual redesign strategies and Chapter 6, delves into the complexities of user access control, privilege management, and audit trails. Chapter 7 explore one of the most prevalent threats to database security – SQL injection attacks. Through an exploration of attack variants and detection/prevention techniques, this chapter equips readers with the knowledge to thwart malicious SQL injection attempts effectively.

The eighth chapter describes the encryption techniques to safeguard data both in transit and at rest. By dissecting vulnerabilities and implementation options for encrypting data, this chapter empowers readers to fortify their databases against unauthorized access and data breaches.

In essence, "Database Security: Protecting against Internal and External Threats" serves as a comprehensive guide for database administrators, security professionals, and IT practitioners tasked with safeguarding critical data assets. Through a meticulous examination of threats, preventive measures, and advanced security techniques, this chapter endeavors to arm readers with the knowledge and tools necessary to uphold the integrity, confidentiality, and availability of databases in an increasingly interconnected world.

—***Author***

CHAPTER 1

INTRODUCTION TO DATABASE SECURITY

LEARNING OBJECTIVES

At the end of this chapter, readers will be able to:

1. Understand the scope and principles of database security;
2. Recognize and mitigate various threats to database security;
3. Understand different access control models, including MAC, DAC, RBAC, and ABAC;
4. Comprehend authentication and authorization mechanisms in database security;
5. Understand the challenges in database security;
6. Understand challenges in managing access to database key fields and foreign keys;
7. Know the methods to handle sensitive information access discreetly within database systems; and
8. Implement essential security measures such as firewalls and digital signatures for database protection.

INTRODUCTORY EXAMPLE

TechSecure Inc. is a reputable company renowned for its expertise in providing secure and efficient database solutions. Currently, TechSecure is undertaking a significant project involving the development of a sophisticated customer relationship management (CRM) system for a large multinational corporation. This CRM system serves as the central hub for storing and managing a vast array of critical customer data, ranging from basic contact information to detailed purchase histories and personalized preferences.

In predicting the complexities of this project, one cannot overlook the paramount importance of ensuring the security and integrity of the data housed within the CRM system. Imagine a scenario where unauthorized access or tampering with this sensitive information could lead to severe repercussions for both TechSecure and its esteemed clientele.

To address these challenges, TechSecure employs a comprehensive approach to database security. This includes implementing robust encryption protocols to safeguard data both at rest and in transit. Additionally, stringent access controls are put in place to ensure that only authorized personnel have access to sensitive information within the CRM system.

Moreover, TechSecure remains vigilant in monitoring for potential vulnerabilities and staying abreast of emerging threats in the cybersecurity landscape. Regular security audits and updates are conducted to fortify the CRM system against evolving risks.

UNIT INTRODUCTION

Security is a vast and pervasive subject that is present in every aspect of an information system. Database security encompasses a range of measures aimed at safeguarding databases from both unintended and deliberate threats. The primary goal of database security is to ensure the protection of valuable information and uphold the utmost confidentiality, availability, and integrity of the database. Ensuring the security of databases goes beyond safeguarding the data stored within them. It also involves protecting the database management system, as well as the various applications, systems, servers (both physical and virtual), and network infrastructure that are associated with it (Bertino & Sandhu, 2005).

Understanding the concept of database security requires acknowledging the existence of various security risks. Ensuring the security of databases requires a comprehensive approach that addresses various potential vulnerabilities. These include protecting against human error, minimizing excessive employee privileges, defending against hacker and insider attacks, mitigating the risks of malware, safeguarding backup storage media, preventing physical damage to database servers, and fortifying vulnerable databases. Examples of vulnerable databases include those that are unpatched or have an excessive amount of data in buffers (Lunt & Fernandez, 1990).

Readers may encounter conce□ts and a□□roaches that can be classified as security measures. For example, the process of recovery, whether after partial or total failure, should be viewed as having a security component. Almost all work on concurrency is focused on another aspect of security (Pernul, 1994).

This chapter primarily focuses on database security, s□ecifically ex□laining into the principles of security theory and practice in relation to database security, rather than discussing security in a broader sense. These technical aspects of security concentrate on details rather than the broader perspective. The chapter is divided into two sections. The first □art covers security □rinci□les and models, itself divided into two parts. It starts with the foundational principles and then addresses s□ecific technical as□ects of database security. The next section focuses on logical access control in structured query language (SQL) databases (Malik & Patel, 2016).

The primary focus will be on the practical aspects of access control. Once the principles are thoroughly addressed, the complex details of access control in SQL databases will be discussed. Additional resources, including textbooks and online materials, are provided for further exploration of the subject matter (Denning et al., 1987).

The topics of database administration, transaction recovery, and catastrophe recovery are not discussed in this chapter, but they are covered in other sections of the module. The first as□ect relates directly to the management rules governing operation and development. The second issue is closely linked to the integrity and consistency of the database, making it mostly an internal concern. The third is more com□rehensible when viewed as a continuation of the first and second, but all three are security-based. (Li et al., 2016).

1.1. THE SCOPE OF DATABASE SECURITY

Learning Objectives

- Understand the scope and principles of database security; and
- Identify various threats and effective security measures for databases.

1.1.1. Overview of Database Security

Every system possesses valuable assets that require protection, and security measures are implemented to safeguard these assets. It is crucial to have a clear understanding of your assets and their respective value (Scott, 2008). Focus on the various components of databases, such as tables, views, and rows, as well as the mechanisms that control access to these objects and the system that supervises them. It is important to keep in mind that not all data is sensitive, therefore not all data requires extensive protection measures (Lv et al., 2017).

Another important aspect to consider is understanding the potential threat that might harm the valuable assets. These factors encompass issues like power outages and instances of employee fraud. It is important to acknowledge that threats in the field of database security are often speculative, constantly evolving, and never fully understood. Measures taken are focused on safeguarding the system against potential threats and vulnerabilities (Weber, 2010).

If a threat seems potential, it must be allowed to become an actuality. Once it becomes actual, there is a significant im□act. It is im□ortant to be ready for possible impact. However, in the worst-case scenario, there may be Loss. Efforts are focused on reducing potential loss and restoring the database to minimize any losses, while also enhancing its protection against recurring or similar threats (Gupta et al., 2022).

A comprehensive development mechanism is:

- Understand the nature of assets and their inherent value.
- Identify potential threats, assess their likelihood, and evaluate the potential impact if they were to occur.
- Identify potential threats for each asset.
- Develop strategies to safeguard each asset based on its value and associated cost of protection. Implement measures to identify any security breaches and reduce the resulting losses. Additionally, establish protocols to restore normal operations in the event of an incident (Sarker et al., 2023).

1.1.2. Threats to the Database

Developing security skills can be approached from two different angles. One aspect comes from recognizing and understanding evolving threats, while the other arises from implementing technical solutions to address them (Senator et al., 2013). Threats are discussed in the following subsections.

1.1.2.1. Unauthorized Modification

Altering data values for malicious purposes, illegal activities, or lack of knowledge, can occur due to insufficient security measures or the unauthorized sharing of passwords, among other factors. Unauthorized disclosure occurs when sensitive information is revealed without proper authorization. A primary issue of great importance, which can occur by chance or with purpose (Van & Wurster, 2011).

1.1.2.2. Loss of Availability

Occasionally referred to as denial of service. In the absence of the database, it incurs a loss (otherwise, life is better without the system). Hence, it is necessary to avoid any potential threat that may result in time offline, even if it is just to verify if an event has occurred (Rosato, 2016).

1.1.2.3. Commercial Sensitivity

Most financial losses resulting from fraudulent activities are caused by employees. Access controls offer a dual benefit by protecting against unlawful activities and serving as proof of any malicious attempts to harm the organization, such as fraud, unauthorized data access, or disruption of services (Lynge & Zumwalt, 1980).

- *Personal Privacy and Data Protection:* Globally, regulations are in place to govern the handling of personal data. Personal data refers to information that can be used to identify a s□ecific individual. In many cases, it is necessary for the person to be alive, although the s□ecific method of identification is not s□ecified. Hence, the postal code of a residence can potentially reveals the identity of an individual, particularly when only one person resides at an address with that postal code. Proper management and control are crucial when dealing with such information (Picu et al., 2005).

Numerous complex issues require in-depth analysis, but it is important to acknowledge the significant im□lications. It is crucial to □ro□erly identify personal data. There should be strict controls in place to regulate the usage of the data, which might limit the ability to perform adhoc queries. It is crucial to maintain a record of all instances where the information has been accessed or disclosed, as this serves as valuable evidence (Vehovar et al., 2001).

1.1.2.4. Computer Misuse

Legislation regarding the misuse of computers is also commonly found. Instances of misuse involve breaching access controls and attempting to cause harm by altering the database state or introducing malicious software to disrupt its normal functioning. These offenses can sometimes be subject to extradition. If unauthorized access occurs in Hong Kong, utilizing computers in France to access databases in Germany, which refer to databases in America could potentially result in extradition to France, Germany, or the USA (Kerr, 2003).

1.1.2.5. Audit Requirements

These operational constraints revolve around the importance of identifying the actions taken, attempted actions, as well as the location and timing of all actions (Fichtner, 2010). They encompass the identification of various events (such as CONNECT and GRANT transactions), offering supporting evidence for detection, ensuring security, and serving as a basis for either defense or prosecution (Van Linden & Hardies, 2018).

When considering logical access to the database, it is important to remember that any system access carries inherent risks. Accessing operating system utilities enables direct access to disk storage, allowing for the copying or damaging of the entire database or its components. A comprehensive assessment must consider all forms of access. Analysts typically aim to reduce communication channels (such as direct, network, and telecommunications) and protect the system from avoidable risks (Johnson et al., 2003).

It is highly probable that encryption would be used for both the data and the schema. Encryption involves transforming text and data into a format that is readable only by the intended recipient, who possesses the knowledge to reverse the process and retrieve the original message. It is important to approach security and auditing as distinct concerns, regardless of how they are incorporated into the database system. Consider conceptualizing the security server and audit servers as distinct functional modules (Thinggaard & Kiertzner, 2008).

1.1.3. Principles of Database Security

To effectively organize ideas surrounding security, it is essential to have a well-defined security model. There are different variations available based on different roles, levels of detail, and objectives. There are several key areas to consider when it comes to database security, including the various threats that can arise, the potential impact and loss that can occur, and the necessary actions to address these issues (Bertino & Sandhu, 2005).

Security risks should be considered in terms of asset loss. These resources include:

- Hardware
- Software
- Data
- Data Quality
- Credibility
- Availability
- Business Benefit

Our focus is on the risks that can affect the security and quality of data. However, it is important to note that a threat to one asset can also have a significant influence on other assets (Sandhu & Jajodia, 1991). It is crucial to have a clear understanding of which asset always requires protection. It is important to acknowledge that achieving absolute security is an unattainable goal. There is always a certain level of risk involved, thus it is necessary to prepare to handle the worst possible outcome. This includes taking measures to reduce the impact and successfully recover from any loss or damage to assets (Jones et al., 2000). Following are the factors to keep in mind:

- *Appropriate Security:* It is important to ensure that the amount spent on security is proportional to the value of the asset.
- It is important to ensure that security measures do not disrupt the normal operation of the system unnecessarily (Wood, 1990) (Figure 1.1).

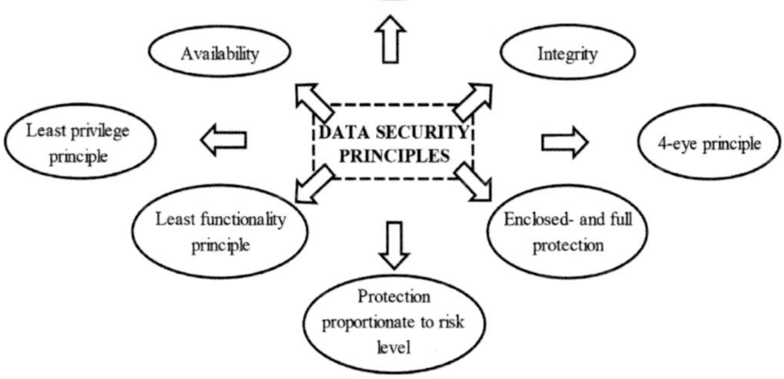

Figure 1.1. *Illustration of data security principles.*

Source: Pal-Michelberger, Creative Commons License.

1.2. SECURITY MODELS AND CONTROLS

Learning Objectives

- Understand the importance and role of security models in database security;
- Identify and differentiate between various access control models; and
- Comprehend the concepts of authentication and authorization in database systems.

Understanding the importance of security models is crucial when it comes to examining and addressing security issues. These models not only provide a framework for considering database implementation and operation but also set the standards for evaluating security concerns in a broader sense. The security models of different DBMSs play a crucial role in the design and operation of systems. Consider the Sea view model as an example. One will come to understand that security models provide an explanation of the functionalities within a DBMS that are necessary for the creation and implementation of effective security systems (Denning & Denning, 1979).

They encompass ideas, execute protocols, and offer servers for such o□erations. Any flaws in the security model can result in either insecure o□eration or inefficient systems.

1.2.1. Access Control Model

It is essential to have a clear understanding of the purpose of access control. Implementing access control measures can be quite costly, both in terms of the resources required for analysis, design, and day-to-day operations. It is utilized in known situations, to known standards, to accomplish specific objectives (Ouaddah et al., 2017). It is crucial to have a comprehensive understanding before implementing any controls. It is important to ensure that the level of control is suitable for the given circumstances. (Goguen & Meseguer, 1982) (Figure 1.2).

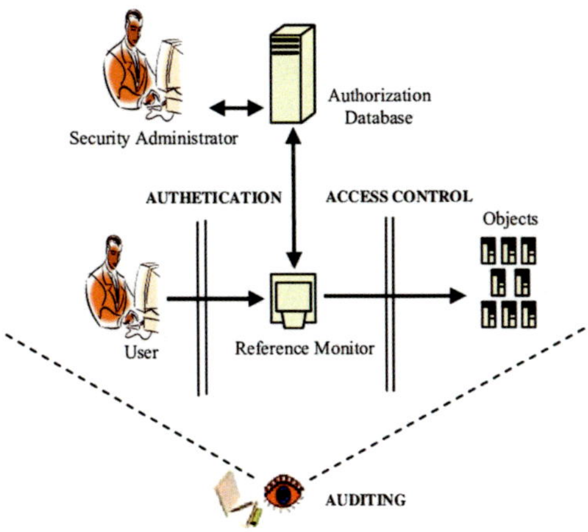

Figure 1.2. *Illustration of access control and other security services.*

Source: Sanjay Kumar, Creative Commons License.

1.2.1.1. Mandatory Access Control (MAC)

Mandatory access control (MAC) is a security strategy that restricts the ability individual resource owners have to grant or deny access to resource objects in a file system. MAC criteria are defined by the system administrator, strictly enforced by the operating system (OS) or security kernel, and cannot be altered by end users.

MAC is a method or access control policy aimed at restricting access to a resource (also known as an object) based on two key factors: the sensitivity of the information contained in that resource and the authorization level of the user trying to access that resource and its information (Ouaddah et al., 2017). Often employed in government and military facilities, mandatory access control works by assigning a classification label to each file system object. In addition, each user is assigned a security or clearance level. They may access the object or resource only if their security level is equal to or greater than the resource's classification label ("Restricted," "Confidential," etc.).

1.2.1.2. Discretionary Access Control Access

Discretionary control refers to the distribution of certain privileges based on specific assets, granting authorized users the ability to utilize them in a particular manner. The security database management system (DBMS) is responsible for creating an access matrix that includes various objects such as relations, records, views, and operations for each user. Each element in the matrix specifies the privileges for creation, read, insert, and update. The complexity of this matrix increases significantly, as authorizations will differ for each object (Singh, 2005).

The matrix can also grow to a significant size, which often requires the use of physical implementation methods commonly used for sparse matrices. Storing the matrix in the computer's main memory might pose some challenges. By delving deeper into this topic, one will come across various additional rights that must be documented, including the rights of the owners and the grant rights (Miles & Snow, 1995).

Authorization by role or level is known as mandatory control. The four-level government classification system of open, secret, most secret, and top secret is a commonly mandated method. Applying security restrictions to roles rather than to people is a related concept. For example, the pay clerk's privileges are based on their employment position rather than their characteristics.

The database implementation involves assigning a classification to each data item for read, create, update, and delete operations, as well as assigning a corresponding classification to each allowed user. An algorithm grants access to objects based on a clearance level that is less than or equal to the assigned level. For example, a user with a clearance level of 3 to read things will also have access to items with clearance levels 0, 1, and 2 (Pestka et al., 2018).

The Bell-LaPadula model, established in 2005, describes a mandatory approach that is commonly mentioned:

- Access to certain data is restricted based on the security classification of the user, account, or program attempting to read it. The subject must have a security classification that is equal to or higher than the object they are trying to access, whether it's a relation, tuple, or view.
- Writing an object is strictly prohibited unless the subject's security classification is equal to or lower than that of the object (Antelman, 2004).

It is important to understand that having a high level of clearance to read means having a low level of clearance to write. This is because information should flow from high levels to low levels. In highly secure systems, this is not allowed. Understanding and managing mandatory security schemes is relatively simple, making them easier to audit. Managing discretionary security can be a challenging task, as it is prone to errors and oversights that can be hard to identify. This challenge can result in financial consequences (Langenberg & Wesseling, 2016).

1.2.1.3. Role-Based Access Control

In database security, role-based access control (RBAC) or role-based security is an approach to restricting system access to authorized users, and to implementing mandatory access control (MAC) or discretionary access control (DAC).

RBAC is a policy-neutral access control mechanism defined around roles and privileges. The components of RBAC such as role-permissions, user-role and role-role relationships make it simple to perform user assignments (Antelman, 2004). A study by NIST has demonstrated that RBAC addresses many needs of commercial and government organizations RBAC can be used to facilitate administration of security in large organizations with hundreds of users and thousands of permissions. Although RBAC is different from MAC and DAC access control frameworks, it can enforce these policies without any complication.

1.2.1.4. Attribute-Based Access Control

Attribute-based access control (ABAC), also known as policy-based access control for identity and access management (IAM), defines an access control paradigm whereby a subject's authorization to perform a set of operations is determined by evaluating attributes associated with the subject, object, requested operations, and, in some cases, environment attributes (Langenberg & Wesseling, 2016).

ABAC is a method of implementing access control policies that is highly adaptable and can be customized using a wide range of attributes, making it suitable for use in distributed or rapidly changing environments. The only limitations on the policies that can be implemented with ABAC are the capabilities of the computational language and the availability of relevant attributes. ABAC policy rules are generated as Boolean functions of the subject's attributes, the object's attributes, and the environment attributes.

1.2.2. Authentication and Authorization Control

Users are generally familiar with the login requirements of most systems. Typically, gaining access to IT resources necessitates a login procedure that is counted to be safe. This topic provides an overview of the process of accessing database management systems from the perspective of a database administrator (DBA). Most of the subsequent content relates directly to Relational client-server systems. Other system models may vary to varying degrees, but the fundamental ideas remain valid. Authentication and authorization are fundamental elements in database systems (Kim & Lee, 2017).

1.2.2.1. Authentication

It is necessary for the client to verify the identification of the server, and for the server to verify the identity of the client. This is frequently accomplished using shared secrets, such as a combination of a password and user ID, or the sharing of biographic and/or biometric data. Alternatively, it can be accomplished through a hierarchical system that has already implemented authentication protocols. In distributed client-server systems, where data is shared but not necessarily the database, authentication can be performed by a peer system. It should be noted that authentication can be transmitted between different systems (Harn, 2012).

The outcome, from the perspective of the DBMS, is an authorization identifier. Authentication does not grant any □rivileges for certain tasks. The statement confirms that the DBMS relies on the user's declared identity and the user's confidence in the DBMS as the intended system. Authentication is a necessary condition for authorization (Wayman et al., 2005).

1.2.2.2. Authorization

Authorization relates to the permissions given to an authorized user to do specific operations, which can involve modifying the database (write-item transactions) and/or retrieving data from the database (read-item transactions). The outcome of authorization, which must occur on a transactional basis, is represented by a vector: Authorization (item, auth-id, operation). A vector is an ordered collection of data elements located at specific positions inside a system. The implementation of this is determined on the functionality of the DBMS (Pearlman et al., 2002) (Figure 1.3).

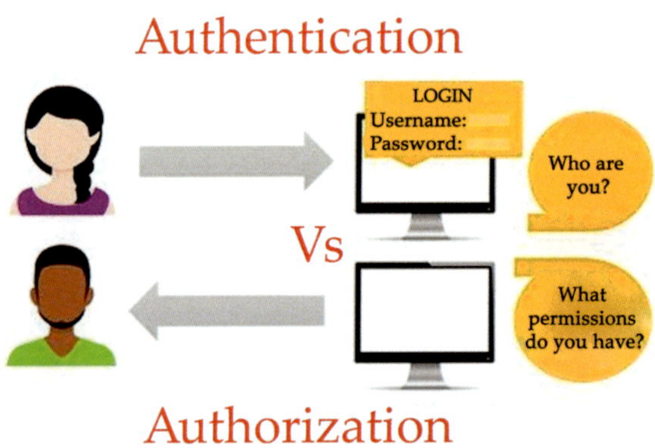

Figure 1.3. *Illustration of authentication and authorization.*

Source: okta.com, Creative Commons License.

At a conceptual level, the system architecture requires an authorization server that must collaborate with an auditing server. The server-to-server security is compromised due to the transmission of authorization between systems, leading to an am□lification □roblem. Am□lification in this context refers to the phenomenon where security problems increase in magnitude when more DBMS servers are involved in the transaction (Ahn & Sandhu, 2000).

Many organizations often fail to properly implement audit requirements. To ensure safety, it is necessary to record every single case of access and document all authorization information along with transaction identifiers. Regular auditing and maintaining a comprehensive audit trail are necessary, typically for an extended duration (Griffiths & Wade, 1976).

1.3. DATABASE SECURITY CHALLENGES

Learning Objectives

- Understand the challenges and solutions in implementing database security measures; and
- Gain knowledge of access control, discretionary security, schema management, and data protection in SQL.

This section discusses the challenges that arise while determining the security requirements and implementation of a database system (Bertino & Sandhu, 2005).

1.3.1. Access to Key Fields

Imagine having a user role that grants access to table A and table C, while intentionally excluding access to table B. There is an issue with the foreign key in C as it incorporates columns from B (Figure 1.4). The following questions arise:

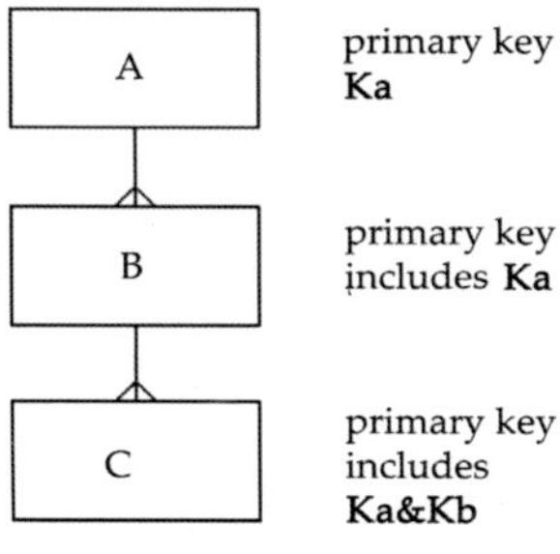

Figure 1.4 *Illustration of access keys.*

Source: Walter Pan, Creative Commons License.

Can you provide information on accessing the foreign key in C? If you engage in this practice, you are aware that there is a tuple present in B and that there is certain information about B that is being withheld from you. Is it possible to make updates to the foreign key columns? If that's the case, it needs to cascade, resulting in an update to B without any granted privileges (Field et al., 2003).

These issues do not occur immediately when the database is implemented using internal pointers. As a user, you do not have to possess any understanding of the connections between the data you are retrieving. They occur because relationships are represented as data values. Frequently, possessing a knowledge of the foreign key will not necessarily be sensitive. If that is the case, then the definition of a view might □rovide a solution to the □roblem (O'Brien et al., 2010).

1.3.2. Access to Surrogate Information

There are situations where the data accessible to a user role extends beyond the internal system. Let's see an example that will help clarify the issue.

In a retail setting, pilferage is a common issue that often arises. To address these issues, private investigators operate secretly. They function as employees of the company and are involved in regular business tasks, just like other staff members. They receive their paychecks or slips at the same time as everyone else, and their information appears in management reports, such as salary analysis, similarly. Individuals assume false identities and hold job titles within the system (Kneebone et al., 2022). The store manager is not informed about the situation, just like everyone else except the corporate security manager. When the store manager accesses the database, the detective needs to blend in and appear like any other employee. Queries might include:

- What is the reason for the leave?
- The security personnel have various inquiries.
- Is there someone present?

One may encounter various complexities. The detective should be included in the distribution of pay slips along with everyone else, although their compensation may differ from the standard salary for the position.

It may be advisable to address these situations on separate databases. While this solution may be suitable, the complexity of the problem can lead to potential confusion. An alternative approach is to consider poly instantiation of tuples, where a single individual is represented by multiple tuples. The data retrieved will be determined by the security classification of the user. It is crucial to ensure that tuples with seemingly identical primary keys have different primary keys. Additionally, it is crucial to effortlessly connect all applications with the security system (Kelly & Wendler, 2012).

1.3.3. Problems with Data Extraction

The issue arises when data access is shown visually, as it becomes evident that the main concern is to guarantee that authenticated users can only access data items that they have been permitted to use for the specific reason at hand. When attention transitions from the data itself to the implications that can be derived from that data, further challenges emerge (Ferrara et al., 2014) (Figure 1.5). Again, an example should make things clear.

Figure 1.5. *Illustration of data extraction challenges.*

Source: xtract.io, Creative Commons License.

You are interested in finding out the salary of the CEO. You have been granted access to the table, exce□t for the MONTHLY-PAY field within this tuple. So, you execute a SQL query to calculate the sum of monthly payments across the entire table. Next, you can create a view that selects the monthly pay and then perform a sum operation on this view. Is it expected to obtain identical results in both scenarios? If not, you can accomplish your goal by subtracting the two totals. If you were to display the monthly salary for all individuals, what would you assume looking at for all the records except the one that is restricted? Would you anticipate receiving alerts with asterisks indicating missing data that you were not permitted to view (Taylor et al., 2021)?

1.3.4. Access Control in SQL

This section focuses on the practical aspects of incorporating security measures into SQL. SQL-92 provides the foundational knowledge, but it's important to note that database security heavily relies on the specific DBMS and hardware being used. When required, the SQL of Oracle provides the necessary specifics. It is crucial to familiarize yourself with the details. The implementation of the access requirements specification will be done using these statements. Another goal is to gain a deeper understanding of the issue by exploring its implications for the management and audit functions of an operating system (Bertino et al., 2011). Firstly, the fundamental statements are presented, followed by a discussion of the managerial functions. The first half of the course will cover the SQL necessary for user management, while the second part will provide an introduction to the SQL required for system management (Roichman & Gudes, 2007).

1.3.5. Discretionary Security in SQL

This section introduces the SQL statements required for implementing access control. It is important to get a comprehensive understanding of this particular aspect of SQL to effectively convert a basic specification into an SQL script. It is important to be aware of the inherent limitations of this script, as it incorporates passwords directly into the text (Winkler, 1992).

The fundamentals of SQL are fundamentally discretionary. Access rights to utilize a database resource are allocated and withdrawn on an individual basis. The primary concern relates to the individuals who possess the authorization to do specific actions within the security subsystem. To implement security measures, one must possess a significant amount of privilege. Unfortunately, these roles are not defined in the SQL standard and differ across different database management systems (DBMS). A role is a set of privileges (Pan et al., 2024).

For example, the jobs provided in Oracle include (among others):

- SYSOPER: Start and stop the DBMS.
- DBA: Permission to create and manage existing users as well as the database.
- SYSDBA: All the DBA's authority plus the authority to create, start, stop, and recover.

It is important to recognize the existence of numerous predefined roles with varying privileges that require proper control. Ensuring that the SQL defaults do not behave unexpectedly is of utmost importance (Farooqui & Furkan, 2014).

1.3.6. Schema Level

One of the initial steps in ensuring security is to establish the schema. In the following example, the authorization is set up using the schema. If the authorization is not specified, it will default to the current user, making it an optional feature. Manipulating the schema is limited to its owner. Here is an example where a user is granted permission to create tables. The privileges for the tables created remain intact by the creator (Arbib, 1992).

Develop a schema for a student database. For the authorization process, it is essential to ensure that the user has the necessary privileges to create specific database objects, such as a schema for a new database. The authorization identifier, referred to as U1, is used to identify the user in question. If the authorization is verified, then others can be granted access to the database using the schema (Lodge & Hamill, 1986).

1.3.7. Mandatory Security in SQL

First, it is important to categorize the individuals (users and their agents) and the specific elements of the database that are involved. Discuss the various methods used to assign a numerical value to indicate the level of security, as set by the implemented regulations.

The classification must be applied to tables, tuples, attributes, and attribute values as needed for the specific requirement. It may be necessary to establish distinct categories to address permissions for creating (INSERT), reading (SELECT), updating, and deleting data. However, the specific rules to be implemented will determine the approach. The rules themselves may connect these options as they do in the model mentioned (Bertino et al., 2007).

There may be a need for extra measures to address statistical security concerns. These measures could include limitations on the number of tuples that can be retrieved, introducing inaccuracies in the retrieved data, or implementing controls on query sequences to prevent users from conducting unnecessary extractive analysis. When it comes to designing databases, one important factor to consider is whether or not to store sensitive tuples. If the decision is made to store them, it is crucial to determine the best approach for doing so (Stachour & Thuraisingham, 1990).

This process involves transforming obligatory security measures into the structure of a security database, where all the above data must be recorded in tables. Additionally, it requires designing transactions to enforce access rules and regulate access to the security tables. Compulsory security must be constructed using the discretionary SQL tools (George & Valeva, 2006).

1.3.8. Data Protection

Consider the following principles from a more theoretical point of view. Every company that has implemented data protection has followed these guidelines, but as always, the key lies in the s□ecifics. If your com□any can ensure that your database system adheres to these requirements, you have accomplished a commendable task (Koops, 2014).

It is essential to ensure that the information contained in personal data is obtained and processed fairly and lawfully.

a) Personal data must only be held for s□ecific and legal □ur□oses.

b) Personal data held for any purpose or purposes should not be utilized or disclosed in any way that is inconsistent with the intended purpose or purposes (Lynskey, 2014).

c) Personal data must be relevant and not excessive for the intended purpose it is being held for.

d) It is important to ensure that personal data is accurate and regularly updated.

e) Personal data should only be kept for as long as it is required for the intended purpose (Martin & Murphy, 2017).

1.4. DATABASE SECURITY AND THE INTERNET

Learning Objectives

- Understand the role of □roxy servers and firewalls in enhancing database security; and
- Understand the conce□t of firewall and im□ortance of digital signatures in verifying database data integrity.

The issues surrounding the protection of internet transmissions and the importance of ensuring privacy align closely with the considerations for database security. Ensuring the security and integrity of sensitive data, such as credit card information or access to internal systems, is crucial when transmitting it over the internet. Database security procedures, such as encrypting data while it is being transferred and when it is stored, are crucial in protecting this information from being intercepted by malicious individuals who may use packet sniffing software or other illegal methods to get access (Jeffery, 2009).

In addition, various authentication mechanisms can be used to enhance the security of communications and prevent senders from denying their actions. These mechanisms include digital signatures and multi-factor authentication. Enhancing database security involves implementing strong access controls and intrusion detection systems to safeguard the integrity and confidentiality of stored data, effectively protecting against potential attacks. In order to ensure trust and protect sensitive information from ever-changing cyber threats, it is crucial to implement thorough database security protocols (Adam & Worthmann, 1989) (Figure 1.6).

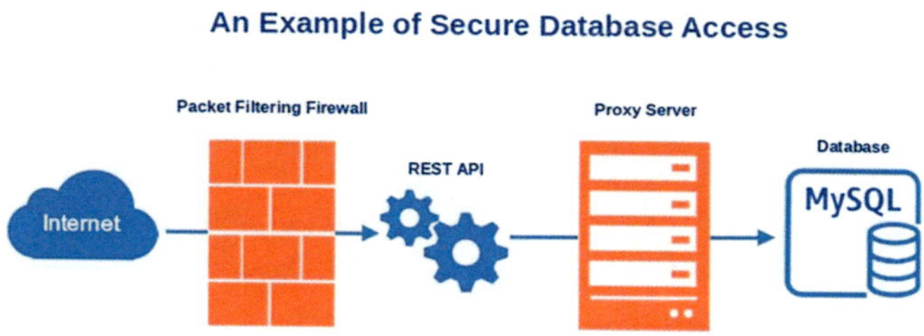

Figure 1.6. *Illustration of secure database access.*

Source: Davy Jones, Creative Commons License.

1.4.1. Proxy Servers

A proxy server serves as a middleman between users and the internet, enabling smooth communication while also enhancing the security of databases. Through the implementation of access control measures, users are authenticated and authorized prior to being granted access to the database. This effectively minimizes the potential for unauthorized data breaches. In addition, it enhances privacy protection by masking real IP addresses, thus anonymizing user interactions and thwarting potential attackers.

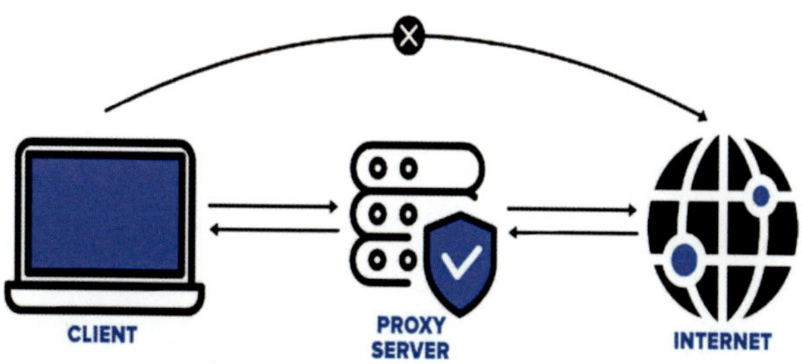

Figure 1.7. *Illustration of proxy server.*

Source: Ben Natan, Creative Commons License.

In order to protect sensitive information like login credentials and personal data, the proxy server utilizes data encryption to ensure that unauthorized parties are unable to read transmitted data (Gautam, 2002). In addition, it keeps track of and monitors database transactions, allowing for the early identification of potentially suspicious activities and making it easier to take immediate action to address them. Through the distribution of database requests and the optimization of performance, the proxy server plays a vital role in upholding system stability and dependability, which are essential for safeguarding the overall security of the database (Wu & Liao, 1997) (Figure 1.7).

1.4.2. Firewalls

Protecting databases is of the greatest significance, and one way to achieve this is through the use of a firewall. This essential tool helps regulate access to databases, whether it is from within the organization or from external networks. It serves as a safeguard between the database servers and the internet, ensuring that only authorized traffic can access the database environment by enforcing security policies. Through the examination of incoming and outgoing data packets, the firewall (Figure 1.8) can detect and prevent any malicious efforts to gain access to or exploit database resources. This includes unauthorized login attempts and SQL injection attacks (Bellovin & Cheswick, 1994).

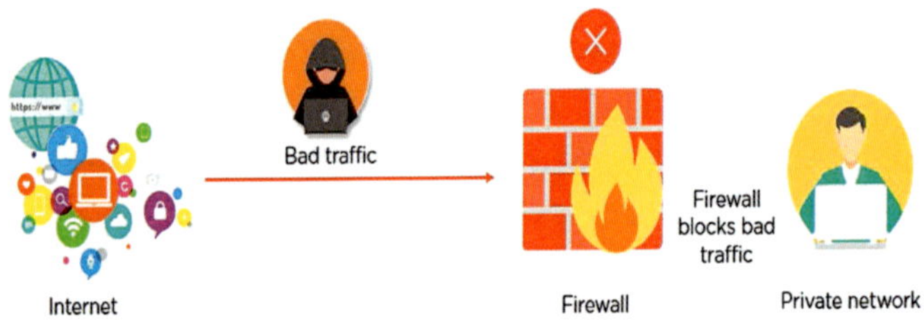

Figure 1.8. *Illustration of firewall.*

Source: Michel Gertz, Creative Commons License.

Practice Problem

As the Chief Information Security Officer (CISO) of HiCO, a prominent healthcare organization, your responsibility is to enhance the security of the com□any's database system that houses confidential □atient medical records. Create and execute a firewall setu□to safeguard the database servers against online dangers, while also enabling authorized healthcare professionals and administrators to securely access the system. Your solution must adhere to HIPAA compliance regulations and effectively reduce the risk of data breaches or unauthorized access to patient information.

Solutions to Practice Problem

In order to improve the security of the database infrastructure of the HiCO firm, a strong firewall configuration that com□lies with industry-s□ecific requirements should be □ut in □lace. Set u□the firewall to □revent unauthorized IP ranges connected to administrative offices and healthcare facilities from accessing critical services like HTTPS and secure VPN connections. Use dee□ □acket ins□ection (DPI) and intrusion □revention systems (IPS) to find and sto□threatening traffic aimed at database a□□lication vulnerabilities. Use logging and monitoring tools to kee□tabs on firewall activities and guarantee that access control and data protection comply with HIPAA rules. Maintain the integrity and privacy of patient medical records kept on database servers by routinely auditing and u□dating firewall rules to counter new threats.

1.4.3. Digital Signatures

The use of digital signatures is essential in enhancing database security, as it guarantees the authenticity and unaffected state of electronic records and transactions stored in the database. Through the implementation of digital signatures, organizations can ensure the authenticity and integrity of database records or documents (Aki, 1983). This allows for verification of the signer's identity and origin, providing confidence that the data remains unaltered since the signing process. By implementing robust security measures, potential unauthorized alterations to valuable data stored in the database can be effectively prevented (Figure 1.9). This proactive approach significantly reduces the possibility of data tampering and fraudulent activities (Rivest et al., 1983).

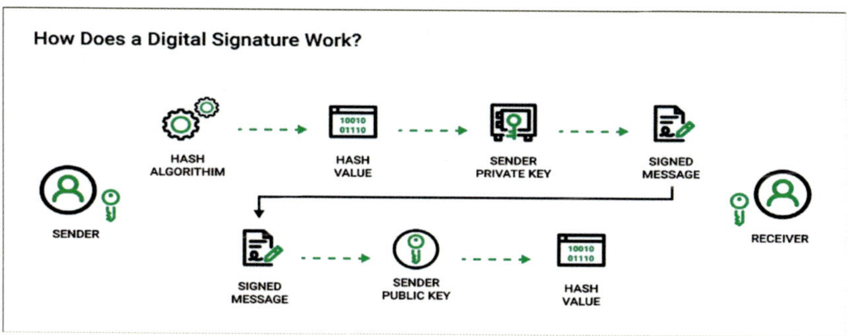

Figure 1.9. *Illustration of the working of digital signatures.*

Source: Sushil Jajodia, Creative Commons License.

SUMMARY

- The chapter titled "Introduction to Database Security" offers a comprehensive overview of the fundamental concepts, principles, and challenges in this field. It ex□lores the sco□e of database security, highlighting its significance in □reserving the integrity and confidentiality of data.
- The importance of implementing strong security measures is emphasized through an examination of different threats, such as unauthorized access and data breaches. Principles such as confidentiality and integrity serve as guiding □rinci□les for database security, providing a solid basis for successful implementation.
- The chapter explores various security models, including access control, authentication, and authorization mechanisms. The chapter delves into various aspects of database security, including the complexities of SQL access control and data extraction, as well as effective data protection strategies.
- This chapter discusses security risks associated with the Internet, s□ecifically focusing on □roxy servers and firewalls. It emphasizes the significance of dealing with these dangers.
- The chapter highlights the crucial importance of database security in protecting sensitive data and provides valuable insights into effective security techniques.

REVIEW QUESTIONS

1. Distinguish discretionary from mandatory security.
2. Explain the nature and use of surrogate information.
3. Explain the implementation of access control in a distributed database.
4. What are the main objectives of database security, and why are they important in modern information systems?
5. Can you provide an example of a real-world scenario where a lack of database security led to a significant breach or data loss?
6. Explain the difference between authentication and authorization in the context of database security.
7. What are the key principles guiding database security measures, and how do they contribute to overall data protection?

8. How does statistical database security differ from traditional approaches to database security, and what are some techniques used to protect statistical data?

MULTIPLE CHOICE QUESTIONS

1. What is the primary objective of database security?

a. Ensuring data availability
b. Maximizing data redundancy
c. Minimizing data integrity
d. Enhancing data transparency

2. Which of the following is NOT a common threat to databases?

a. Unauthorized access
b. Data breaches
c. System redundancy
d. Data manipulation

3. What are the key principles guiding database security measures?

a. Confidentiality, integrity, and accountability
b. Reliability, durability, and redundancy
c. Scalability, availability, and consistency
d. Confidentiality, integrity, and availability

4. What is the purpose of access control in database security?

a. To restrict physical access to databases
b. To control who can access what data and actions within a database
c. To optimize database performance
d. To encrypt database backups

5. What does authentication refer to in the context of database security?

a. Verifying the identity of users
b. Determining the appropriate access level for users
c. Encrypting data during transmission
d. Auditing database activities

6. Which aspect of database security deals with protecting sensitive statistical data?

a. Access control
b. Statistical database security

c. Authentication

d. Database auditing

Answers to Multiple Choice Questions

1. (a); 2. (c); 3. (d); 4. (b); 5. (a); 6. (b)

REFERENCES

1. Adam, N. R., & Worthmann, J. C. (1989). Security-control methods for statistical databases: A comparative study. *ACM Computing Surveys (CSUR)*, *21*(4), 515–556.
2. Ahn, G. J., & Sandhu, R. (2000). Role-based authorization constraints s□ecification. *ACM Transactions on Information and System Security (TISSEC)*, *3*(4), 207–226.
3. Aki. (1983). Digital signatures: A tutorial survey. *Computer*, *16*(2), 15–24.
4. Antelman, K. (2004). Do open-access articles have a greater research impact? *College & Research Libraries*, *65*(5), 372–382.
5. Arbib, M. A. (1992). Schema theory. In *The Encyclopedia of Artificial Intelligence* (2nd ed., pp. 1427–1443).
6. Beck, L. L. (1980). A security mechanism for statistical databases. *ACM Transactions on Database Systems (TODS)*, *5*(3), 316–338.
7. Bellovin, S. M., & Cheswick, W. R. (1994). Network firewalls. *IEEE Communications Magazine*, *32*(9), 50–57.
8. Bertino, E., & Sandhu, R. (2005). Database security-concepts, approaches, and challenges. *IEEE Transactions on Dependable and Secure Computing*, *2*(1), 2–19.
9. Bertino, E., Byun, J. W., & Kamra, A. (2007). Database security. In *Security, Privacy, and Trust in Modern Data Management* (pp. 87–101).
10. Bertino, E., Ghinita, G., & Kamra, A. (2011). Access control for databases: Concepts and systems. *Foundations and Trends® in Databases*, *3*(1–2), 1–148.
11. Denning, D. E., & Denning, P. J. (1979). Data security. *ACM Computing Surveys (CSUR)*, *11*(3), 227–249.
12. Denning, D. E., Akl, S. G., Heckman, M., Lunt, T. F., Morgenstern, M., Neumann, P. G., & Schell, R. R. (1987). Views for multilevel database security. *IEEE Transactions on Software Engineering*, *SE-13*(2), 129–140.
13. Farooqui, M. A., & Furkan, M. (2014). An empirical view of database security measurements. *International Journal of Electrical, Electronics and Computer Engineering*, *3*(2), 107–112.

14. Ferrara, E., De Meo, P., Fiumara, G., & Baumgartner, R. (2014). Web data extraction, applications and techniques: A survey. *Knowledge-Based Systems*, *70*, 301–323.
15. Fichtner, J. R. (2010). The recent international growth of mandatory audit committee requirements. *International Journal of Disclosure and Governance*, *7*, 227–243.
16. Field, S., Sarver, M. D., & Shaw, S. F. (2003). Self-determination: A key to success in postsecondary education for students with learning disabilities. *Remedial and Special Education*, *24*(6), 339–349.
17. Gautam, N. (2002). Performance analysis and optimization of web proxy servers and mirror sites. *European Journal of Operational Research*, *142*(2), 396–418.
18. George, B., & Valeva, A. (2006). A database security course on a shoestring. *ACM SIGCSE Bulletin*, *38*(1), 7–11.
19. Goguen, J. A., & Meseguer, J. (1982). Security policies and security models. In *1982 IEEE Symposium on Security and Privacy* (pp. 11–11).
20. Gøtzsche, P. C., Hróbjartsson, A., Marić, K., & Tendal, B. (2007). Data extraction errors in meta-analyses that use standardized mean differences. *JAMA*, *298*(4), 430–437.
21. Griffiths, P. P., & Wade, B. W. (1976). An authorization mechanism for a relational database system. *ACM Transactions on Database Systems (TODS)*, *1*(3), 242–255.
22. Harn, L. (2012). Group authentication. *IEEE Transactions on Computers*, *62*(9), 1893–1898.
23. Imrie, R. (2012). Universalism, universal design and equitable access to the built environment. *Disability and Rehabilitation*, *34*(10), 873–882.
24. Jeffery, K. G. (2009). The Internet of Things: The death of a traditional database? *IETE Technical Review*, *26*(5), 313–319.
25. Johnson, L. E., Freeman, R. J., & Davies, S. P. (2003). Local government audit procurement requirements, audit effort, and audit fees. *Research in Accounting Regulation*, *16*, 197–207.
26. Jones, C., Hall, J., & Hale, J. (2000). Secure distributed database mining: Principles of design. *Advances in Distributed and Parallel Knowledge Discovery*, *2*(1), 277–294.
27. Kelly, B., Rid, A., & Wendler, D. (2012). Systematic review: Individuals' goals for surrogate decision-making. *Journal of the American Geriatrics Society*, *60*(5), 884–895.
28. Kerr, O. S. (2003). Cybercrime's scope: Interpreting access and

authorization in computer misuse statutes. *New York University Law Review, 78*, 1596.

29. Kim, H., & Lee, E. A. (2017). Authentication and authorization for the Internet of Things. *IT Professional, 19*(5), 27–33.
30. Kneebone, E., Beilby, K., & Hammarberg, K. (2022). Experiences of surrogates and intended parents of surrogacy arrangements: A systematic review. *Reproductive BioMedicine Online, 45*(4), 815–830.
31. Koops, B. J. (2014). The trouble with European data protection law. *International Data Privacy Law, 4*(4), 250–261.
32. Langenberg, S., & Wesseling, H. (2016). Making sense of Weick's organizing: A philosophical exploration. *Philosophy of Management, 15*(3), 221–240.
33. Lodge, M., & Hamill, R. (1986). A partisan schema for political information processing. *American Political Science Review, 80*(2), 505–519.
34. Lunt, T. F., & Fernandez, E. B. (1990). Database security. *ACM SIGMOD Record, 19*(4), 90–97.
35. Lv, Z., Song, H., Basanta-Val, P., Steed, A., & Jo, M. (2017). Next-generation big data analytics: State of the art, challenges, and future research topics. *IEEE Transactions on Industrial Informatics, 13*(4), 1891–1899.
36. Lynge, M. J., & Zumwalt, J. K. (1980). An empirical study of the interest rate sensitivity of commercial bank returns: A multi-index approach. *Journal of Financial and Quantitative Analysis, 15*(3), 731–742.
37. Lynskey, O. (2014). Deconstructing data protection: The 'added-value' of a right to data protection in the EU legal order. *International & Comparative Law Quarterly, 63*(3), 569–597.
38. Malik, M., & Patel, T. (2016). Database security-attacks and control methods. *International Journal of Information, 6*(1/2), 175–183.
39. Martin, K. D., & Murphy, P. E. (2017). The role of data privacy in marketing. *Journal of the Academy of Marketing Science, 45*, 135–155.
40. Matyas, S. M. (1979). Digital signatures—An overview. *Computer Networks (1976), 3*(2), 87–94.
41. Miles, R. E., & Snow, C. C. (1995). The new network firm: A s□herical structure built on a human investment philosophy. *Organizational Dynamics, 23*(4), 5–18.
42. O'Brien, K., Wilkins, A., Zack, E., & Solomon, P. (2010). Scoping the field: Identifying key research □riorities in HIV and rehabilitation. *AIDS and Behavior, 14*, 448–458.

43. Oppliger, R. (1997). Internet security: Firewalls and beyond. *Communications of the ACM, 40*(5), 92–102.

44. Ouaddah, A., Mousannif, H., Abou Elkalam, A., & Ouahman, A. A. (2017). Access control in the Internet of Things: Big challenges and new opportunities. *Computer Networks, 112*, 237–262.

45. Pan, X., Obahiaghon, A., Makar, B., Wilson, S., & Beard, C. (2024). Analysis of database security. *Open Access Library Journal, 11*(4), 1–19.

46. Pearlman, L., Welch, V., Foster, I., Kesselman, C., & Tuecke, S. (2002). A community authorization service for group collaboration. In *Proceedings Third International Workshop on Policies for Distributed Systems and Networks* (Vol. 2, pp. 50–59).

47. Pernul, G. (1994). Database security. In *Advances in Computers* (Vol. 38, pp. 1–72).

48. Picu, R. C., Vincze, G., Ozturk, F., Gracio, J. J., Barlat, F., & Maniatty, A. M. (2005). Strain rate sensitivity of the commercial aluminum alloy AA5182-O. *Materials Science and Engineering: A, 390*(1–2), 334–343.

49. Pointcheval, D., & Stern, J. (2000). Security arguments for digital signatures and blind signatures. *Journal of Cryptology, 13*, 361–396.

50. Rivest, R. L., Shamir, A., & Adleman, L. (1983). A method for obtaining digital signatures and public-key cryptosystems. *Communications of the ACM, 26*(1), 96–99.

51. Roichman, A., & Gudes, E. (2007). Fine-grained access control to web databases. In *Proceedings of the 12th ACM Symposium on Access Control Models and Technologies* (Vol. 2, pp. 31–40).

52. Rosato, A. (2016). Selling substitute goods to loss-averse consumers: Limited availability, bargains, and rip-offs. *The RAND Journal of Economics, 47*(3), 709–733.

53. Sandhu, R., & Jajodia, S. (1991). Integrity principles and mechanisms in database management systems. *Computers & Security, 10*(5), 413–427.

54. Sarker, I. H., Khan, A. I., Abushark, Y. B., & Alsolami, F. (2023). Internet of Things (IoT) security intelligence: A comprehensive overview, machine learning solutions, and research directions. *Mobile Networks and Applications, 28*(1), 296–312.

55. Scott, M. D. (2008). The FTC, the unfairness doctrine, and data security breach litigation: Has the commission gone too far? *Administrative Law Review, 60*(2), 127–156.

56. Singh, A. K. (2005). HRD practices and philosophy of management in Indian organizations. *Vikalpa, 30*(2), 71–80.

57. Stachour, P., & Thuraisingham, B. (1990). SQL extensions for security assertions. *Computer Standards & Interfaces, 11*(1), 5–14.
58. Taylor, K. S., Mahtani, K. R., & Aronson, J. K. (2021). Summarizing good practice guidelines for data extraction for systematic reviews and meta-analysis. *BMJ Evidence-Based Medicine, 26*(3), 88–90.
59. Thinggaard, F., & Kiertzner, L. (2008). Determinants of audit fees: Evidence from a small capital market with a joint audit requirement. *International Journal of Auditing, 12*(2), 141–158.
60. Traub, J. F., Yemini, Y., & Woźniakowski, H. (1984). The statistical security of a statistical database. *ACM Transactions on Database Systems (TODS), 9*(4), 672–679.
61. Van Linden, C., & Hardies, K. (2018). Entrance requirements to the audit profession within the EU and audit quality. *International Journal of Auditing, 22*(3), 360–373.
62. Van Oorschot, P. C., & Wurster, G. (2011). Reducing unauthorized modification of digital objects. *IEEE Transactions on Software Engineering, 38*(1), 191–204.
63. Vehovar, V., Manfreda, K. L., & Batagelj, Z. (2001). Sensitivity of electronic commerce measurement to the survey instrument. *International Journal of Electronic Commerce, 6*(1), 31–51.
64. Wayman, J., Jain, A., Maltoni, D., & Maio, D. (2005). An introduction to biometric authentication systems. In *Biometric Systems: Technology, Design and Performance Evaluation* (Vol. 1, pp. 1–20).
65. Weber, R. H. (2010). Internet of Things–New security and privacy challenges. *Computer Law & Security Review, 26*(1), 23–30.
66. Winkler, H. (1992). Sybase Secure SQL Server. In *Research Directions in Database Security* (Vol. 2, pp. 81–89).
67. Wood, C. C. (1990). Principles of secure information systems design. *Computers & Security, 9*(1), 13–24.
68. Wu, S., & Liao, C. C. (1997). Virtual proxy servers for WWW and intelligent agents on the Internet. In *Proceedings of the Thirtieth Hawaii International Conference on System Sciences* (Vol. 4, pp. 200–209).

CHAPTER 2

DATABASE SECURITY FUNDAMENTALS

LEARNING OBJECTIVES

At the end of this chapter, readers will be able to:

1. Understand database security management and its importance;
2. Understand the three levels of the database security framework: DBMS security, operating system security, and network security;
3. Explore IAM features and their integration with GaussDB (for MySQL);
4. Understand GaussDB (for MySQL) permission types and their application levels;
5. Learn how to manage database users and assign appropriate permissions;
6. Explore the role-based permission management and authorization processes; and
7. Gain insight into cloud audit services for logging and tracking database operations.ecurity measures such as firewalls and digital signatures for database protection.

INTRODUCTORY EXAMPLE

DataGuard Solutions, a leading provider of cybersecurity solutions, recently collaborated with a regional bank facing escalating cyber threats and data breaches. The bank's existing security measures were proving inadequate in safeguarding sensitive customer data and financial information from sophisticated cyber-attacks. Recognizing the urgent need for enhanced data protection, DataGuard Solutions proposed the implementation of a comprehensive cyber security framework tailored to the bank's specific needs.

To address this challenge, DataGuard Solutions recommended deploying advanced encryption techniques, multi-factor authentication protocols, and real-time threat monitoring systems. By leveraging cutting-edge technologies and industry best practices, DataGuard Solutions aimed to fortify the bank's defenses against cyber threats and ensure compliance with regulatory requirements.

Through a series of security assessments and penetration tests, DataGuard Solutions identified vulnerabilities in the bank's network infrastructure and developed customized mitigation strategies to address them effectively. By prioritizing proactive security measures and continuous monitoring, DataGuard Solutions sought to bolster the bank's resilience to cyber threats and minimize the risk of data breaches.

As DataGuard Solutions continues to collaborate with the bank in enhancing its cyber security posture, the company remains committed to delivering robust, scalable solutions that protect sensitive data assets and maintain customer trust. This introductory example underscores the critical role of cyber security firms like DataGuard Solutions in mitigating cyber risks and safeguarding organizations against evolving threats in today's digital landscape.

UNIT INTRODUCTION

The primary objective of managing database security is to secure the data stored within the database system, reducing the risks of unauthorized access, data manipulation, and data loss. When it comes to database security, ensuring the proper permissions are in place for different users is crucial. A database system is responsible for storing a wide range of important and sensitive data, making it mandatory to prioritize the protection of this information (Elmasri et al., 2020).

In this chapter, we will explore the fundamental techniques used in managing security in databases. These techniques include object permissions, user management, access control, cloud audit services and permission management.

A comprehensive exploration of these techniques, examining them from three distinct perspectives e.g., foundational principles, practical techniques, and real-world situations will be discussed (Davidson & Davidson, 2021).

2.1. OVERVIEW OF DATABASE SECURITY FEATURES

Learning Objectives

- Understand the three-level framework of database security: network, OS, and DBMS; and
- Understand database security features like access control, user rights management, and security audits.

2.1.1. Database Security Management

Ensuring the protection of databases is essential in protecting sensitive information, preventing unauthorized access, and decreasing the risk of data loss caused by various factors such as network vulnerabilities, system weaknesses, and software errors. It includes a range of measures that focus on protecting valuable data and preventing any unauthorized disclosure (Wang & Cheng, 2021).

2.1.2. Database Security Framework

The security framework of database can be categorized into three levels as shown in Figure 2.1:

- Network Security
- Operating System Security
- DBMS Security (Bertino, & Sandhu, 2005).

2.1.2.1. Network Security

Several key technologies play a crucial role in ensuring network security. These technologies include encryption, digital signatures, intrusion detection systems and firewalls. Network-level security primarily emphasizes the encryption of transmission contents. Encrypting content before sending it over a network is essential to guaranteeing data security during transmission. The receiver must then decrypt the data upon receiving it (Pawar & Anuradha, 2015).

2.1.2.2. Operating System Security

Data files included in the operating system are encrypted as part of the encryption process used to secure the operating system. The primary objective is to safeguard the server's security, particularly concerning user accounts, passwords, access privileges, and other related aspects. Data security primarily includes encryption technology, as well as the security of data storage and transmission. Examples of technologies used for data transmission security include Kerberos, IPsec, SSL, and VPN (Grampp & Morris, 1984).

2.1.2.3. DBMS Security

DBMS security encryption involves the use of custom or built-in methods to encrypt and decode data throughout the process of reading and writing. It includes data access control, security audits, database encryption, and data backup (Neto & Vieira, 2008).

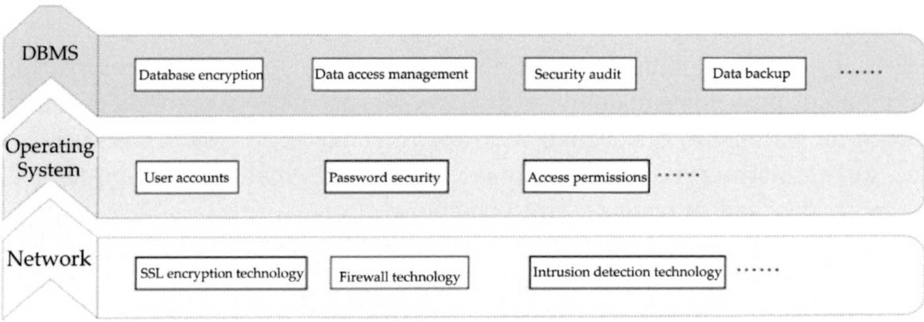

Figure 2.1. *Illustration of database security framework.*

Source: Huawei Tech Creative Commons License.

2.1.3. Feature of Database Security

GaussDB (for my structured query language (MySQL)) incorporates several robust security measures to protect against both intentional and unintentional breaches.

- The initial layer of protection is established by implementing access control and SSL connection, which effectively protects against information leakage, client counterfeiting, and tampering with interactive messages (Pernul, 1994).
- The second layer of protection prioritizes user rights management, improving the database server to minimize threats such as illegal □ermission modifications.

- The third line of defense is established by security audit management, which enables the tracking of all activities performed on the database (Denning et al., 1987).

GaussDB (for MySQL) provides a robust defense mechanism to safeguard against potential DOS attacks. It effectively prevents any attempts by clients to maliciously exploit server-side session resources, ensuring the integrity and security of the system. The server will immediately close a connection and release any session resources it is using if the connection cannot authenticate within the allotted authentication time. Ensuring the protection of connection session resources is of utmost importance to mitigate the potential risks posed by malicious TCP connections. It is highly effective in preventing Denial of Service (DOS) attacks (Jiang et al., 2018).

This chapter will discuss primary methodologies for managing database security, focusing on three key areas: user rights management, access control, and cloud audit service.

Practice Problem

A com□any manages a database housing confidential customer data on a server operating on the UNIX platform. The IT department intends to enhance database security by implementing strong operating system protections. Provide a detailed security □lan that covers user authentication, file system permissions, network security, and audit trails to ensure effective protection of the database.

Solutions to Practice Problem

Develop strong password policies, use role-based access management, and impose two-factor authentication. Implement the principle of least privilege for file system □ermissions, use encry□tion for sensitive information, and actively monitor file integrity. Incor□orate firewalls, intrusion detection systems, and SSL encryption, to ensure network security. Implement database auditing, thoroughly examine logs for any signs of suspicious actions, and frequently create backups of logs to ensure compliance and facilitate forensic investigations.

2.2. MANAGEMENT IN DATABASE SECURITY

Learning Objectives

- Understand the components and deployment models of Identity and Access Management (IAM);
- Know how IAM features enhance secure access and manage permissions; and
- Explore the integration and use of GaussDB (for MySQL) with IAM for database security.

2.2.1. Identity and Access Management

A comprehensive system called identity and access management (IAM) helps businesses effectively manage electronic or digital identities. It includes a range of business processes, policies, and technologies to ensure secure access to sensitive information. By establishing an IAM architecture, IT administrators get the power to effectively control user access to critical information within their organizations. Various systems are used for IAM, such as two-factor authentication, single sign-on systems, privileged access management, and multifactor authentication.

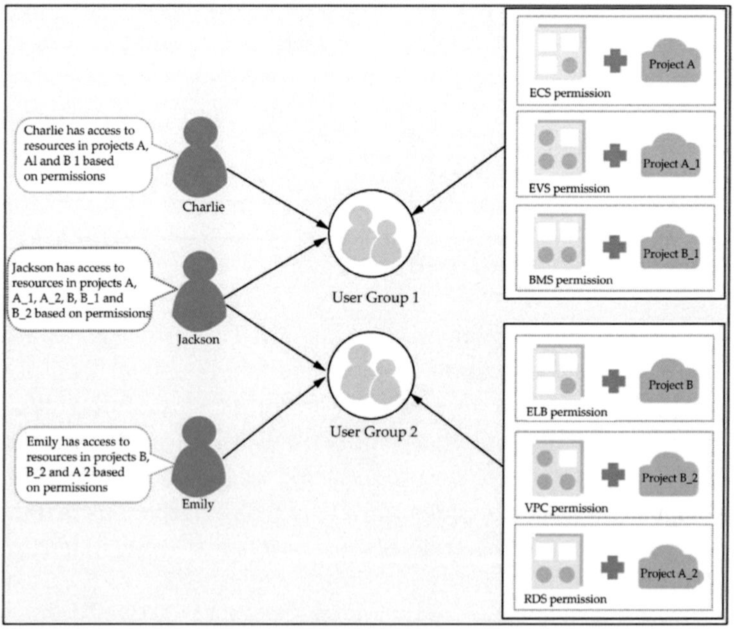

Figure 2.2. *Description of the use of IAM.*

Source: Alfred Basta, Creative Commons License.

These systems also include data governance features to guarantee that only relevant and necessary information is shared, and the ability to securely maintain identity and □rofile data (Mohammed et al., 2013).

There are various options available for using IAM systems, including on-premises deployment, cloud-based subscription models provided by third-party vendors, or a hybrid model. Figure 2.2 shows the implementation of IAM (Parker et al., 2002).

2.2.2. IAM Features

IAM offers precise control over permission management, ensuring secure access and protection of sensitive operations. The system enables the effective administration of user permissions by user groups and guarantees the separation of resources within a specified region. IAM also facilitates joint authentication and allows for transfer of resource management to cloud services or other accounts. In addition, it allows for the establishment of account security policies and guarantees complete uniformity (Daniels, 2013).

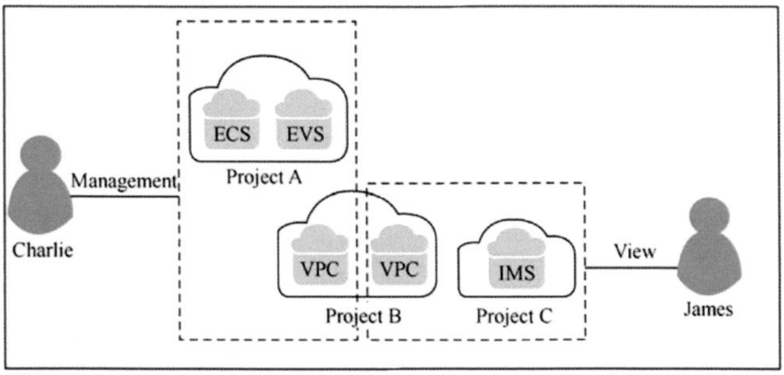

Figure 2.3. *Representation of the example of fine-grained permission management.*

Source: Thomas L. Creative Commons License.

- *Fine Grained Permission Management:* With IAM, it is possible to assign various resources to IAM users in order to achieve precise permission management, as shown in Figure 2.3.
  - *Secure Access:* One option is to use IAM to create identity credentials for individuals or applications, eliminating the need to share account passwords with others. This system ensures that users can securely access account resources by carrying permission information within their identity credentials (Marti & Bunke, 2002).
  - *Sensitive Operations:* IAM offers strong protections for sensitive operations, that includes measures to protect logins

and operations. For enhanced security measures, the system requires a secondary authentication process when accessing the console or conducting sensitive operations. This involves providing a verification code through cell phone, email or virtual MFA. Such measures are taken to ensure an increased level of protection for both account and the associated resources (Ziaratban et al., 2009)

- *Managing User Permissions in Bulk:* Instead of demanding unique authorization for each user, it is advisable to categorize users into user groups and assign relevant permissions to these groups. By adding users to the appropriate user group, they can inherit the permissions assigned to that group. When there are changes in user permissions, one can easily manage them by removing the user from the user group or adding them to different user groups. This will help ensure efficient user authorization (Ermondi et al., 2018).
- *Resources Isolated Within a Region:* By establishing sub-projects inside a specific region, the resources of projects located in that region can be separated from each other.
- *Joint Authentication:* Consumers can avoid creating new Huawei Cloud user accounts by using an existing authentication mechanism. Instead, they can utilize the identity provider feature to directly access the Cloud, enabling single sign-on (Ermondi et al., 2018).
- *Managing Resource Delegation:* By utilizing the delegate trust function, users can assign operation control to other Huawei Cloud accounts or cloud services that possess advanced knowledge and effectiveness. Then using the given authority, these selected accounts or services will perform everyday tasks on behalf of the users (Iam-On, et al., 2010).
- *Creating Account Security Policies:* Enhance the protection of user information and system data by implementing robust password policies, strict login authentication policies, and comprehensive access control lists (Barbato, 2006).

2.2.3. Identity and Access Management Authorization

For a variety of Huawei Cloud services, IAM provides authorization and authentication capabilities. Users who are created in IAM have the ability to utilize various services within the system, based on their permissions, once they have been authorized. For services that do not support IAM authorization, the

IAM user created in the account must log in to the account in order to use the cloud services. Here is an explanation of the key terms in IAM authorization (Indu & Anand, 2016).

- *Service:* IAM authorization is frequently used by cloud services, giving users easy access to and viewing of the permissions linked to each service. By clicking on the service name, users can explore the various permissions available and understand the differences between them.
- *Region:* The region chosen for authorization by the cloud service when implementing IAM authorization (Salecha, 2022).
- *Global Region:* The service is globally deployed without identifying a s□ecific □hysical area. This means that it o□erates at a worldwide level and is permitted in a global project. Users can access the service without the need to switch between different regions.
- *Other Regions:* The service is implemented by assigning a physical geographic area, which is a service at the project level. Authorization is performed in regions other than the global region and only applies inside the authorized region. This enables access to cloud services that necessitate switching to the correct area (Sharma et al., 2016).
- *Console:* Whether permission management in the IAM console is supported by the cloud service.
- *API:* If the cloud service allows requesting permission control over an API.
- *Delegation:* The user grants operation permissions to the service, allowing it to use other cloud services on its behalf and carry out daily tasks (Singh et al., 2023).
- *Policy:* Can the cloud service effectively handle permission management through policies? These policies are written in JSON format and describe a s□ecific set of □ermissions, allowing or denying users to perform certain operations on the service's resource types (Talluri & Makani, 2023).

2.2.4. Relationship Between IAM and GaussDB (for MySQL) Usages

The following actions can be performed by IAM if fine-grained permission control is required for the user-owned cloud database GaussDB (for MySQL).

- Enterprises typically establish IAM users in their cloud accounts to assign unique security credentials to employees based on their roles within the organization. This allows employees to access and utilize GaussDB (for MySQL) resources with the necessary security measures in place.

- By assigning different access rights based on the functions of enterprise users, the goal of isolating rights between users can be achieved (Huawei, 2022).

Outsource GaussDB (for MySQL) resources to other Huawei cloud accounts or cloud services that have s□ecialized ex□ertise and higher efficiency. This allows for smooth operation and maintenance on behalf of users, in accordance with their authorized permissions (Lin et al., 2022).

2.2.5. How to Use GaussDB (for MySQL) with IAM?

Figure 2.4 shows how IAM works with GaussDB (for MySQL).

- Establish a user group and provide it authorization. Grant the group the "GaussDB Read Only Access" permission in the IAM interface to create a user group with read-only access to GaussDB (for MySQL).
- Establish user accounts and join their user groups. Generate user accounts in the IAM console and assign them to the user group established in the previous phase (Ma et al., 2022).
- Users are required to log in and verify their permissions. Proceed to the authorization section within the recently developed user login interface and ensure that the □ermissions are correctly configured. To access the main interface of GaussDB (for MySQL), choose GaussDB (for MySQL) from the "Service List." To proceed with purchasing an instance of GaussDB (for MySQL), select the "Purchase a database instance" option situated in the upper right corner. If the purchase failed (assuming that the current permission only allows for GaussDB Read Only Access), it indicates that the "GaussDB Read Only Access" is currently in effect (Marathe et al., 2022).
- Choose a service from the "Service List" other than cloud database GaussDB (for MySQL). If you receive a message about insufficient permissions, it means that the current policy only allows GaussDB Read Only Access (Lin et al., 2022).

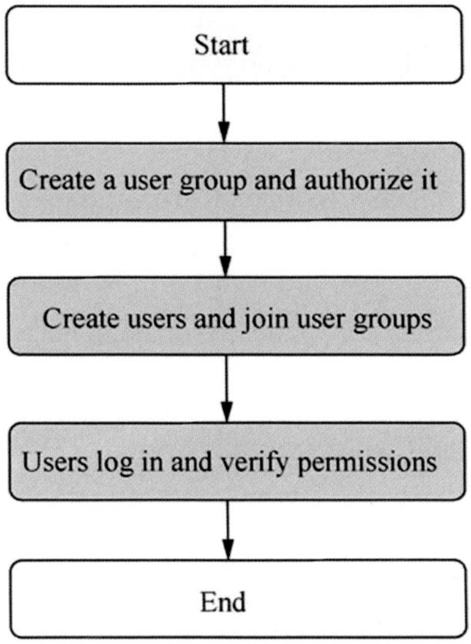

Figure 2.4. *Description of flow of IAM using GaussDB (for MySQL).*

Source: Mellisa Zgola Creative Commons License.

2.3. USER PERMISSION CONTROL

Learning Objectives

- Understand GaussDB (for MySQL) permission concepts and management;
- Know user creation, alteration, and deletion commands; and
- Comprehend role-based permission assignment and recovery processes.

2.3.1. Permission Concept

Permissions mean the capability of executing specific SQL statements and accessing or managing specific objects. Managing a small village with a few dozen households is undoubtedly easier compared to the challenges of overseeing a bustling metropolis with millions of residents. Ensuring proper permission control for users is important when it comes to managing database resources and maintaining security (Bannon et al., 2002).

GaussDB (for MySQL) provides adequate assistance for managing user permissions, enabling you to control the operational access of users to database objects and the utilization of database functions. The operations that can be performed by GaussDB (for MySQL) accounts are determined by the permissions granted to them. The following shows how the various GaussDB (for MySQL) permissions vary in the contexts and operation levels to which they apply (Kromann & Kromann, F., 2018).

- *Administrative Permission:* allows users to supervise and manage the operations of the GaussDB (for MySQL) server; the permission is applied universally and is not limited to a single database.
- *Database Permission:* The permission is applicable to the entire database and all of its items. The funding might be given either s□ecifically for a certain database or universally, de□ending on the unique needs (Denton & Peace, 2003).
- *Object Permission:* Access can be allowed to s□ecific database items, all objects in the database of a certain kind (like all tables), or all objects in the database in general (like tables, indexes, views, and stored routines).

GaussDB (for MySQL) offers support for both static and dynamic permissions, with the server incorporating static permissions. User accounts can always be granted permissions and cannot be cancelled. Permissions that are dynamic can be added or removed during the execution of a program, but doing so will impact their accessibility. Unregistered dynamic permissions cannot be granted (Kardava et al., 2021).

The GaussDB (for MySQL) server manages user access to the database by utilizing permission tables. These tables are stored in the GaussDB (for MySQL) database and are initialized during the database initialization process. Table 2.1 shows permission table example.

Table 2.1. An Example of Permission Table

Permission Table	Permission Description
db	Database-level permissions
Global grants	Dynamic global permissions
User	User account, static global permissions and other non-permission columns
Tables_priv	Table-level permissions
Procs_priv	Stored procedure and function permissions
Columns_priv	Column-level permissions

Source: Mellisa Zgola Creative Commons License.

2.3.2. Users

As a database administrator, it is important to establish a separate database user for every individual requiring access to the database. When accessing the database, the user is required to provide their username and password for authentication purposes. Here, the user takes the role of a database user with the ability to manipulate database objects and access data. This includes tasks like accessing tables, creating tables and executing SQL statements (Rawat & Purnama, 2021).

There are three distinct categories of users for the GaussDB (MySQL) database by default.

- The system administrator holds the highest level of authority over the database, e.g., by users such as SYS and SYSDBA.
- The security administrator possesses the CREATE USER permission.
- *Ordinary User:* By default, the ordinary user is granted the PUBLIC object permission and is only allowed to access the objects they have created. If additional permissions are required, the user must be granted them by the system administrator using the GRANT statement.

The SYSDBA user has the privilege to access the database without requiring a password. To establish a connection with the database, one can use the login "zsql/ AS SYSDBA." The creation of users can be achieved through the use of the CREATE USER statement. It is important to keep in mind the following three points when using this statement (Christudas & Christudas, 2019).

- In order to create a new user, it is essential for the user executing this statement to have the necessary system permissions. Without the required permissions, the creation of a new user will not be possible.
- When setting up a user, it is necessary to provide the user's name and password. These credentials will be used when the user connects to the database (Győrödi et al., 2015).
- Creating the root user is □rohibited as it is a □re-defined user within the system. Here is a common syntax format to create users:

```
CREATE USER user_name IDENTIFIED BY password;
```

Please ensure that the user name is provided as "user_name" and the password is enclosed in single quotes. Once the user has been successfully created, a connection to the database using the right credentials can easily be established. Please note that certain special characters cannot be used in the user name (Maesaroh et al., 2022).

Here are some characters commonly used in writing: vertical line, semicolon, dollar sign, backquote, bit operator, less than sign, double quote, greater than sign, exclamation mark, single quote, spaces, and the copyright symbol. Quotation marks or backticks are also prohibited. When it comes to user names, it's important to note that any special characters, except for the ones mentioned above, should be enclosed in either double quotation marks ("“") or back quotes (“).

When creating a password for a user name, certain criteria need to be fulfilled.

- The password must be at least eight characters long (Dipina et al., 2016).
- When creating a password, it is important to enclose the password in single quotes.
- *Example:* You can run the following statement to create a user with the username "smith" and the password "database_123."

```
CREATE USER smith IDENTIFIED BY ‘database_123’;
```

The username is composed of letters, while the password includes letters, special symbols, and numbers. These meet the necessary criteria and can be successfully generated. The password provided meets all the necessary criteria for a secure password (Madyatmadja & Adora, 2019).

2.3.3. Altering a User

To edit users, use the ALTER USER command and be mindful of the following considerations:

- The user running this command must have ALTER USER system access, which are similar to CREATE USER privileges.
- If the s□ecified user does not exist, an error message will be dis□layed. Modifications can only be a□□lied to a □re-existing user (Liu et al., 2012).

User modification is □rimarily utilized in the following situations:

- Change the user password.
- Enable or disable user access manually. For example, if a user has been denied access after a certain number of failed login attempts, the user will need to go through the process of being unlocked (Simeone et al., 2017).

The recommended syntax for modifying the user password is as follows:

```
ALTER USER user_name IDENTIFIED BY new_password;
```

The variable "user_name" represents the current user's username, while the variable "new password" represents the desired new password for the user (Hagan et al., 1995). To modify the password of user smith to "database_456." The administrator has the ability to modify it directly using the following command (Larson & Chang, 2016).

```
ALTER USER user_name IDENTIFIED BY new_password;
```

2.3.4. Dropping a User

Eliminating a user from the system when they are no longer needed is crucial. This will result in the deletion of every object associated with that user. The DROP USER statement can be used to delete a user. It is important to realize that, in order to DROP USER, the user performing the statement must have the necessary system permissions, just like they would need to CREATE USER (Ainsworth & Jones, 2020)

Here is the syntax format for deleting a userP:

```
DROP USER [IF EXISTS] user_name;
```

The variable "user_name" s□ecifies the username that is to be removed. The IF EXISTS statement is employed to verify if the user to be deleted exists (Ellickson et al., 1998). If the IF EXISTS option is removed, an error message will be displayed if the user being deleted is not found. However, when the IF EXISTS option is applied, the command will provide a successful execution outcome regardless of whether the user exists or not. If the user does exist, they will be removed (Modest et al., 2018).

For example: Following command can be used to remove smith:

```
DROP USER IF EXISTS smith;
```

2.3.5. Roles

A collection of privileges known as a role enables a database to partition rights according to the level of the organization. The introduction of roles did not occur until MySQL 8. To facilitate management, a database can be accessible by numerous users. To achieve this, permissions can be grouped and assigned to roles, with each role having a corresponding set of permissions. To accommodate users with varying permission levels, one may have the option to assign different roles to users. This allows to grant the necessary permissions to users collectively, rather than individually (Shin et al., 2003).

For exam□le, a com□any may have various financial roles that come with different permissions, such as the ability to process payroll and allocate funds. It is important to note that a role is not exclusive to any particular user. Rather, it can be shared among multiple users, making it an organizational unit. For exam□le, the role of finance is not limited to a single em□loyee, but can be shared among multiple employees. Imagine if a user named Smith creates a role called "staffs," then the access to "smith.staffs" is restricted to Smith only. Access or operation on "smith.staffs" is limited to the smith user, unless other users have been granted the necessary permissions (Jeong et al., 2003).

The CREATE ROLE statement is used to create roles. It is important to mention that the user running the statement must possess the CREATE ROLE system □ermission. The □osition isn't s□ecific to any user and cannot be used to log into the database or perform SQL statement operations. Additionally, the role must be unique inside the system (Kuji Kosuge et al., 2010).

GaussDB (for MySQL) includes the following four system-□reconfigured roles as □art of its basic configuration.

- A database administrator has full system permissions that are unchangeable.
- The RESOURCE role is responsible for creating basic objects and has the authority to create stored procedures, functions, triggers, and table sequences.
- The "CONNECT" role has the authorization to establish a connection with the database.
- STATISTICE, a statistical role (Litchfield, 2005).

The syntax format for role creation is as follows:

```
CREATE ROLE role_name;
```

The term "role_name" refers to name assigned to the role that has been formed.

Example: To create the teacher role:

```
CREATE ROLE teacher;
```

DROP ROLE statement can be used to remove the role. In order to delete a role, certain conditions must be met. The user performing the statement needs to be the one who created the role, have the DROP ANY ROLE system permission, or have been given the role with the WITH GRANT OPTION attribute. If the designated role is not present, an error message will be shown. When a role is eliminated, the permissions associated with that position are transferred back to either the user or another role to which the role was originally issued. Thus, the user or role linked to the removed role will lose the ability to use the permissions they had before in that position (Becchetti & Trovato, 2002).

The deleting role syntax format is as follows:

```
DROP ROLE role_name;
```

role_name represents the role name. Example: To delete the role teacher.

Here is the relationship between user permissions and roles.

- Users can create roles and assign varying levels of permissions to them. These roles serve as a collection of various permissions.
- When a user or another role assigns a role, the granted object inherits all the permissions of that role.
- Role permissions can be inherited.

GaussDB (for MySQL) offers strong assistance for role-based permission management. Users have the ability to establish roles, and once a user is assigned a position, they are automatically given all the required permissions that come with that role (Dong et al., 2017).

The role shown in Figure 2.5 only has the authority to process wage payments and distribute funds, whereas the director's privileges are limited to inspecting the budget and accessing the income statements. Once the director is given the financial role, they gain the necessary permissions to audit the budget, access income statements, and handle payroll and fund allocation.

2.3.6. Authorization

Authorization involves the assignment of permissions or responsibilities to users or other roles, ensuring that they have the necessary permissions. For example, a recently established user lacks the necessary authorization to execute any actions on the database or establish a connection to it. Granting the CREATE SESSION permission allows them to establish a connection to the database. To create a table, the user must possess the necessary permission to do so. This permission, known as the CREATE TABLE permission, grants the user the ability to create tables (Kudo & Hada, 2000).

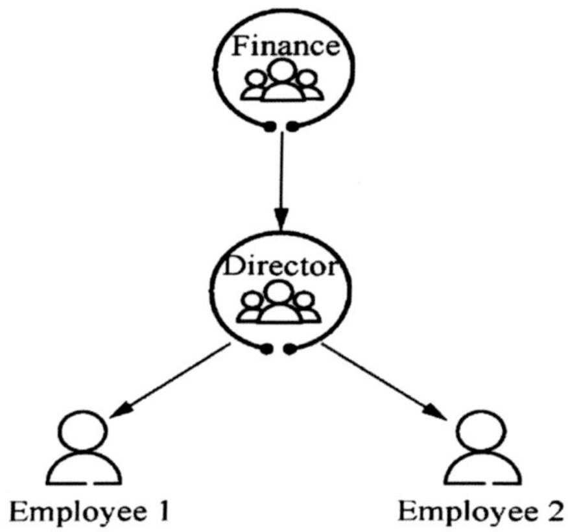

Figure 2.5. *Illustration of 2 user, role, and permission.*

Source: Davies Creative Commons License.

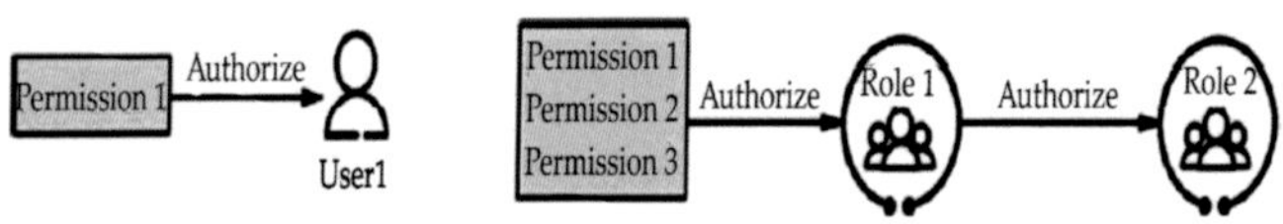

Figure 2.6. *Illustration of authorization.*

Source: Dana Bullaboy Creative Commons License.

The table created by the user is associated with their object, granting them the ability to perform operations such as adding, deleting, modifying, and checking data within the table. Authorization can be accomplished using the GRANT statement, which allows granting permissions to users or roles, either individually or in bulk (Shehab et al., 2011). User 1 may be granted permission 1, and Role 1 may be granted permissions 1, 2, and 3. Role 1 has the ability to grant these permissions to Role 2, and ultimately, the user can be granted the permissions of Role 2, as shown in Figure 2.6.

Here is a typical syntax format for granting permissions:

```
GRANT privilege_name ON db/objects TO grantee [ WITH GRANT OPTION ];
```

- **Permission_name:** Refers to the name assigned to a s□ecific permission.
- **db/objects:** An authorized database or object for use.
- **Grantee:** The role or individual that will be granted authorization (Sato, 2017).

- **With Grant Option:** This optional feature allows the user or role with permissions to grant them to others.

In order to grant the permission, the user executing the grant statement must possess the WITH GRANT OPTION attribute and already have the necessary permission. For instance, to enable smith to grant the CREATE USER permission to other users or roles and to authorize smith to grant this permission to other people (Shehab & Marouf, 2012).

```
GRANT CREATE USER ON *.* TO smith WITH GRANT OP-
TION;
```

The syntax format for granting roles closely matches the format for granting permissions, as shown below:

```
GRANT role_name TO grantee [WITH GRANT OPTION];
```

When it comes to granting permissions, it's important to understand the role_name and the grantee. The role_name refers to the s□ecific role name, while the grantee represents the user or role that will be granted. When the option WITH GRANT OPTION is enabled, users or roles who have been granted a role can then pass on that role to others. To successfully grant the role, the user executing the granting role statement must meet one of the s□ecified conditions:

- The role has been granted and possesses the attribute of WITH GRANT OPTION.
- The individual responsible for creating the role.
- *Example:* To authorize Smith as an instructor and enable Smith to delegate this authorization to other users or roles. Enabling the WITH GRANT OPTION property gives authorized users the ability to pass on their permissions or responsibilities to other users or roles (Satoto et al., 2016).

```
GRANT teacher TO smith WITH GRANT OPTION;
```

2.3.7. Permission Recovery

Regaining access to a certain permission or position from the authorized person is known as permission recovery. Upon completion of the recovery process, the role or user in question will be deprived of that permission. For instance, if there is a need to prevent a user from creating a table, one can terminate the CREATE TABLE system permission from that user. If one wants to prevent user access to the database, it is possible to disable the CREATE SESSION permission from the user. Recovering permissions involves restoring system permissions, role permissions and object permissions, which can all be accomplished using REVOKE statement (Carnevale et al., 2013).

Here is a typical syntax format for permission recovery:

```
REVOKE privilege_name ON db/objects FROM revokee;
```

Permissions can be revoked by the authorizer using the REVOKE command. The □erson or role whose □ermissions are to be revoked is identified by the revokee o□tion, while the □ermission_name o□tion s□ecifies the name of the permission to be revoked. A maximum of sixty-three users or roles may be assigned at once (Pierce & Politis, 1990).

The user executing the grant statement must already have the attribute WITH GRANT OPTION and be granted permission in order to provide a permission. The authorized user can assign the acquired role or permission to other users or roles if the WITH GRANT OPTION attribute is present. For example: To enable the user Smith to once again create users (Hahn et al., 1976).

```
REVOKE CREATE USER ON *.* FROM smith;
```

If a user no longer needs the permissions that are linked to their assigned role, their role permissions should be revoked. For example, in the scenario where Em□loyee A is a finance □ersonnel who has authorization to utilize the com□any's financial assets, if this individual de□arts, it becomes necessary to redistribute their finance-related duties to other em□loyees. The system administrator, also known as the SYS user and assigned the database administrator role, possesses all system privileges, including the GRANT ANY ROLE system privilege. Consequently, the role recover statement can be executed by the system administrator (Zhang et al., 2016).

To get back the role, the user executing the REVOKE operation must satisfy one of the following conditions.

- It has been assigned the role and possesses the WITH GRANT OPTION characteristic.
- The role is being restored by its creator.

The following is the standard syntax format for obtaining a role:

```
REVOKE role_name FROM revokee;
```

The term "role_name" refers to the s□ecific name assigned to a role, whereas "revokee" refers to the user or role from which permissions are being restored. A maximum of 63 users or roles can be allocated simultaneously. Please be aware that it is strictly prohibited to restore the authority of the database administrator role. At the time the database is created, the permissions for the database administrator role are set. The database administrator position then gets additional permissions that you can give it, but you can't take those permissions back (Archer et al., 1984).

The principle of minimization should guide the use of permissions, and roles and permissions must be immediately recovered when not in usage to maintain database security (Jenkins, 1984).

The following is an example of how users, roles, and permissions are applied. To setup the user "smith," using database_123 as the password:

```
CREATE USER smith IDENTIFIED BY 'database_123';
```

Establish the role manager; the CREATE ROLE statement does this.

```
CREATE ROLE manager;
```

Authorize the role manager to have the CREATE USER permission.

```
GRANT CREATE USER ON *.* TO manager;
```

Authorize the manager to have query and insertion access for the grant object.

```
GRANT SELECT, INSERT ON mysql.staffs TO manager;
```

2.4. CLOUD AUDIT SERVICES

Learning Objectives

- Understand key o□erations and benefits of cloud audit services for security.

2.4.1. What are Cloud Audit Services?

Businesses and organizations rely on the log audit module to ensure the effectiveness of their information security audit function and to manage the risks associated with information system security. Various international organizations responsible for managing information and data security have released numerous standards in this field, aligning with the ongoing transition of information systems towards cloud-based platforms. These standards include

GB/T 20945-2013, COBIT ISO IEC27000, COSO, NISTSP800, ITIL, and others (Ryoo et al., 2013).

Huawei's cloud security solution includes a log auditing service called Cloud Trace Service (CTS). It offers functions for collecting, storing, and querying various operation records related to cloud resources (Li et al., 2015). This service is designed to support a range of application scenarios, including security analysis, resource tracking, compliance audit, and problem location, as shown in Figure 2.7.

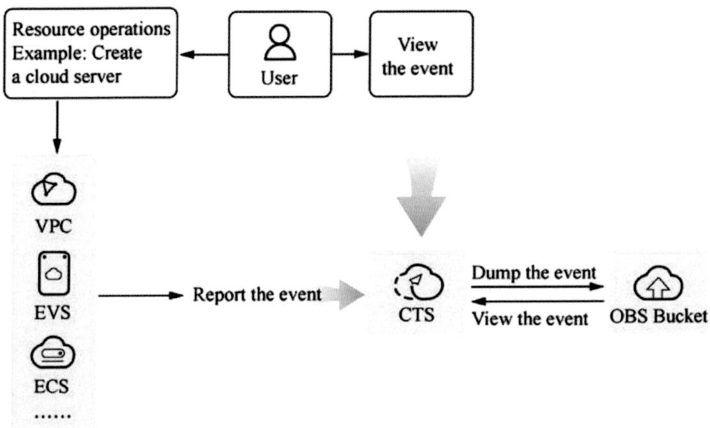

Figure 2.7. *Illustration of cloud audit service.*

Source: Thomas L. Creative Commons License.

The cloud audit service primary purposes are as follows:

- *Record Audit Logs:* The application-programming interface (API) and management console actions carried out by users, as well as any automatic actions carried out by each service, are captured and logged by the system (Khodakivska et al., 2019).
- *Audit Log Query:* enables users to easily access and analyze operation records within a seven-day timeframe through the management console. The records can be queried based on various dimensions including ty□e of event, resource ty□e, source of event, filter ty□e, event level and operation user.
- *Audit Log Dumping:* enables the dumping of audit logs to OBS containers on a periodic basis via the object storage service (OBS), that com□resses audit logs into service-dimensional event files (Mangiuc, 2014).

- *Event File Encryption:* Allows the encry□tion of the event file during dump using the Data Encryption Workshop (DEW) key (BENDOVSCHI & IONESCU, 2015).

2.4.2. Key Operations for Cloud Audit Services

Operational events connected to GaussDB (for MySQL) events can be logged using the cloud audit service, making searches, audits, and trackbacks simpler (Moghadasi et al., 2018). The cloud audit service manages the major operating events as depicted in Table 2.2.

Table 2.2. Range of Key Operations Events Supported by Cloud Audit Service

Operation	**Resource Type**	**Event**
Create an instance	Instance	createInstance
Restart an instance	Instance	restartinstance
Modify an instance port	Instance	changeInstancePort
Delete a read-only node	Instance	deleteNode
Adds a read-only node	Instance	addNodes
Upgrade a read-only instance to a primary instance	Instance	instanceFailOver
Modify an instance security group	Instance	modifySecurityGroup
Bind or unbind a public IP	Instance	setOrResetPublicIP
Modify the node priority	Instance	modifyPriority
Modify the s□ecification	Instance	instanceAction
Rename an instance	Instance	renameInstance
Remove an instance	Instance	deleteInstance
Backup and restore to a new instance	Instance	restoreInstance
Reset the password	Instance	resetPassword
Delete a backup	Backup	deleteManualSnapshot
Create a backup	Backup	createManualSnapshot
Delete a parameter template	parameterGroup	deleteParameterGroup
Create a parameter template	parameterGroup	createParameterGroup
Copy a parameter template	parameterGroup	copyParameterGroup
Reset a parameter template	parameterGroup	resetParameterGroup
Compare parameter templates	parameterGroup	compareParameterGroup

Modify a parameter template	parameterGroup	updateParameterGroup
Apply a parameter template	parameterGroup	applyParameterGroup

Source: Paul Beynon. Creative Commons License.

After the cloud audit service is turned on, the system starts to record cloud service resources through a procedure called track event viewing. A log of the last seven days of activities is kept by the cloud audit service management console. To access the cloud audit service's information page, navigate to the administrative interface and choose "Manage & Deploy > Cloud Audit Service" from the "All Services" or "Service List" section. Then, by choosing the "Event List" option from the left navigation tree, you can examine the details about the event list. It is □ossible to filter the event list and obtain the □ertinent o□eration events (Yu et al., 2016). Four aspects of the combined query are supported by the current event list, with the necessary information provided below:

- **Type of Resource, Type of Event, and Type of Filter:** From the dropdown menu, you can select the relevant query conditions. Select "CloudTable" as the event source by default. You have two options for the resource type: either choose "All Resource Types" or enter a single resource ty□e. You have two □ossibilities for the filter ty□e: "All Filter Types" or one of the following: "By Event Name," "By Resource ID," or "By Resource Name."
- **The User for Operations:** From the dropdown menu, you can select a s□ecific o□eration user that is at the user level rather than the tenant level (Torkura et al., 2021).
- **Event Level:** "All Event Levels," "Normal," "Warning," and "Incident" are the options offered. One can only select one of them (Yu et al., 2015).
- **The Start and Finish Times:** You can obtain operation events by giving a suitable time interval.

SUMMARY

- Database security involves implementing different measures to protect databases against data breaches, unauthorized access, and other potential security risks.
- Managing database security requires the establishment and enforcement of policies, the implementation of controls, and the prompt response to security incidents in order to protect valuable database assets.
- The database security framework encompasses various aspects such as network security, operating system security, and database management system (DBMS) security to ensure a comprehensive level of protection.
- DBMS vendors offer a range of security features that improve database security. These include access controls, encryption, audit trails, and fine-grained access controls. These measures are designed to enhance the overall security of the database.
- Access control is responsible for managing user access to database resources. This is done through various mechanisms such as authentication, authorization, and access rights management.
- Managing user permissions within a database involves the control of user access to database objects, including defining, modifying, and controlling access.
- Cloud audit services provide functionalities to monitor and analyze activities in cloud-based databases, enabling compliance, threat detection, and incident investigation.

REVIEW QUESTIONS

1. What are the primary components of database security features, and how do they contribute to overall security?
2. Explain the concept of database security management and its significance in □rotecting sensitive data.
3. Describe the database security framework and its role in establishing a comprehensive security strategy.
4. Discuss the key features of database security mechanisms and their im□lementation in safeguarding data integrity and confidentiality.
5. How does access control work in database security, and what are the different methods of controlling access to database resources?

6. What is user permission control, and why is it essential for managing user access in database systems?
7. Explain the concept of cloud audit services and their importance in ensuring compliance and security in cloud-based databases

MULTIPLE CHOICE QUESTIONS

1. What is the primary goal of database security?

a. Maximizing data redundancy
b. Ensuring data confidentiality, integrity, and availability
c. Minimizing database performance
d. Increasing data volatility

2. Which of the following is NOT a component of database security?

a. Network Security
b. Operating System Security
c. Database Management System (DBMS) Security
d. Data Encryption

3. What is the purpose of Identity and Access Management (IAM) in database security?

a. Managing user permissions and authentication
b. Optimizing database performance
c. Encrypting database backups
d. Securing network connections

4. Which type of permission allows users to execute specific SQL statements and access or maintain particular database objects?

a. Administrative permission
b. Database permission
c. Object permission
d. System permission

5. What is the main function of Cloud Audit Services?

a. Data encryption
b. Database backup
c. Log auditing and monitoring
d. Network firewall management

6. Which of the following operations is not supported by IAM in relation to GaussDB (for MySQL)?

a. Fine-grained permission management

b. User authentication

c. Delegating resource management

d. Creating database instances

Answers to Multiple Choice Questions

1. (b); 2. (d); 3. (a); 4. (c); 5. (c); 6. (d)

REFERENCES

1. Ainsworth, S., & Jones, T. M. (2020). MarkUs: Drop-in use-after-free prevention for low-level languages. In *2020 IEEE Symposium on Security and Privacy (SP)* (Vol. 1, pp. 578–591).
2. Archer Jr, J. E., Conway, R., & Schneider, F. B. (1984). User recovery and reversal in interactive systems. *ACM Transactions on Programming Languages and Systems (TOPLAS), 6*(1), 1–19.
3. Bannon, R., Chin, A., Kassam, F., Roszko, A., & Holt, R. (2002). MySQL conceptual architecture. *Technical Report*, University of Waterloo, *3*(1), 100–200.
4. Davidson, L., & Davidson, L. (2021). Database Security and Security Patterns. Pro SQL Server Relational Database Design and Implementation: Best Practices for Scalability and Performance, 647-771.
5. Barbato, F. (2006). The use of immobilized artificial membrane (IAM) chromatography for determination of lipophilicity. *Current Computer-Aided Drug Design, 2*(4), 341–352.
6. Becchetti, L., & Trovato, G. (2002). The determinants of growth for small and medium sized firms. The role of the availability of external finance. *Small Business Economics, 19*, 291–306.
7. Bendovschi, A. C., & Ionescu, B. Ș. (2015). The ga□ between cloud computing technology and the audit and information security. *Audit Financiar, 13*, 125–390.
8. Bertino, E., & Sandhu, R. (2005). Database security: Concepts, approaches, and challenges. *IEEE Transactions on Dependable and Secure Computing, 2*(1), 2–19.
9. Carnevale, A., Smith, N., & Strohl, J. (2013). The road to recovery. *Community College Journal, 84*(3), 26–200.

10. Christudas, B., & Christudas, B. (2019). MySQL. *Vol 1*, 877–884.
11. Daniels, Z. A., & Baird, H. S. (2013). Discriminating features for writer identification. In *2013 12th International Conference on Document Analysis and Recognition* (Vol. 2, pp. 1385–1389).
12. Denton, J. W., & Peace, A. G. (2003). Selection and use of MySQL in a database management course. *Journal of Information Systems Education, 14*(4), 401.
13. Dipina Damodaran, B., Salim, S., & Vargese, S. M. (2016). Performance evaluation of MySQL and MongoDB databases. *International Journal of Cybernetics and Informatics (IJCI), 5*, 387–394.
14. Dong, H., Wu, C., Wei, Z., & Guo, Y. (2017). Dropping activation outputs with localized first-layer dee□ network for enhancing user □rivacy and data security. *IEEE Transactions on Information Forensics and Security, 13*(3), 662–670.
15. Ellickson, P., Bui, K., Bell, R., & McGuigan, K. A. (1998). Does early drug use increase the risk of dropping out of high school? *Journal of Drug Issues, 28*(2), 357–380.
16. Ermondi, G., Vallaro, M., & Caron, G. (2018). Learning how to use IAM chromatography for predicting permeability. *European Journal of Pharmaceutical Sciences, 114*, 385–390.
17. Hagan, H., Jarlais, D. C., Friedman, S. R., Purchase, D., & Alter, M. J. (1995). Reduced risk of hepatitis B and hepatitis C among injection drug users in the Tacoma syringe exchange program. *American Journal of Public Health, 85*(11), 1531–1537.
18. Huawei Technologies Co., Ltd. (2022). Database security fundamentals. In *Database Principles and Technologies–Based on Huawei GaussDB* (Vol. 2, pp. 167–187).
19. Iam-On, N., Boongeon, T., Garrett, S., & Price, C. (2010). A link-based cluster ensemble approach for categorical data clustering. *IEEE Transactions on Knowledge and Data Engineering, 24*(3), 413–425.
20. Indu, I., & Anand, P. R. (2016). Hybrid authentication and authorization model for web-based applications. In *2016 International Conference on Wireless Communications, Signal Processing and Networking (WiSPNET)* (Vol. 3, pp. 1187–1191).
21. Khodakivska, L., Plaksiienko, V., & Hrybovska, Y. (2019). Internal audit and cloud information security. *Економіка та Держава*, (10), 26–30.
22. Kosuge, T., Mizuguchi, Y., Shimizu, T., Arima, Y., Yokomuro, S., Yoshida, H., & Takizawa, T. (2010). Identification of obstructive jaundice-related microRNAs in mouse liver. *Hepato-Gastroenterology, 57*, 1013–1023.

23. Kromann, F. M., & Kromann, F. M. (2018). MySQL views. In *Beginning PHP and MySQL: From Novice to Professional* (Vol. 3, pp. 733–750).

24. Kudo, M., & Hada, S. (2000). XML document security based on provisional authorization. In *Proceedings of the 7th ACM Conference on Computer and Communications Security* (Vol. 1, pp. 87–96).

25. Larson, D., & Chang, V. (2016). A review and future direction of agile, business intelligence, analytics and data science. *International Journal of Information Management, 36*(5), 700–710.

26. Li, J., Li, J., Xie, D., & Cai, Z. (2015). Secure auditing and deduplicating data in the cloud. *IEEE Transactions on Computers, 65*(8), 2386–2396.

27. Lin, S., Marathe, A. P., Larson, P. Å., Chen, C., Sun, C., Lee, P., & Zhuxii, Q. (2022). Near data processing in Taurus database. In *2022 IEEE 38th International Conference on Data Engineering (ICDE)* (Vol. 1, pp. 1662–1674).

28. Ma, Y., Xie, S., Zhong, H., Lee, L., & Lv, K. (2022). Hiengine: How to architect a cloud-native memory-optimized database engine. In *Proceedings of the 2022 International Conference on Management of Data* (Vol. 5, pp. 2177–2190).

29. Madyatmadja, E. D., & Adora, C. (2019). Designing and using a MySQL database for human resource management. *Advances in Science, Technology and Engineering Systems, 4*(6), 285–290.

30. Maesaroh, S., Gunawan, H., Lestari, A., Tsaurie, M. S. A., & Fauji, M. (2022). Query optimization in MySQL database using index. *International Journal of Cyber and IT Service Management, 2*(2), 104–110.

31. Mangiuc, D. M. (2014). Adapting audit to the cloud: A proposal. In *Proceedings of the 9th International Conference Accounting and Management Information Systems (AMIS 2014)* (Vol. 1, pp. 285–298). Editura ASE, București.

32. Marathe, A. P., Lin, S., Yu, W., El Gebaly, K., Larson, P. Å., & Sun, C. (2022). Integrating the Orca optimizer into MySQL. In *EDBT* (Vol. 3, pp. 2–511).

33. Marti, U. V., & Bunke, H. (2002). The IAM-database: An English sentence database for offline handwriting recognition. *International Journal on Document Analysis and Recognition, 5*, 39–46.

34. Modest, A. M., Wise, L. A., Fox, M. P., Weuve, J., Penzias, A. S., & Hacker, M. R. (2018). IVF success corrected for drop-out: Use of inverse probability weighting. *Human Reproduction, 33*(12), 2295–2301.

35. Moghadasi, M., Mousavi, S. M., & Fazekas, G. (2018). Cloud computing

auditing. *International Journal of Advanced Computer Science and Applications, 9*(12), 23–100.

36. Mohammed, I. A. (2013). Intelligent authentication for identity and access management: A review paper. *International Journal of Management, IT and Engineering (IJMIE), 3*(1), 696–705.
37. Neto, A. A., & Vieira, M. (2008). Towards assessing the security of DBMS configurations. In *2008 IEEE International Conference on Dependable Systems and Networks with FTCS and DCC (DSN)* (Vol. 1, pp. 90–95).
38. Parker, P., Letcher, R., Jakeman, A., Beck, M. B., Harris, G., Argent, R. M., & Bin, S. (2002). Progress in integrated assessment and modelling. *Environmental Modelling & Software, 17*(3), 209–217.
39. Pawar, M. V., & Anuradha, J. (2015). Network security and types of attacks in network. *Procedia Computer Science, 48*, 503–506.
40. Pernul, G. (1994). Database security. In *Advances in Computers* (Vol. 38, pp. 1–72).
41. Pierce, S. K., & Politis, A. D. (1990). Ca^{2+}-activated cell volume recovery mechanisms. *Annual Review of Physiology, 52*(1), 27–42.
42. Polychronaki, M., Kogias, D. G., Leligkou, H. C., & Karkazis, P. A. (2023). Blockchain technology for access and authorization management in the Internet of Things. *Electronics, 12*(22), 4606.
43. Rawat, B., & Purnama, S. (2021). MySQL Database Management System (DBMS) on FTP Site LAPAN Bandung. *International Journal of Cyber and IT Service Management, 1*(2), 173–179.
44. Sharma, D. H., Dhote, C. A., & Potey, M. M. (2016). Identity and access management as security-as-a-service from clouds. *Procedia Computer Science, 79*, 170–174.
45. Shehab, M., & Marouf, S. (2012). Recommendation models for open authorization. *IEEE Transactions on Dependable and Secure Computing, 9*(4), 583–596.
46. Shehab, M., Marouf, S., & Hudel, C. (2011). ROAuth: Recommendation based open authorization. In *Proceedings of the Seventh Symposium on Usable Privacy and Security* (Vol. 8, pp. 1–12).
47. Simeone, A. L., Mavridou, I., & Powell, W. (2017). Altering user movement behavior in virtual environments. *IEEE Transactions on Visualization and Computer Graphics, 23*(4), 1312–1321.
48. Singh, C., Thakkar, R., & Warraich, J. (2023). IAM identity access management—Importance in maintaining security systems within

organizations. *European Journal of Engineering and Technology Research, 8*(4), 30–38.

49. Torkura, K. A., Sukmana, M. I., Cheng, F., & Meinel, C. (2021). Continuous auditing and threat detection in multi-cloud infrastructure. *Computers & Security, 102*, 102–124.
50. Wang, Y., Xi, J., & Cheng, T. (2021). The overview of database security threats' solutions: Traditional and machine learning. *Journal of Information Security, 12*(01), 34.
51. Yu, J., Ren, K., & Wang, C. (2016). Enabling cloud storage auditing with verifiable outsourcing of key u□dates. *IEEE Transactions on Information Forensics and Security, 11*(6), 1362–1375.
52. Yu, J., Ren, K., Wang, C., & Varadharajan, V. (2015). Enabling cloud storage auditing with key-exposure resistance. *IEEE Transactions on Information Forensics and Security, 10*(6), 1167–1179.
53. Zhang, H., Ramakrishnan, T. S., Nikolov, A., & Wasan, D. (2016). Enhanced oil recovery driven by nanofilm structural disjoining □ressure: Flooding experiments and micro visualization. *Energy & Fuels, 30*(4), 2771–2779.
54. Ziaratban, M., Faez, K., & Bagheri, F. (2009). FHT: An unconstraint Farsi handwritten text database. In *2009 10th International Conference on Document Analysis and Recognition* (pp. 281–285).

CHAPTER 3

DATABASE SECURITY THREATS AND PREVENTION

LEARNING OBJECTIVES

At the end of this chapter, readers will be able to:

1. Understand the key aspects of database security: confidentiality, integrity, and availability;
2. Understand common security threats to databases and their origins;
3. Understand the top 10 security threats in databases and how they operate;
4. Know preventive measures for addressing SQL injection attacks;
5. Explore strategies for preventing privilege abuse and escalation; and
6. Gain insights into mitigating vulnerabilities in vulnerable or incorrectly configured databases.

INTRODUCTORY EXAMPLE

TechSecure Inc. is a leading technology firm renowned for its innovative database solutions. However, despite its stellar reputation, the company recently faced a significant setback due to a security breach in its database system.

In a recent incident, hackers exploited a vulnerability in TechSecure's web application, gaining unauthorized access to its customer database. Through a sophisticated SQL injection attack, the attackers managed to bypass authentication measures and extract sensitive customer information, including names, addresses, and payment details.

This breach not only resulted in financial losses for TechSecure but also severely tarnished its reputation as a provider of secure database solutions. In the aftermath of the attack, TechSecure's team scrambled to investigate the breach, assess the extent of the damage, and implement robust preventive measures to fortify its database security defenses.

This incident serves as a reminder of the critical importance of database security in safeguarding sensitive information and maintaining the trust of customers and stakeholders. As organizations increasingly rely on databases to store and manage vast amounts of data, ensuring robust security measures becomes imperative to mitigate the risks posed by evolving security threats. Through proactive measures and diligent security practices, companies like TechSecure can strengthen their database security posture and defend against potential breaches.

UNIT INTRODUCTION

In today's modern era, data has become a powerful catalyst, completely altering the way people and institutions function. Over time, it has become a valuable strategic asset that can generate valuable insights and promote innovation. Whether it's managing personal finances or making informed business decisions, data plays a crucial role in today's world. At the center of this data ecosystem lies the database, an administrative center that stores interconnected datasets crucial to an organization's operations and goals. The database enables firms to enhance productivity and explore new possibilities by utilizing the abundance of information available to them (Sarmah, 2019).

However, as data-driven practices become more prevalent, a multitude of security challenges arise. Fraudulent individuals are constantly on alert to look for weaknesses in databases, with the intention of compromising the security and privacy of sensitive information. Ensuring proper security measures is crucial to safeguarding valuable data and protecting it from unauthorized access. Failure to do so can result in severe consequences, such as data breaches and the exposure of sensitive information to external threats. In addition, the unauthorized disclosure of sensitive data can have significant implications, putting the organization's competitive edge at risk and eroding trust among stakeholder (Patil et al., 2020).

Considering possible risks, it is absolutely crucial to prioritize the protection and maintenance of the database's integrity and security. When it comes to database security, there are various aspects to consider preventing unauthorized access, minimizing the chances of errors, and protecting against data loss or corruption. Similar to the way valuable possessions are protected with strict security measures, the organization must implement strong safeguards to protect the integrity and confidentiality of their data assets stored in the database (Hutchings et al., 2013).

At various levels, database security covers physical, data, network, application, and host aspects. Every layer of security has been carefully created to strengthen the database against any potential threats and vulnerabilities, guaranteeing complete safeguarding of valuable information assets. Organizations can enhance the security of their database infrastructure and protect against malicious activities by implementing strict access controls, encryption protocols, and intrusion detection systems (Deshpande et al., 2015).

3.1. ASPECTS OF DATABASE SECURITY

Learning Objective

- Understand the CIA Triad model and its significance in database security.

The CIA Triad, consisting of Confidentiality, Integrity, and Availability, is a model used to establish security rules for databases. It helps detect potential threats and determine suitable solutions to assure information security (Denning, 1988). A comprehensive data security(Figure 3.1) solution must fulfill the following three requirements:

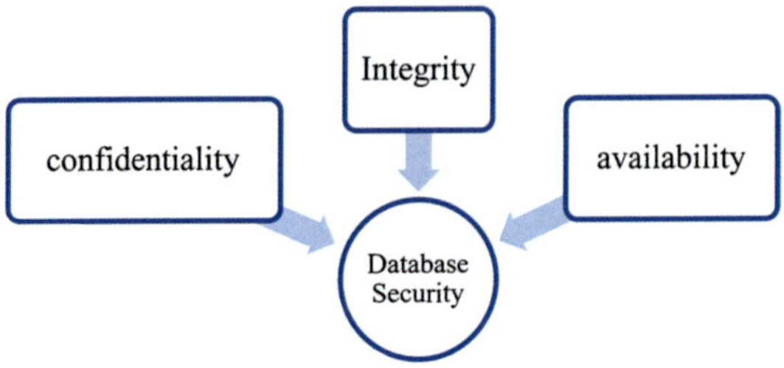

Figure 3.1. *Illustration of database security aspects.*

Source: Sandeep Reddy Creative Commons License.

3.1.1. Confidentiality

Confidentiality ensures authorized individuals or entities can only access that information. It involves protecting confidential information against unlawful entry, disclosure, or exposure. Confidentiality measures are taken to maintain the privacy and confidentiality of information, protecting it from unauthorized access, hackers, or harmful individuals (Kaiser, 2012). Implementing confidentiality involves using a range of tactics and procedures, which may include:

- **Access Control:** Access control mechanisms are used to limit access to sensitive information, following the principle of least privilege. It is essential to establish a system that grants access to specific information or resources only to authorized users (Gillon, 1985).
- **Encryption:** Encryption involves the transformation of plain data into unreadable ciphertext through the use of cryptographic algorithms. Database security is crucial in safeguarding data from unauthorized access. It ensures that data remains secure during storage, transmission, and processing, making it unreadable to anyone without the proper decryption key (Fischel, 1998).
- **Data Masking:** One important aspect of data security is the practice of data masking. This technique involves the replacement of sensitive information with fictional or altered data. The purpose is to ensure the confidentiality of the data while still allowing authorized users to access and utilize it. This technique is frequently used in non-production environments to protect against unauthorized access to sensitive data (Paulsson & Rawding, 1995).

3.1.2. Integrity

Integrity guarantees that information maintains its accuracy, dependability, and coherence during its entire lifespan. Data security include safeguarding information from unlawful modification, alteration, or manipulation. Preserving data integrity is essential for guaranteeing the credibility and dependability of information (Taylor, G., & Gaita, R. (1981).

Effective strategies for maintaining the accuracy and reliability of data encompass:

- **Data Validation:** Data validation procedures are used to validate the accuracy and authenticity of data input. This helps reduce errors, discrepancies, or malevolent inputs that have the potential to compromise the integrity of the data (Cox et al., 2014).
- **Checksums and Hashing:** Checksums and hashing techniques are utilized to provide distinct IDs (checksums or hashes) for sets of data. These identifiers can be utilized to authenticate data integrity by comparing the computed checksum or hash value with the original value.
- **Digital Signatures:** Digital signatures are cryptographic techniques used to verify the originality and authenticity of digital documents or messages. They offer a means to authenticate that a communication or document has remained unaltered or untampered with during its transit (Clark & Fujimoto, 1990).

3.1.3. Availability

Availability ensures that authorized users can access information and resources promptly and without interruption when necessary. It involves the prevention or reduction of disruptions or downtime that could affect the availability of essential systems or services (Bhagwan et al., 2003).

Strategies for guaranteeing availability include:

a) **Redundancy:** Redundancy refers to the act of replicating essential systems, components, or resources in order to guarantee the uninterrupted functioning of activities in case of hardware failures or other disturbances. Redundancy can be used at many levels, such as network infrastructure, hardware, and information storage (Kantor, 1976).

b) **Failover Systems:** Failover systems are designed to effortlessly redirect traffic or resources to backu□systems or servers in case of any failure or outage. This ensures minimal downtime and guarantees uninterrupted access to services.

c) **Backups and Disaster Recovery:** It is important to have regular backups and disaster recovery plans in place to minimize the consequences of data loss or system failures. Offsite storage of backup copies ensures that data and systems can be readily restored in case of any unforeseen disasters or failures (Kestin, 1980).

Understanding the CIA triad is essential for evaluating and implementing security measures to safeguard information assets. Organizations may efficiently reduce security risks and threats by □rioritizing confidentiality, integrity, and availability. This approach ensures the protection of sensitive data and the uninterrupted operation of critical systems and services (Chalmers, 1997).

3.2. ORIGIN OF SECURITY THREATS

Learning Objective

- Understand the different sources of security threats: internal, external.

There are multiple sources from which security threats can originate, including both internal and external factors.

3.2.1. Internal

These incidents arise internally within the business and involve persons who have authorized access to the database. Internal dangers encompass behaviors such as staff fraud, insider assaults, and negligence. Employee misconduct can include activities such as unauthorized access or data theft, whereas insider attacks may include harmful actions carried out by persons who possess privileged access. Negligence include unintentional actions or omissions that weaken the security of a database, such as misconfigurations or failure to adhere to security guidelines (Bartnik, 2021).

3.2.2. External

External threats originate from sources outside the organization and are caused by individuals or entities aiming to take advantage of weaknesses in the database or its infrastructure. Examples include breaches of data, and denial-of-service (DoS) attacks. Cyberattacks include a range of methods that try to illegally access systems, take confidential information, or disrupt normal operations. Data breaches occur when attackers effectively access the database to extract valuable information with malicious goals. Denial-of-service attacks have the objective of overflowing the database's server or its infrastructure with an excessive number of requests, resulting in service outages or periods of inactivity (Myrick, 2021).

3.3. DATABASE SECURITY THREATS

Learning Objectives

- Understand the top 10 security threats in databases;
- Learn how SQL injection, excessive privilege abuse, and other threats work; and
- Comprehend the vulnerabilities in database communication protocols and their prevention.

Usually, the primary risk associated with an attack is determined by three factors: threats, vulnerabilities, and impacts (Al-Sayid & Aldlaeen, 2013) (Figure 3.2). This section presents the top 10 security threats in databases and provides an explanation of how they operate:

- SQL Injection
- Excessive Privilege Abuse
- Abuse of Legitimate Privilege
- Privilege Escalation

Figure 3.2. *Representation of database security threats.*

Source: Hassan Bediar Creative Commons License

- Exploitation of Vulnerabilities in Vulnerable or Incorrectly Configured Databases
- Weakness of the Native Audit
- Denial of Service
- Vulnerabilities of Database Communication Protocols
- Unauthorized Copying of Sensitive Data
- Exposure of Backup Data (Mousa et al., 2020)

3.3.1. SQL Injection

During a SQL injection attack, the attacker usually inserts unauthorized database information into a vulnerable SQL data string, bypassing security measures. In many cases, the data strings that are affected are the stored procedures and input settings used in web applications. The injected information is transmitted to the database and subsequently executed. Through the exploitation of SQL injection (Figure 3.3) vulnerabilities, malicious individuals can obtain full access to an entire database (Halfond et al., 2006).

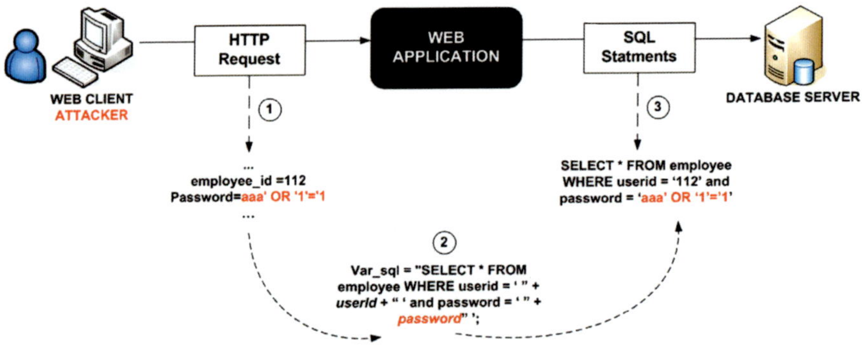

Figure 3.3. *Illustration of SQL injection attack.*

Source: Klassen Ed. Creative Commons License.

3.3.2. Excessive Privilege Abuse

When individuals or applications have access to databases beyond what is necessary for their professional requirements, it creates opportunities for misuse. For example, a university dean who is responsible for keeping student contact information up to date. However, if given extensive privileges to the database, individuals could potentially misuse this access to manipulate grades. Many times, users find themselves with privileges they don't need due to database administrators not having enough time to customize access controls for each person (Strassberg, 2006). As a result, access privileges are often too broad, applying to entire user groups instead of specific functions. Lacking attention to this matter exposes databases to potential misuse, as certain individuals could take advantage of excessive permissions for malicious intentions. To address this potential risk, administrators must establish and consistently maintain accurate access controls that are specifically designed to meet the professional needs of users. This will help create a more secure environment for the database (Dalton, 2012).

3.3.3. Abuse of Legitimate Privilege

It is important to note that individuals with authorized access to a database may sometimes misuse their privileges for unauthorized activities. Consider a hypothetical scenario where a health official, who possesses certain privileges, gains access to patients' medical records via a specialized web application. In most cases, the access of users in a web application are restricted to only being able to view the medical record of one patient at a time and are unable to view multiple folders at the same time, as well as electronic copies are prohibited. However, the potential attackers can bypass these restrictions by establishing a connection to the database through alternative methods like MS-Excel (Aravindharamanan et al., 2019).

By utilizing MS-Excel and the appropriate login credentials, employees can access and modify patient medical records. It is uncertain whether these personal copies of patient record databases follow the regulations set by medical institutions for safeguarding patient data. It is important to take into consideration two potential risks (Higgins, 1985). One example is a fraudulent individual who attem□ts to □rofit from selling □atients' medical records. Another common scenario involves an employee who, for legitimate business reasons, retrieves and backs u□a significant amount of data on their client's com□uter. However, due to negligence, this action can pose a security risk. Once data is backed up on another computer, it becomes susceptible to various security risks such as Trojan horses and laptop theft (Strassberg, 2006).

3.3.4. Privilege Escalation

Attackers can exploit weaknesses in database platform software, using them to give regular users the same access privileges as administrators. Such vulnerabilities often appear in stored processes, protocol implementations, and sometimes within SQL data structures (Yamauchi et al., 2021).

Consider a situation where a software develo□er working at a financial institution comes across a function that has a vulnerability. This vulnerability gives them the ability to gain access to the database with administrator privileges. Given the elevated permissions, the developer with malicious intentions can disable auditing mechanisms, create ghost accounts without detection, mani□ulate financial data, and carry out unauthorized fund transfers (Kujanpää et al., 2021).

In addition, the □otential consequences of such ex□loitation are significant, financial losses, encom□assing breaches of data, and com□romised confidentiality of sensitive information. Therefore, organizations must take proactive measures in identifying and addressing potential vulnerabilities. This is essential to protect against potential exploitation and minimize the risks posed by malicious individuals (Song et al., 2006).

3.3.5. Exploitation of Vulnerabilities in Vulnerable or Incorrectly Configured Databases

Database security is an important concern, as databases can be prone to vulnerabilities, lack of updates, and default account and configuration settings. Despite efforts by vendors to address system weaknesses with patch packs, enterprise databases continue to be vulnerable to exploitation. After the release of a hotfix, it may take some time before it becomes accessible. When it comes to applying a hotfix to a database, there are various factors that need to be taken into account (Martin, 2001).

Before implementation, the organization should assess the system repair a□□roach by examining how the fix would im□act the system. Occasionally, a solution may clash with preexisting code or need additional processes. Then, the system encounters a period of inactivity due to the failure of the database server to deliver the necessary service to users. Finally, major corporations with several databases must establish an improvement strategy, giving priority to the databases that require corrections first (Bisho□, 1999).

Therefore, it is predictable to observe that the correction procedure for numerous firms s□ans several months, often ranging from 6 to 9 months (as determined by research done by the independent group of Oracle users known as IOUG). The fixing □rocess involves the □artici□ation of individuals such as database administrators, system administrators, IT administrators, and developers. Despite the limited availability of resources and time, servers continue to be susceptible to vulnerabilities for an extended period of time following the implementation of a patch (Nayak et al., 2014).

An attacker may take advantage of default account and configuration options that are always enabled on a production database. A potential intruder may try to gain unauthorized access to the database by exploiting a default account. An inadequate audit configuration could enable the attacker to by□ass audit trails or eliminate any evidence of their actions. Attackers may use weak identification □atterns to □retend as authorized users of databases by stealing or acquiring login credentials (Medeiros et al., 2014).

3.3.6. Weakness of the Native Audit

It is important to have a system in place that automatically registers all sensitive and/or unusual database transactions as the foundation of any database deployment. A weak database auditing rule can pose a significant risk to an organization at various levels (Ettredge & Sun, 2006).

3.3.6.1. Regulatory Risk

Organizations that lack proper database auditing mechanisms are increasingly dealing with legal challenges related to government regulations. For example, the Sarbanes-Oxley (SOX) Act regulates financial services and requires strict auditing practices to guarantee the integrity and accountability of data. In the healthcare sector, there are strict auditing standards imposed by the Healthcare Information Portability and Accountability Act (HIPAA) to ensure the protection of patient information (Black, 2006). Failure to implement strong auditing measures not only puts regulatory compliance at risk but also leaves organizations vulnerable to potential legal consequences and harm to their reputation. Therefore, organizations need to strengthen their database auditing mechanisms to comply with changing regulatory requirements and safeguard sensitive data efficiently (Larsen & Bunn, 1999).

3.3.6.2. Deterrence

Similar to how surveillance cameras keep an eye on people going into a bank, auditing of database mechanisms serves as an obstacle to potential attackers. These systems highlight the importance of monitoring database audits, as they provide investigators with valuable forensic insights into the individuals responsible for a crime (Geerken & Gove, 1974). Similar to how visible security measures can discourage potential intruders, implementing thorough database auditing can act as a digital deterrent, significantly improving data security and preventing malicious individuals from gaining unauthorized access or tampering with sensitive information (Jacobs, 2010).

3.3.6.3. Detection and Recovery

Ensuring the security of databases requires a strong focus on detection and recovery, with auditing playing a crucial role as the final line of defense. If initial defense systems are compromised by attackers, audits play a crucial role in detecting violations after the attack (Horning et al., 1985). Through careful examination of audit results, organizations can track down any violations to individual users and take the appropriate steps to fix any issues within the system. While many database software options do have basic auditing capabilities, they often have vulnerabilities that may hinder their successful implementation. These vulnerabilities can vary from limited functionalities to complete prevention of deployment, requiring organizations to enhance native auditing skills with specialized tools or solutions to ensure thorough detection and recovery strategies. Improving these procedures strengthens the security of databases, reduces the risk of potential harm, and boosts overall resistance to cyber threats (Strickland & Hahn, 1997).

3.3.6.4. Lack of User Accountability

Ensuring user accountability becomes a major hurdle, especially when it comes to accessing databases using web applications such as Oracle, SAP, or PeopleSoft. Commonly, audit mechanisms that are native to systems may not possess the ability to distinguish the specific identities of users. As a result, the account name of the web application is responsible for all user activities, making it difficult to determine who should be held accountable (Vance et al., 2015). When investigating native audit findings that identify deceptive database transactions, the lack of ability to connect these actions to individual users adds complexity to the investigation and attribution process. This restriction weakens the ability of audit trails to ensure individual accountability in the database environment. To tackle this problem, organizations might consider implementing additional measures, such as user authentication protocols or improved audit logging mechanisms, to guarantee precise user identification and accountability for database activities (Koh & Heng, 1996).

3.3.6.5. Performance Degradation

Native database auditing mechanisms often lead to performance degradation due to their heavy consumption of CPU and hard disk resources. Implementing auditing features can result in significant performance consequences, causing organizations to consider reducing the frequency of audits or disabling them entirely (Lee, 1996). The delicate balance between performance and security highlights the importance of implementing efficient auditing solutions that optimize resource usage while ensuring strong defense against potential risks (Jamil et al., 2017).

3.3.6.6. Feature Separation

Administrative users, whether obtained legally or through malicious methods, can deactivate audit features on the database server, hiding any fraudulent activities. For enhanced security measures, it is essential to ensure that audit functions are separate from the access rights of database administrators and the functionalities of the server platform (Zuo et al., 2005). Through a separation of roles, organizations can strengthen transparency and accountability, guaranteeing the preservation of crucial audit trails, even when administrative access is present (Lin & Zhang, 2005).

3.3.6.7. Limited Granularity

Several native auditing mechanisms do not possess the necessary data recording capabilities that are essential for identifying attacks and aiding in forensic analysis and recovery. It is quite common for important information, such as details about database client applications, source IP addresses, query response items, and failed queries (which can be a strong indicator of potential attacks), to go unnoticed and remain unregistered (Kuwano & Hatano, 2011). The lack of these functionalities significantly reduces the ability of native mechanisms to detect and respond to security breaches. This emphasizes the need to enhance auditing systems with additional features in order to ensure strong threat detection and mitigation capabilities (Du & Lowery, 2011).

3.3.6.8. Owner

The auditing mechanisms are closely linked to the database server platform, such as Oracle, MS-SQL, Sybase, and others, which produce unique outcomes. The variability in database settings can be quite challenging for organizations that need to manage multiple databases. It can make it difficult to implement standardized and scalable auditing procedures across the entire enterprise (Winch & Leiringer, 2016). The absence of consistency adds complexity to streamlining security practices and undermines the capacity to efficiently collect and evaluate audit data. As a result, organizations might find it challenging to ensure consistent oversight and response capabilities. This highlights the significance of implementing flexible auditing solutions that can adapt to various database environments (Down, 1999).

3.3.7. Denial of Service

Denial of Service (DOS) is a broad category of attacks that restricts certain users from accessing network applications. Various techniques can be used to create denial of service conditions, many of which are linked to the vulnerabilities mentioned earlier. As an example, a server can be compromised by exploiting a vulnerability in a database platform, resulting in a denial of service. Additional denial of service techniques involve data corruption, network congestion, and the strain on server resources such as memory and CPU (Needham, 1993).

Overloading resources is a widely used technique in database environments. There is a wide range of motivations behind denial of service attacks. Denial of service attacks are often associated with attempts to demand money, where a hacker installs servers remotely until the victim transfers funds to an international bank account. Denial of service can also be associated with a computer worm infection. Regardless of the origin, denial of service poses a significant threat to numerous organizations (Borisov et al., 2007).

Practice Problems

TeHN Corporation, a leading provider in the technology sector, s currently facing a significant issue with its database server, resulting in a noticeable decrease in performance. This has caused inconvenience for users who are struggling to access crucial information. After careful examination, it has been determined that the server is being inundated with an excessive number of requests, leading to a denial of service (DoS) attack. This incident has severely impacted the regular functioning of the business and has put critical data at risk.

Solutions to Practice Problems

In order to address the issue of denial of service (DoS) attacks, TeHN Corporation has implemented a number of preventive measures. Initially, intrusion prevention systems (IPS) are used to identify and prevent any harmful traffic that may be directed toward the database server. In addition, access control mechanisms are configured to limit unauthorized access and prevent excessive resource consumption. The company implements resource limits to minimize the impact of DoS attacks, ensuring that the database server can maintain optimal performance even during high-traffic periods. Implementing regular security updates and monitoring is crucial in identifying and addressing potential vulnerabilities, which strengthens the resilience of the database infrastructure against DoS attacks.

3.3.8. Vulnerabilities of Database Communication Protocols

Database communication protocols designed by various database providers are increasingly being found to have security vulnerabilities. Various malicious activities may take advantage of these vulnerabilities, leading to unauthorized access to data, manipulation of data, and disruption of services. A case that exemplifies this is the SQL slammer2 computer worm, which took advantage of a vulnerability in the Microsoft SQL server protocol to induce a denial of service. It is important to note that the lack of documentation on these specific instances of fraud in audit journalism further complicates matters (Geneiatakis et al., 2006). This is due to the fact that most native database audit mechanisms do not encompass all protocol operations. Protecting against attacks on database communication protocols. Protocol validation is a technology that can effectively address database communication protocol attacks. Protocol validation technology disassembles database traffic and compares it to traffic predictions. If the actual traffic does not align with the forecasts, it may be necessary to implement alerts or blocking actions (Imtiaz & Arshad, 2019).

3.3.9. Unauthorized Copying of Sensitive Data

Numerous organizations are working carefully to identify and effectively manage a comprehensive list of their databases. Creating new databases without the knowledge of the security team can lead to potential risks, as sensitive data copied to these databases may be vulnerable if proper controls are not implemented. These concealed databases may contain sensitive information, including transaction details and contact information of customers and employees. Nevertheless, without a comprehensive understanding of the database contents, it becomes challenging to guarantee the implementation of essential security measures (Hansen & Walden, 2013).

Whether it's done deliberately or accidentally, unauthorized individuals, be it em□loyees or hackers, can gain illegal access to valuable and confidential information. An example would be databases that have been neglected and overlooked over time. Without proper management, the databases are vulnerable to unauthorized access, exposing sensitive data to potential threats (Hsieh & Yeh, 2012).

3.3.10. Exposure of Backup Data

It is common for auxiliary database backup devices to lack protection against potential attacks. Due to various security breaches, there have been instances of hard disks and database backup tapes being stolen (Karame et al., 2017).

3.4. PREVENTIVE MEASURE FOR DATABASE SECURITY

Learning objectives

- Understand preventive measures for common database security threats.
- Understand strategies to prevent SQL injection and excessive privilege abuse.
- Explore methods to mitigate vulnerabilities and prevent privilege escalation.
- Discover techniques to prevent denial of service attacks and unauthorized data copying.

A database is an essential component of any company, serving as its foundation. Hence, the firm must choose any security solution. The use of threat prevention measures can guarantee the security of both the data stored within the system and the physical components of the database, including hardware, software, and human resources. Detailed descriptions of preventive measures for data threats are provided (Anwar et al., 2007).

3.4.1. Prevention of SQL Injection

To effectively resist SQL injection, three strategies can be combined: Intrusion Prevention Technology (IPS), Request Access Control (specifically Excessive Privilege Override), and Event Correlation. The IPS system can detect the most susceptible stored processes or SQL injection strings. Relying only on an IPS (Intrusion Prevention System) is not reliable due to the high number of false positives generated by SQL injection attacks. Security officials who exclusively depend on IPS technology would receive a constant stream of alerts regarding potential SQL injections (Alwan & Younis, 2017).

In practical terms, it is possible to accurately identify a real attack by constructing a SQL injection signature with a different type of violation, such as a request access control violation. It is extremely unlikely for a typical business operation to have both a SQL injection signature and another type of violation in the same query (Ghafarian, 2017).

3.4.2. Prevention of Excessive Privilege Abuse

An effective approach to addressing the issue of excessive privilege abuses is by eliminating unnecessary rights. It is essential to recognize and address unnecessary user rights, which go beyond what is required for their specific tasks. This process involves extracting the permissions from the databases, matching them with the corresponding business users, and then analyzing these permissions. This process can be quite challenging and time-consuming, especially when performed manually. It demands a significant investment of both time and resources. A streamlined solution can greatly decrease the time and resources required and expedite the analysis process (Mousa et al., 2020).

To improve the execution of access rights, it is necessary to implement access restrictions s□ecifically for detailed inquiries. Query access control is a method that limits access privileges to databases to only essential SQL operations such as SELECT and UPDATE. The level of detail in the data access control has to be expanded beyond the entire table to include individual rows and columns within the same table. An adequately detailed query access control mechanism would permit the previously mentioned malevolent university principal to change student contact information, while simultaneously activating a notification if the student tried to alter the notes. Query access control serves the purpose of not only identifying and addressing instances of unauthorized privilege exploitation by envious employees but also mitigating the majority of the top 10 threats (Lee et al., 2019).

3.4.3. Prevention of Abuse of Legitimate Privilege

Database access control is a crucial solution to address the issue of legitimate privilege abuse. It not only focuses on the specific access requests mentioned earlier but also takes into account the overall context of database access. Through the implementation of a control rule for client applications, along with considering factors such as the time and location of access requests, it becomes feasible to detect users who may be utilizing their authorized database access privileges suspiciously (Rozell, 1984).

3.4.4. Prevention of Privilege Escalation

To prevent privilege escalation abuses, it is recommended to utilize a combination of a traditional Intrusion Prevention System (IPS) and request access control. This approach helps in mitigating the risks associated with excessive privilege abuse, as discussed earlier. An IPS is used to analyze database traffic and detect any patterns that may indicate the presence of known vulnerabilities. For example, when dealing with a susceptible function, an IPS technology has the capability to either restrict all access to the vulnerable procedure or, if feasible, restrict only procedures that contain intentional attacks (Jaafar et al., 2016).

Unfortunately, it can be challenging to s□ecifically target database access requests with s□ecifically integrated attacks using only IPS. Several database functions that are susceptible to security breaches are often used for legitimate reasons. Avoiding the complete blocking of these functions is advisable. PS technology effectively distinguishes between legitimate functions and functions that may contain malicious attacks. It is often challenging to differentiate between attacks with their countless variations (Qiang et al., 2018).

In such circumstances, it is advisable to utilize IPS systems only in alert mode, rather than blocking mode, due to the possibility of encountering false positives. Enhancing precision can be achieved by integrating IPS technology with additional attack indicators, like query access control. An Intrusion Prevention System (IPS) can be utilized to verify if the database access request relies on a susceptible function, whereas request access control manages whether the query aligns with a standard user profile. If a single request suggests access to a vulnerable function or an uncommon user profile, it is highly likely that an attack is underway (Lee et al., 2016).

3.4.5. Prevention of Exploitation of Vulnerabilities in Vulnerable Databases

To reduce the risk posed by unprotected and susceptible databases, it is necessary to initially evaluate the security posture of the databases and fix any detected vulnerabilities and security weaknesses. It is advisable for companies to regularly conduct database scans to identify any existing vulnerabilities and ensure that all necessary patches are installed. The configuration assessments should offer a concise and comprehensive summary of the present configuration status of the data systems. These evaluations should also detect databases that do not adhere to the specified configuration standards (Priyanka & Smruthi, 2020).

It is important to immediately use any security patches that are lacking. If a vulnerability is identified before the patch is ready, either due to the vendor not releasing it or it not being deployed yet, a virtual fix should be established. This method effectively prevents any attempts to take advantage of these vulnerabilities. Applying a virtual patch can reduce the exposure window, so safeguarding the database from exploitation attempts until an official patch is implemented (Mohosina & Zulkernine, 2012).

3.4.6. Prevention of Weakness of Native Audit

Network-quality auditing systems effectively tackle the vulnerabilities commonly found in native auditing tools. Efficient devices that rely on network quality can effortlessly maintain line speed while ensuring optimal database performance. By delegating the task of auditing procedures to network applications, organizations can potentially enhance the performance of databases.

Network-based auditing devices offer the advantage of operating independently from database administrators, ensuring a clear separation between audit and administrative functions. In addition, network devices remain unaffected by privilege escalation attacks from non-administrator users due to their independence from the network (Rahimi & Zargham, 2013).

Network-based auditing devices commonly support popular database platforms, allowing for consistent criteria and centralized auditing procedures across diverse database environments. When these features are combined, they effectively lower the expenses associated with operating the database server, managing the workload distribution, and handling administrative tasks (Kim et al., 2017).

Additionally, they offer enhanced security measures. It is crucial to consistently monitor logs in order to detect potential risks and threats that may pose a threat to databases. Consider a scenario where a malicious individual, commonly referred to as an attacker, manages to surpass existing defense mechanisms. In such cases, audits play a crucial role in detecting violations post-attack. Additionally, logs and audits can aid in system restoration through updates, while also assisting in tracing the origin of the attack back to its perpetrator (Pelechrinis et al., 2010).

3.4.7. Prevention of Denial of Service

Preventing denial of service attacks necessitates implementing protections across various layers. This chapter focuses on the specific security measures required for databases, as well as the necessary protections for networks, applications, and databases.

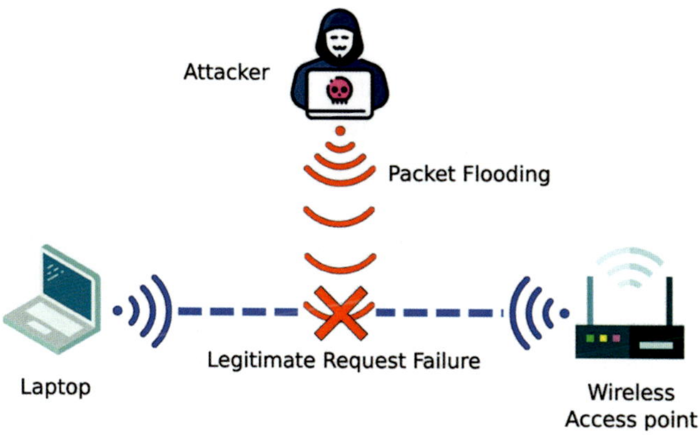

Figure 3.4. *Illustration of denial-of-service attack.*

Source: Edward Staddon Creative Commons License.

It is highly recommended to de□loy a control flow connection, IPS technology, access control applications, and control response time in this □articular scenario. By carefully selecting and configuring the necessary components for a database, it is possible to mitigate the risk of denial of service (DoS) attacks (Figure 3.4). Implementing resource limits is an effective □reventive measure that can significantly hinder attackers from targeting the system. Regularly applying security patches and running security reports are essential practices for administrators to ensure the prevention of DoS attacks and the identification of security vulnerabilities (Mahjabin et al., 2017).

3.4.8. Prevention of Vulnerabilities of Database Communication Protocols

Using protocol validation technology can be a valuable approach in addressing the vulnerabilities associated with database communication protocols. In this technology, the analysis of database traffic involves the examination and comparison of the actual data with the expected data. Scientists are currently developing a mechanism that can offer proactive validation of protocol messages as they travel from clients to servers. Any suspicious message that deviates from the expected pattern are immediately flagged and discarded. This mechanism is highly effective in detecting bugs and worms, as well as preventing both known and unknown vulnerabilities (Xu et al., 2017).

3.4.9. Prevention of Unauthorized Copying of Sensitive Data

For organizations to ensure the authenticity of their inventory of databases and the security of sensitive data, it is crucial to identify all databases on the network that store such information. Next, it is important to determine the specific types of sensitive or classified data that are stored within the objects in the databases. Identifying sensitive data within a vast array of tables poses a significant challenge in data classification (Takebayashi et al., 2010).

One challenge is identifying combinations of data that may seem harmless on their own, but become sensitive when combined with other data. To ensure the proper safeguarding of sensitive information, it is crucial to establish appropriate controls that align with the organization's data access policies. This should be done once a com□rehensive inventory of databases and the identification of sensitive data locations have been completed (Kaur et al., 2017).

3.4.10. Prevention of Exposure of Backup Data

It is crucial to ensure that all database backups are encrypted. In fact, certain vendors have proposed that available database management systems should no longer facilitate the generation of unencrypted backups (Newton, 1985). Many experts recommend encrypting information from online production databases. However, the challenges of managing cryptographic keys can make this solution impractical and it is generally seen as a limited alternative to copyright controls. The access control discussed earlier is highly detailed and specific (Lee et al., 2018).

SUMMARY

- Data is the foundation of the twenty-first century, fueling discoveries and improving operations across a range of industries. Database security, which includes the CIA Triad of confidentiality, integrity, and availability, must be guaranteed. Threats to database security can come from both internal and external sources, presenting hazards at various database infrastructure levels.
- The top 10 security risks encompass SQL injection, privilege abuse, and vulnerability exploitation. To counter these threats, preventive methods such as Intrusion Prevention Technology (IPS), authorization, and vulnerability assessments are necessary.
- Protocol validation and encryption are crucial techniques for reducing the dangers of unwanted data access and exposure.
- Taking proactive measures, such as identifying sensitive data and encrypting backups, is vital for enhancing database security. Organizations can protect their databases from potential risks and guarantee the security, privacy, and accessibility of their valuable data assets by implementing these preventive steps.

REVIEW QUESTIONS

1. How does database security contribute to an organization's overall security posture?
2. Ex□lain the significance of the CIA Triad in database security and how it is implemented.
3. What are the differences between internal and external sources of security threats to databases?
4. Discuss the potential risks associated with SQL injection attacks and how organizations can prevent them.
5. How can organizations address the issue of excessive privilege abuse in their databases?
6. Describe the importance of preventive measures in mitigating vulnerabilities in vulnerable or incorrectly configured databases.
7. What are some key considerations for preventing unauthorized copying of sensitive data from databases?

MULTIPLE CHOICE QUESTIONS

1. **What is one of the main aspects of database security, according to the table of contents?**
   a. Confidentiality
   b. Availability
   c. Integrity
   d. Authorization
2. **Which section of the content discusses the prevention of SQL Injection?**
   a. Origin of Security Threats
   b. Database Security Threats
   c. Aspects of Database Security
   d. Preventive Measure for Database Security
3. **Which type of security threat involves users or applications having access privileges exceeding their professional function?**
   a. SQL Injection
   b. Privilege Escalation
   c. Excessive Privilege Abuse
   d. Denial of Service
4. **What is recommended as a preventive measure for the weakness of the native audit?**
   a Regular monitoring of logs
   b. Database communication protocols validation
   c. Intrusion Prevention Technology
   d. Implementing granular access controls
5. **Which section discusses the origin of security threats, distinguishing between internal and external sources?**
   a. Aspects of Database Security
   b. Database Security Threats
   c. Origin of Security Threats
   d. Preventive Measure for Database Security
6. **What preventive measure is suggested to prevent the exposure of backup data?**
   a. Regular monitoring of logs
   b. Encryption of backup data

c. Implementing access controls

d. Protocol validation

Answers to Multiple Choice Questions

1. (a); 2. (d); 3. (c); 4. (b); 5. (c); 6. (b)

REFERENCES

1. Al-Sayid, N. A., & Aldlaeen, D. (2013). Database security threats: A survey study. In *2013 5th International Conference on Computer Science and Information Technology* (Vol. 1, pp. 60–64).
2. Alwan, Z. S., & Younis, M. F. (2017). Detection and prevention of SQL injection attack: A survey. *International Journal of Computer Science and Mobile Computing, 6*(8), 5–17.
3. Anwar, M. M., Zafar, M. F., & Ahmed, Z. (2007). A proposed preventive information security system. In *2007 International Conference on Electrical Engineering* (Vol. 2, pp. 1–6).
4. Aravindharamanan, S., Ramasubbareddy, S., & Govinda, K. (2019). Legitimate privilege abuse and data security in database. In *Innovations in Computer Science and Engineering: Proceedings of the Sixth ICICSE 2018* (Vol. 3, pp. 175–181).
5. Bartnik, R. (2021). Diagnosis of threats to the European Union's internal security. *Humanities and Social Sciences, 28*(3), 7–18.
6. Black, J. (2006). Managing regulatory risks and defining the □arameters of blame: A focus on the Australian Prudential Regulation Authority. *Law & Policy, 28*(1), 1–30.
7. Borisov, N., Danezis, G., Mittal, P., & Tabriz, P. (2007). Denial of service or denial of security? In *Proceedings of the 14th ACM Conference on Computer and Communications Security* (Vol. 2, pp. 92–102).
8. Chalmers, D. J. (1997). Availability: The cognitive basis of experience. *Behavioral and Brain Sciences, 20*(1), 148–149.
9. Clark, K. B., & Fujimoto, T. (1990). The power of product integrity. *Harvard Business Review, 68*(6), 107–118.
10. Cox, D., La Caze, M., & Levine, M. (2014). Integrity. In *The Handbook of Virtue Ethics* (Vol. 4, pp. 200–209).
11. Dalton, K. M. (2012). The Priest-Penitent Privilege v. Child Abuse Re□orting Statutes: How to avoid the conflict and serve society. *Widener Law Review, 18*, 1–100.

12. Denning, D. E. (1988). Database security. *Annual Review of Computer Science, 3*(1), 1–22.

13. Deshpande, P., Sharma, S. C., & Kumar, P. S. (2015). Security threats in cloud computing. In *International Conference on Computing, Communication & Automation* (Vol. 1, pp. 632–636).

14. Down, S. (1999). Owner manager learning in small firms. *Journal of Small Business and Enterprise Development, 6*(3), 267–280.

15. Du, L. B., & Lowery, A. J. (2011). Optimizing the subcarrier granularity of coherent optical communications systems. *Optics Express, 19*(9), 8079–8084.

16. Ettredge, M. L., Li, C., & Sun, L. (2006). The impact of SOX Section 404 internal control quality assessment on audit delay in the SOX era. *Auditing: A Journal of Practice & Theory, 25*(2), 1–23.

17. Fischel, D. R. (1998). Lawyers and confidentiality. *The University of Chicago Law Review, 65*(1), 1–33.

18. Geerken, M. R., & Gove, W. R. (1974). Deterrence: Some theoretical considerations. *Law & Society Review, 9*, 300–497.

19. Gillon, R. (1985). Confidentiality. *British Medical Journal (Clinical Research Ed.), 291*(6509), 1634.

20. Higgins, R. (1985). The abuse of diplomatic privileges and immunities: Recent United Kingdom experience. *American Journal of International Law, 79*(3), 641–651.

21. Hsieh, P. H., & Yeh, K. C. M. (2012). Cultural effects on perceptions of unauthorized software copying. *Journal of Computer Information Systems, 53*(1), 42–47.

22. Hutchings, A., Smith, R. G., & James, L. (2013). Cloud computing for small business: Criminal and security threats and prevention measures. *Trends and Issues in Crime and Criminal Justice,* (456), 1–8.

23. Jaafar, F., Nicolescu, G., & Richard, C. (2016). A systematic approach for privilege escalation prevention. In *2016 IEEE International Conference on Software Quality, Reliability and Security Companion (QRS-C)* (Vol. 1, pp. 101–108).

24. Jacobs, B. A. (2010). Deterrence and deterrability. *Criminology, 48*(2), 417–441.

25. Jamil, W. J., Rahman, H. A., Shaari, S., & Salam, Z. (2017). Performance degradation of photovoltaic power system: Review on mitigation methods. *Renewable and Sustainable Energy Reviews, 67*, 876–891.

26. Kaiser, K. (2012). Protecting confidentiality. In *The SAGE Handbook of Interview Research: The Complexity of the Craft* (2nd ed., pp. 457–464).
27. Kantor, P. B. (1976). Availability analysis. *Journal of the American Society for Information Science, 27*(5), 311–319.
28. Karame, G. O., Soriente, C., Lichota, K., & Capkun, S. (2017). Securing cloud data under key exposure. *IEEE Transactions on Cloud Computing, 7*(3), 838–849.
29. Kaur, K., Gupta, I., & Singh, A. K. (2017). A comparative evaluation of data leakage/loss prevention systems (DLPS). In *Proceedings of the 4th International Conference on Computer Science & Information Technology (CS & IT-CSCP)* (Vol. 2, pp. 87–95).
30. Kestin, J. (1980). Availability: The concept and associated terminology. *Energy, 5*(8–9), 679–692.
31. Kujanpää, K., Victor, W., & Ilin, A. (2021). Automating privilege escalation with deep reinforcement learning. In *Proceedings of the 14th ACM Workshop on Artificial Intelligence and Security* (Vol. 3, pp. 157–168).
32. Kuwano, O., & Hatano, T. (2011). Flash weakening is limited by granular dynamics. *Geophysical Research Letters, 38*(17). 101–200.
33. Larsen, E. R., & Bunn, D. W. (1999). Deregulation in electricity: Understanding strategic and regulatory risk. *Journal of the Operational Research Society, 50*(4), 337–344.
34. Lee, H. T., Kim, D., Park, M., & Cho, S. J. (2016). Protecting data on the Android platform against privilege escalation attacks. *International Journal of Computer Mathematics, 93*(2), 401–414.
35. Lee, J. (1996). Measurement of machine performance degradation using a neural network model. *Computers in Industry, 30*(3), 193–209.
36. Lee, K., Oh, I., Lee, Y., Lee, H., Yim, K., & Seo, J. (2018). A study on a secure USB mechanism that prevents the exposure of authentication information for smart human care services. *Journal of Sensors, 2018, 3*(2), 1–17.
37. Martin, R. A. (2001). Managing vulnerabilities in networked systems. *Computer, 34*(11), 32–38.
38. Mousa, A., Karabatak, M., & Mustafa, T. (2020). Database security threats and challenges. In *2020 8th International Symposium on Digital Forensics and Security (ISDFS)* (Vol. 3, pp. 1–5).
39. Myrick, R. (2021). Do external threats unite or divide? Security crises, rivalries, and polarization in American foreign policy. *International Organization, 75*(4), 921–958.

40. Needham, R. M. (1993). Denial of service. In *Proceedings of the 1st ACM Conference on Computer and Communications Security* (Vol. 3, pp. 151–153).

41. Newton, J. (1985). Strategies for problem prevention. *IBM Systems Journal, 24*(3–4), 248–263.

42. Patil, B. P., Kharade, K. G., & Kamat, R. K. (2020). Investigation on data security threats & solutions. *International Journal of Innovative Science and Research Technology, 5*(1), 79–83.

43. Paulsson, J., & Rawding, N. (1995). The trouble with confidentiality. *Arbitration International, 11*(3), 303–320.

44. Pelechrinis, K., Iliofotou, M., & Krishnamurthy, S. V. (2010). Denial of service attacks in wireless networks: The case of jammers. *IEEE Communications Surveys & Tutorials, 13*(2), 245–257.

45. Rozell, M. (1984). In defense of executive privilege. *International Social Science Review, 59*(2), 67–199.

46. Sarmah, S. S. (2019). Database security–Threats & prevention. *International Journal of Computer Trends and Technology, 67*(5), 46–53.

47. Song, X., Stinson, M., Lee, R., & Albee, P. (2006). A qualitative analysis of privilege escalation. In *2006 IEEE International Conference on Information Reuse & Integration* (Vol. 1, pp. 363–368).

48. Strassberg, M. I. (2006). Privilege can be abused: Exploring the ethical obligation to avoid frivolous claims of attorney-client privilege. *Seton Hall Law Review, 37*, 413–500.

49. Strickland, R. N., & Hahn, H. I. (1997). Wavelet transform methods for object detection and recovery. *IEEE Transactions on Image Processing, 6*(5), 724–735.

50. Takebayashi, T., Tsuda, H., Hasebe, T., & Masuoka, R. (2010). Data loss prevention technologies. *Fujitsu Scientific and Technical Journal, 46*(1), 47–55.

51. Taylor, G., & Gaita, R. (1981). Integrity. *Proceedings of the Aristotelian Society, Supplementary Volumes, 55*, 143–176.

52. Vance, A., Lowry, P. B., & Eggett, D. (2015). Increasing accountability through user-interface design artifacts. *MIS Quarterly, 39*(2), 345–366.

53. Winch, G., & Leiringer, R. (2016). Owner project capabilities for infrastructure development: A review and development of the "strong owner" concept. *International Journal of Project Management, 34*(2), 271–281.

54. Xu, Y., Yang, Y., Li, T., Ju, J., & Wang, Q. (2017). Review on cyber

vulnerabilities of communication protocols in industrial control systems. In *2017 IEEE Conference on Energy Internet and Energy System Integration (EI2)* (Vol. 1, pp. 1–6).

55. Zuo, M. J., Lin, J., & Fan, X. (2005). Feature separation using ICA for a one-dimensional time series and its application in fault detection. *Journal of Sound and Vibration, 287*(3), 614–624.

CHAPTER 4

DATABASE SECURITY POLICIES

LEARNING OBJECTIVES

At the end of this chapter, readers will be able to:

1. Understand the critical role of database security policies in safeguarding data;
2. Comprehend access-control policies and their application in database security;
3. Understand authorization policies, including positive and negative authorizations;
4. Gain insights into role-based access control (RBAC) and its implementation;
5. Understand the roles and responsibilities of Database Administrators (DBAs);
6. Understand the challenges and solutions in identification and authentication processes within discretionary security; and
7. Understand the importance of auditing in database systems for detecting fraud and data misuse.

INTRODUCTORY EXAMPLE

Secure Solutions Ltd. is a reputable cyber security firm specializing in providing cutting-edge security solutions to businesses worldwide. Among its core offerings is a sophisticated database security platform designed to protect sensitive data from cyber threats. In recent months, Secure Solutions Ltd. has witnessed a surge in cyber-attacks targeting databases across various industries. To illustrate the critical importance of database security, consider the following scenario:

Secure Solutions Ltd.'s database security platform safeguards a diverse range of sensitive data, including financial transactions, personal information, and intellectual property, for its clients. Without robust security measures, unauthorized access to this data could lead to significant ramifications, including financial losses, regulatory fines, and reputational damage.

In response to these threats, Secure Solutions Ltd. implements stringent database security policies encompassing access controls, authorization mechanisms, administrative procedures, and auditing protocols. These policies are tailored to ensure the confidentiality, integrity, and availability of its clients' data.

Through proactive measures such as continuous monitoring, regular security assessments, and prompt incident response, Secure Solutions Ltd. reinforces its commitment to protecting client data and maintaining trust in an increasingly hostile cyber landscape. By adhering to these rigorous policies, the company strengthens its position as a trusted leader in database security solutions, safeguarding businesses against emerging cyber threats.

UNIT INTRODUCTION

In the ever-evolving world of technology, where the flow of information is constant, safeguarding the integrity of data stored in databases is of utmost importance. Ensuring the security of databases is of the highest priority, as they are vulnerable to various risks such as unauthorized access, data breaches, and insider misuse. Implementing robust security policies is crucial in protecting this valuable asset. These policies encompass a thorough framework of strategies, controls, and procedures carefully designed to maintain the integrity, availability, and confidentiality of data (Bertino & Sandhu, 2005).

Access-control policies are essential in ensuring the security of databases, as they determine the permissions for accessing, modifying, or deleting data within the system. When it comes to managing user permissions and preventing unauthorized access, organizations are focused on employing either discretionary or mandatory access control mechanisms. The goal is to carefully control access and minimize the risk of data compromise (Lunt & Fernandez, 1990).

Developing a comprehensive grasp of database security policies is crucial for creating strong defense mechanisms. In this introductory section, students will take a broad look at the complex world of database security, setting the stage for a detailed examination of various security mechanisms. The establishment of authorization policies is crucial in defining the □rivileges granted to users or roles within the database ecosystem. Organizations can customize permissions to match individuals' responsibilities, reducing the risk of unauthorized data manipulation or disclosure. This is achieved by defining access rights based on user roles or attributes (Denning, 1988).

In today's interconnected world of systems and distributed data environments, the task of maintaining access control across different platforms presents its own set of challenges. Ensuring the integrity and confidentiality of data across a network poses challenges for distributed access control mechanisms. These mechanisms need to address concerns like data replication, synchronization, and consistency. In addition, role-based access control (RBAC) is a powerful framework that sim□lifies access management by linking □ermissions to □redefined roles instead of individual users. Through the im□lementation of RBAC, organizations can enhance security measures, streamline access control, and mitigate the potential for human error, resulting in reduced administrative burdens (Bertino et al., 1995).

Efficient management □olicies are crucial for the effective execution and maintenance of security measures for databases. Effective administration policies are crucial for maintaining the integrity and effectiveness of database security frameworks (Abramov et al., 2012). These policies encompass various aspects such as user management, □rivilege escalation, security configuration, and monitoring. In addition, im□lementing strong identification and authentication mechanisms is essential in preventing unauthorized access attempts. Through the implementation of various security measures, organizations can enhance their protection against unauthorized access and effectively deter potential intruders (Pernul, 1994).

Auditing plays a crucial role in database security, helping organizations uphold accountability, identify security breaches, and meet regulatory obligations. By carefully examining audit logs, organizations can gain valuable insights into database activities, allowing them to detect any irregularities or unauthorized access attempts (Larrondo et al., 1989). In database security, views have proven to be a powerful tool for organizations. They enable the implementation of security policies by providing controlled access to sensitive data through filtered or abstracted views of the database. Nevertheless, there are certain challenges associated with views, such as the view update problem, which requires careful consideration when implementing them in access-control policies (Malik & Patel, 2016) (Figure 4.1).

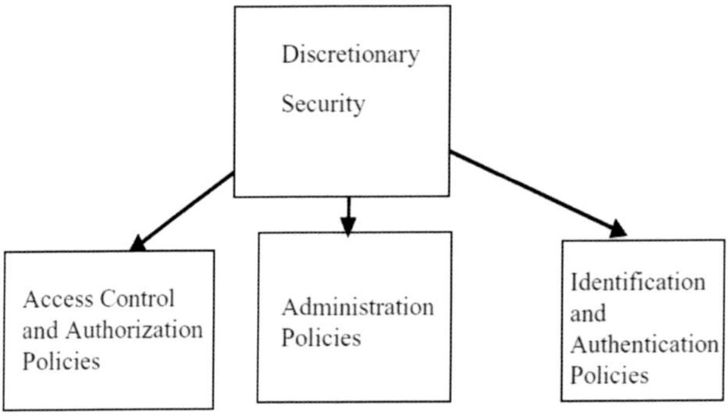

Figure 4.1. *Illustration of discretionary security policies.*

Source: Turasingham Mithal Creative Commons License.

4.1. ACCESS CONTROL POLICIES

Learning Objectives

- Understand the access-control policies from operating systems to database systems;
- Understand the role-based and authorization policies' applications and implications in database security; and
- Understand the challenges and considerations in propagating authorization rules in database environments.

4.1.1. Overview of Control Policies

As previously discussed, access-control policies were first examined for operating systems. One important factor to take into account is whether a process can be granted access to a file. There are two main types of access: write access and read access. Access to modify, include, or delete could be granted. The principles discussed were implemented in database systems such as Ingres and System R. throughout the years, scholars have explored various forms of access-control policies (Bertino et al., 2009).

Several commercial systems have now implemented role-based access-control policies, which have gained recognition. It is crucial to note that access-control policies also include required policies. In the following section, a comprehensive overview of access-control policies based on role-based and authorization and distributed access-control policies will be discussed (Karyda et al., 2005). Many commercial products in the industry are currently using role-based access control. Similar policies are being implemented for various applications, including knowledge management and collaboration. Figure 4.2 shows a visual representation of the different access-control policies (Cholvy & Cuppens, 1997).

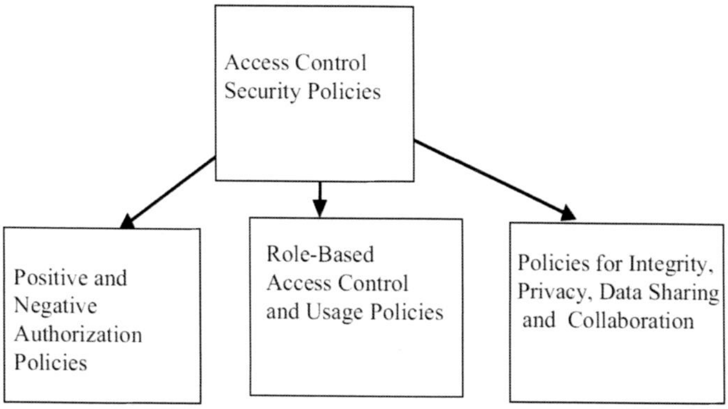

Figure 4.2. *Illustration of access control security policies.*

Source: S. Bhavani Creative Commons License.

4.1.2. Authorization Policies

Many access-control policies depend on authorization policies. This suggests that users are given access to data according to authorization rules. In this section, students will explore different types of rules implemented by authorities (McDaniel, 2003).

a) *Positive Authorizations:* In the early stages, systems primarily emphasized what are now referred to as positive authorization rules. John has been granted access to the EMP relation, while Jane has been granted access to the DEPT relation (Preuveneers & Joosen, 2017). Here are some access-control rules for relations. Access can also be granted to other entities, such as tuples and attributes. For example, John has been granted read access to the attribute salary and write access to the attribute name in the EMP relation. Access to the system can be granted for appending, modifying, or deleting data (Fournet et al., 2005).

b) *Negative Authorization*: Does the absence of a s□ecified access for John indicate that he lacks access to the object in question? There are variations in different systems when it comes to authorization rules. Within certain systems, any rule that is not defined is seen as a form of negative authorization. However, in other systems, negative authorizations are explicitly stated. For example, rules could be implemented to restrict John's access to the EMP relation or Jane's access to the DEPT relation (Thompson et al., 2003).

c) *Conflict Resolutions*: When faced with conflicting rules, it's challenging to find a resolution. How can one effectively navigate and address these conflicts? For exam□le, a rule could be im□lemented to provide John with read access to the EMP relation. However, there is a rule that denies John read access to the salary attribute in EMP. This □resents a conflict. Ty□ically, a system follows the □rinci□le of least privilege, meaning that John has access to EMP data, except salary values (Becker & Nanz, 2010).

d) *Strong and Weak Authorization*: Systems also implement various levels of authorizations. For robust authorization, the rule remains valid even in the face of conflicts. In weak authorizations, the rule doesn't a□□ly when there's a conflict. Consider this scenario: John has been given access to EMP, which is considered a strong authorization rule. However, there is a weak authorization rule in place that denies John access to the salary attribute. As a result, a conflict arises. This indicates that the robust authorization will remain in place (Woo & Lam, 1992).

e) *Propagation of Authorization Rules*: The current issue pertains to the distribution of rules. John's read access to relation EMP does not imply universal read access to every element within EMP. Usually, this statement is true unless there is a regulation that explicitly prohibits the automatic distribution of an authorization rule. If there is a restriction on the automatic dissemination of a regulation, it is necessary to establish authorization rules that specify the objects that John is permitted to access (Kabbani et al., 2014).

f) *Special Rules*: Extensive research has been conducted on the enforcement of content- and context-based constraints in mandatory policy extensions. It is important to understand that security constraints are essentially the rules that govern security. Access can be granted based on the content of the data or the context in which the data is displayed through content and context-based rules (Ganapathy et al., 2006). These guidelines can also be applied to discretionary security measures. For example, when it comes to content-based constraints, John is only granted read access to tuples within DEPT D100. When it comes to context- or association-based constraints, John is unable to access names and salaries together. However, he does have the ability to access individual names and salaries. After the election, John is granted access to all elements to EMP in the case of event-based constraints (Haddad et al., 2012).

g) *Consistency and Completeness of Rules*: One of the key considerations in this area is maintaining the uniformity and thoroughness of constraints. So, in the case of inconsistent constraints or rules, are there conflict resolution rules in place to resolve the conflicts? What measures can be taken to guarantee that access-control rules encompass all entities, including attributes, relations, elements, and more, for a user? Essentially, the question at hand is whether the rules are comprehensive enough (Chapin et al., 2008). Otherwise, what assumptions are made regarding organizations that lack specific authorizations for a particular user or group of users?

Authorization Rules:

* John has read access to employee relation
* John does not have write access to department relation
* Jane has read access to name values in employee relation
* Jane does not have read access to department relation

Figure 4.3. *Description of authorization rules.*

Source: Taylor C. Creative Commons License.

Important aspects regarding authorization rules have been discussed previously. Figure 4.3 provides several examples for reference. In the following section, students will delve into a widely used access-control policy known as distributed access control and role-based access control. These policies have been successfully implemented in various commercial systems (Jøsang, 2017).

Practice Problem

Describe the difference between authentication and authorization using an example of a banking system. Discuss the importance of each in ensuring database security.

Solutions to Practice Problem

Authentication verifies the identity of a user (e.g., username and password), while authorization determines what actions or data the authenticated user is allowed to access based on their roles and permissions. In a banking system, authentication ensures only authorized users (customers, bank employees) can access accounts, while authorization restricts employees to specific functions like transactions or customer service.

4.1.3. Distributed Access Control

First, let's delve into access-control rules. These regulations are strictly applied to data across the various nodes. Implementing and enforcing these rules can be a challenging task, particularly when they are contingent upon the content of fragmented relations. Consider a rule that specifies John's access privileges limited to employee salaries, but only if the employees belong to the math department (Ruj et al., 2011). Consider a scenario where there are two relations in the database, EMP and DEPT. The EMP relation is stored in site A and contains attributes such as E#, Ename, D#, and Salary. The DEPT data is kept at site B and includes the attributes D#, Dname, and Mgr. To retrieve the salary values from the EMP table, a join operation must be conducted between the EMP and DEPT tables, which are located in separate locations. This will establish a connection between the Salary and Dname columns (Almutairi et al., 2011). If the department name (Dname) is MATH, then John is granted permission to view the salary data of the employees inside the mathematics department.

This is shown in Figure 4.4. Let's take another example, where John is granted access to the Employee relation only if the cumulative salaries of employees amount to less than one million dollars. Additionally, let's assume that the employee relationship is divided and stored in locations A and B (Yu et al., 2010). In this scenario, it is necessary to calculate the cumulative pay of all employees across the various locations and after that determine whether John has authorization to access the corresponding data (He et al., 2011).

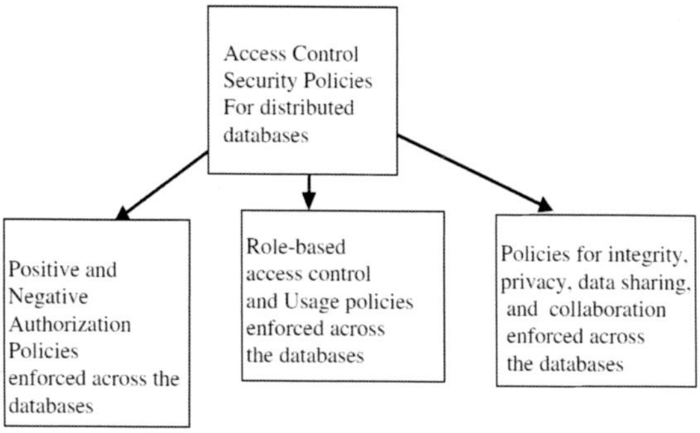

Figure 4.4. *Illustration of access control.*

Source: Campbell John. Creative Commons License.

The access-control rules can either be centralized or copied at each site. An alternative strategy is to spread the regulations. If the system is centralized, every time a query is made, the request is routed to the database that contains the rules (Butun & Österberg, 2020). Re□licating the rules enhances the efficiency of query processing. Nevertheless, it is essential to maintain uniformity in the rules across all locations and ensure that any updates to a regulation are effectively communicated. If the rules have been dispersed, then one must devise a mechanism for their distribution (Bauer et al., 2005).

For example, it may be logical to keep the rules close to the relations on which the rules are applied. Extensive research has been conducted on access control in distributed database systems. The ideas have been used in systems such as R* and Distributed INGRES. Additionally, numerous research prototypes have been built (Lunardi et al., 2018). A significant number of commercial □roducts incorporate access-control regulations for distributed contexts. Nevertheless, a significant □ortion of the regulations that are im□lemented are quite uncomplicated and one still requires effective algorithms to ensure compliance with these regulations across numerous databases (Zhang et al., 2011).

4.1.4. Role-Based Access Control

As an access-control system, role-based access control, or RBAC, has become increasingly common. This methodology has been put into practice in commercial systems such as Trusted Oracle. The objective is to provide users with access based on their assigned roles and responsibilities. Let's delve into the fundamental concept that lies at the core of role-based access control. Data access is necessary for users based on their assigned roles and responsibilities (Sandhu, 1998). For example, a president can have special access to information on her vice president and the board members, and the chief financial officer might have access to financial data and details about people who work for him (Bacon et al., 2002).

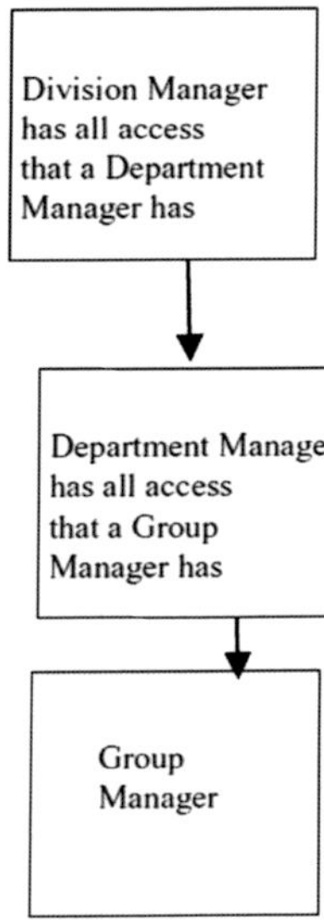

Figure 4.5. *Illustration of role hierarchy.*

Source: Taylor C. Creative Commons License.

The director possesses information regarding the individuals employed within his division, while the human resources director possesses personal data concerning the corporation's employees. Role-based access control is an authorization policy that relies on the user's role and the corresponding activities associated with that role (Park et al., 2001).

The literature has extensively examined various research initiatives on role hierarchies. Additionally, there exists a conference series known as SACMAT (Symposium on Access Control Models and Technologies) that originated from studies focused on role-based access control (Oh & Park, 2003). For example, how is access transmitted or distributed? Is it possible for one role to encompass or incorporate another? Examine the role hierarchy shown in Figure 4.5. (Ni et al., 2010).

Is access granted to a node in the hierarchy propagated upwards? In the given scenario, if a department manager gets access to certain project information, does this access automatically apply to the higher-level parent node, which in this case is the director node? When a section leader has access to personnel information within her section, it is worth investigating whether this access also applies to the department manager, who holds a superior position in the role hierarchy (Ferraiolo et al., 1995). What is the fate of the child nodes? Is access propagated downward in this context? Consider this scenario: Should a department manager have access to a certain piece of information, would their staff members have the same information at their disposal?

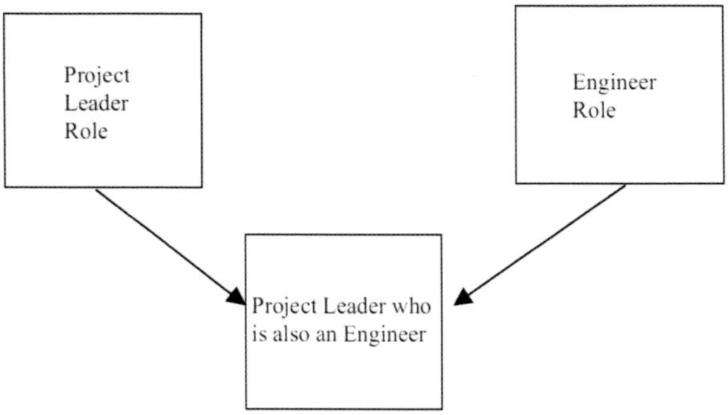

Figure 4.6. *Illustration of multiple parents.*

Source: Turasingham Mithal Creative Commons License.

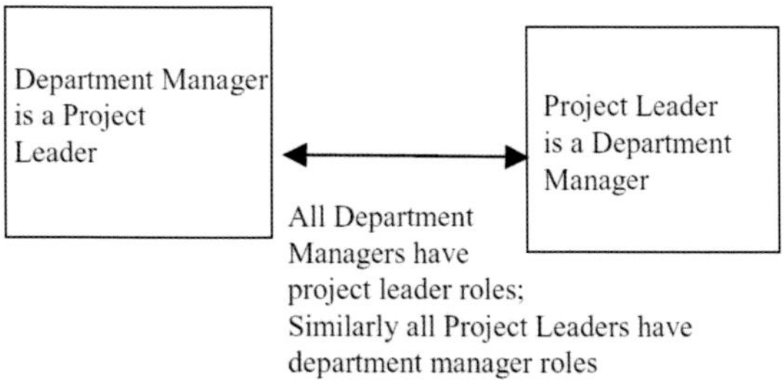

Figure 4.7. Illustration of cyclic graph.

Source: Turasingham Mithal Creative Commons License.

Are cases where lower-level employees are granted access to data that is not accessible to their department manager? What is the protocol when an employee is required to report to two different supervisors, one being their department manager and the other their project manager? What occurs when the department manager is engaged in a project and needs to provide updates to his subordinate, who also happens to be his project leader? Figure 4.6 showcases several parents, while Figure 4.7 shows a cycle (Thomas, 1997).

Role-based access control has been extensively studied in various domains, including relational systems, object systems, distributed systems, and emerging technologies like knowledge management systems, data warehouses, E-commerce systems, digital libraries, and semantic Web. In addition, object models have been utilized to depict activities and roles, as demonstrated by the Proceedings of the IFIP database security conference series (Li & Tripunitara, 2006).

In recent years, Sandhu has introduced a new model called the Usage Control Model, also known as UCON. This model, as seen in the work reported in [PARK04], is another access-control-like model. The UCON model aims to incorporate three policies: (1) trust management, (2) access control, and (3) rights management. The concept aims to establish a level of authority over the utilization of objects. While the concepts are still in the early stages, this model demonstrates great potential (Joshi et al., 2005).

4.2. ADMINISTRATION POLICIES

Learning Objective

- Understand the responsibilities of Database Administrators (DBAs) in managing metadata and access controls.

Access-control policies define the level of access that certain users are granted to the data, while administration policies determine the individuals responsible for managing the data. One responsibility of administration is to maintain the accuracy of the data, ensuring that the metadata is promptly updated whenever changes are made. Additionally, it is crucial to be prepared for any potential failures and to take the necessary steps to recover from them (Moynihan & Soss, 2014).

The database administrator (DBA) is typically responsible for maintaining various components such as metadata, indexes, and access methods. They also ensure that access-control restrictions are effectively implemented. The system security officer (SSO) may also have a function. The SSO and DBA may divide the responsibilities amongst themselves (Christensen et al., 2002). The SSO may be accountable for security-related matters, whereas the DBA may be accountable for data-related matters. Additional administrative procedures under consideration involve the allocation of caretakers (Van Buuren et al., 2020). Typically, owners own authority over the data they generate and can oversee the data throughout its entire lifespan. If owners are unavailable to administer the data, they have the option to assign caretakers (Verma, 2002).

Administration policies can become quite intricate in distributed organizations, especially in a Web environment. When it comes to the online domain, the sharing of information often involves multiple individuals, including the content creator, the publisher, and the individuals who are searching for the data. Determining the legitimate owner of the data is a crucial aspect to consider (Ewalt & Jennings Jr, 2004). Who is responsible for this? The person who owns it or the publisher? When data is transferred from the owner to the publisher, does the publisher then take ownership of the data?

During the shift from a relational database to a distributed, probably Web-based system, numerous important questions must be answered. In addition, there are various aspects to consider such as addressing copyright concerns, ensuring data accuracy and reliability, tracking data origins, and implementing effective governance measures. Several interesting papers have been presented at recent conferences focusing on administration policies (Majone, 1996). Figure 4.8 shows a range of administration policies.

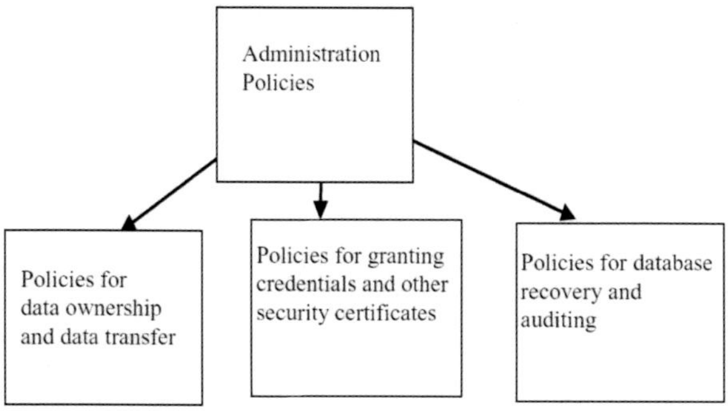

Figure 4.8. *Illustration of administration policies.*

Source: S. Bhavani Creative Commons License.

4.3. IDENTIFICATION AND AUTHENTICATION

Learning Objectives

- Understand the concept of identification and authorization in database security;
- Understand the challenges of password-based authentication and the need for alternatives; and
- Understand the benefits and advancements of biometric authentication in security.

It is crucial to thoroughly discuss the topic of identification and authentication in discretionary security to ensure a comprehensive understanding. Authentication is a crucial step in accessing a system, where users provide their credentials, usually a combination of a user ID and password, to verify their identity. On the other hand, authentication confirms the validity of these credentials, guaranteeing that the user is truly the person they say they are by comparing the given user ID with the associated password (Zviran & Erlich, 2006).

Nevertheless, the widely used password-based authentication scheme has faced numerous obstacles. Unauthorized individuals can gain access to systems by taking advantage of vulnerabilities and obtaining user passwords, which enables them to impersonate legitimate users. In distributed environments, these challenges are increased, presenting significant obstacles to system security. The increasing prevalence of the World Wide Web and E-commerce applications has exacerbated these concerns, as financial institutions struggle with significant losses caused by hackers who impersonate genuine users (Gassend et al., 2004).

As a response to these weaknesses, biometric techniques have come up as a promising alternative. Biometrics utilize distinct physical or behavioral traits of individuals, like facial attributes or voice patterns, for authentication. These techniques provide enhanced security and convenience in comparison to conventional password-based methods. Currently, there is a growing implementation of face and voice recognition technologies, showcasing their immense potential in improving authentication procedures (Idrus et al., 2013).

With the continuous evolution of face recognition technologies, there is a growing expectation for the widespread adoption of biometric techniques. The adoption of biometric authentication represents a significant advancement in enhancing security measures and reducing the vulnerabilities of password-based systems, especially in the face of the ever-changing cyber threat landscape (Garfinkel, 2003).

4.4. AUDITING A DATABASE SYSTEM

Learning Objectives

- Understand the importance of auditing in database systems for detecting fraud and unauthorized activities.

Examining audit data has emerged as a crucial method for identifying instances of fraud and unauthorized use of data. It is important to note that audit trails may contain a wealth of complicated and confidential data about production systems (Little & Misra, 1994). By conducting audits, it becomes possible to identify any unauthorized activities, as well as actions carried out by individuals with proper authorization. It provides insights into the actions taken and the impact they had. Even harmless audit information can be leveraged to deduce other sensitive data through correlation (Noreen et al., 2009).

There are various reasons why databases undergo auditing. For example, audits can be conducted to monitor the frequency of queries, updates, transactions, and secondary storage access to optimize system design. Security audits are an essential aspect of database management. For example, have any access-control rules been bypassed by disclosing information to the users? Is there an issue with the inference problem? Is there a potential breach of privacy? Have there been any unauthorized intrusions?

The role of the auditor involves reviewing predetermined reports that are categorized based on audit events. They are responsible for identifying potential security risks, developing and evaluating alert scenarios, as well as generating and overseeing comprehensive and concise reports on system events. The auditor can generate personalized audit reports and utilize the Data Warehouse service to analyze audit data for patterns, breaches, irregularities, and more (Lu & Miklau, 2008).

Audits generate a trace and the audit data might be saved in a database. The database can be analyzed to identify any abnormal trends or behaviors. Data mining has been extensively employed for auditing and intrusion detection. Given the prevalence of E-commerce transactions on the Web, the analysis of audit trails has become particularly crucial. An organization must possess the capacity to perform an analysis and identify issues such as credit card fraud and identity theft (Malvestuto et al., 2006).

SUMMARY

- The chapter titled "Database Security Policies" examines essential techniques for protecting sensitive data and ensuring the reliability of database systems. The chapter explores access-control rules, which govern user access to data, encompassing discretionary and required access-control procedures.
- An overview em□hasizes the utmost significance of database security rules in reducing risks and safeguarding against unauthorized access. The discussion then focuses on authorization policies, which provide a detailed explanation of how access permissions are provided depending on user roles or qualities.
- Ensuring data security across distributed environments can be quite challenging when it comes to distributed access control. However, access management becomes simpler with role-based access control, which associates □ermissions with □redefined roles.
- Policies set the rules for managing databases, including tasks like updates, metadata maintenance, and recovery procedures. Identification and authentication mechanisms □lay a crucial role in verifying user identities and ensuring secure access to the system.
- Lastly, the cha□ter discusses auditing techniques, with a s□ecific emphasis on analyzing audit data to identify instances of fraud, misuse, and security breaches. Gain a thorough understanding of the necessary knowledge and techniques to successfully implement robust database security measures with this all-encompassing guide.

REVIEW QUESTIONS

1. Describe the role of access-control policies in ensuring database security, and provide examples of different types of access-control mechanisms.
2. How do authorization policies contribute to the overall security of a database system? Explain the concept of role-based access control (RBAC) and its advantages.
3. What are the challenges associated with implementing distributed access control mechanisms in a distributed database environment? How can organizations address these challenges?
4. Compare and contrast discretionary access control (DAC) and mandatory access control (MAC), highlighting their key differences and use cases.

5. Discuss the significance of administration □olicies in database security. What are some essential components of effective administration policies, and how do they contribute to maintaining a secure database environment?
6. Ex□lain the im□ortance of identification and authentication mechanisms in database security. What are some common methods of user identification and authentication, and how do they mitigate the risk of unauthorized access?
7. Describe the role of auditing in database security. Why is auditing important, and what are the steps involved in auditing a database system?

MULTIPLE CHOICE QUESTIONS

1. Which of the following lies at the core of database security, dictating who can access, modify, or delete data within the system?

a. Encryption techniques

b. Authentication mechanisms

c. Access-control policies

d. Auditing procedures

2. What is the primary purpose of authorization policies in a database system?

a. To collect and analyze audit logs

b. To define access rights based on user roles or attributes

c. To encrypt sensitive data at rest and in transit

d. To manage database backups and recovery procedures

3. In a distributed database environment, what challenges do distributed access control mechanisms need to address?

a. User authentication

b. Data replication and synchronization

c. Backup and recovery procedures

d. Role-based access control

4. Which access control framework associates permissions with predefined roles rather than individual users?

a. Discretionary access control (DAC)

b. Mandatory access control (MAC)

c. Role-based access control (RBAC)

d. Attribute-based access control (ABAC)

5. What is a crucial aspect of administration policies in a database security framework?

a. Identification and authentication

b. Encryption of sensitive data

c. Monitoring and auditing procedures

d. User management and privilege escalation

6. Which mechanism forms the first line of defense against unauthorized access attempts in a database system?

a. Auditing

b. Encryption

c. Identification and authentication

d. Views for security

Answers to Multiple Choice Questions

1. (c); 2. (b); 3. (b); 4. (c) 5. (d); 6. (c)

REFERENCES

1. Abramov, J., Anson, O., Dahan, M., Shoval, P., & Sturm, A. (2012). A methodology for integrating access control policies within database development. *Computers & Security, 31*(3), 299–314.
2. Almutairi, A., Sarfraz, M., Basalamah, S., Aref, W., & Ghafoor, A. (2011). A distributed access control architecture for cloud computing. *IEEE Software, 29*(2), 36–44.
3. Bacon, J., Moody, K., & Yao, W. (2002). A model of OASIS role-based access control and its support for active security. *ACM Transactions on Information and System Security (TISSEC), 5*(4), 492–540.
4. Bauer, L., Garriss, S., & Reiter, M. K. (2005). Distributed proving in access-control systems. In *2005 IEEE Symposium on Security and Privacy (S&P'05)* (Vol. 2, pp. 81–95).
5. Becker, M. Y., & Nanz, S. (2010). A logic for state-modifying authorization policies. *ACM Transactions on Information and System Security (TISSEC), 13*(3), 1–28.
6. Bertino, E., & Sandhu, R. (2005). Database security—Concepts, approaches, and challenges. *IEEE Transactions on Dependable and Secure Computing, 2*(1), 2–19.

7. Bertino, E., Brodie, C., Calo, S. B., Cranor, L. F., Karat, C. M., Karat, J., & Wang, X. (2009). Analysis of privacy and security policies. *IBM Journal of Research and Development, 53*(2), 3–1.
8. Bertino, E., Jajodia, S., & Samarati, P. (1995). Database security: Research and practice. *Information Systems, 20*(7), 537–556.
9. Butun, I., & Österberg, P. (2020). A review of distributed access control for blockchain systems towards securing the Internet of Things. *IEEE Access, 9*, 5428–5441.
10. Chapin, P. C., Skalka, C., & Wang, X. S. (2008). Authorization in trust management: Features and foundations. *ACM Computing Surveys (CSUR), 40*(3), 1–48.
11. Denning, D. E. (1988). Database security. *Annual Review of Computer Science, 3*(1), 1–22.
12. Ewalt, J. A. G., & Jennings Jr, E. T. (2004). Administration, governance, and policy tools in welfare policy implementation. *Public Administration Review, 64*(4), 449–462.
13. Ferraiolo, D., Cugini, J., & Kuhn, D. R. (1995). Role-based access control (RBAC): Features and motivations. In *Proceedings of the 11th Annual Computer Security Application Conference* (Vol. 2, pp. 241–248).
14. Fournet, C., Gordon, A. D., & Maffeis, S. (2005). A type discipline for authorization policies. In *European Symposium on Programming* (Vol. 3, pp. 141–156).
15. Gana□athy, V., Jaeger, T., & Jha, S. (2006). Retrofitting legacy code for authorization policy enforcement. In *2006 IEEE Symposium on Security and Privacy (S&P'06)* (Vol. 2, pp. 15-pp).
16. Garfinkel, S. L. (2003). Email-based identification and authentication: An alternative to PKI? *IEEE Security & Privacy, 1*(6), 20–26.
17. Gassend, B., Lim, D., Clarke, D., Van Dijk, M., & Devadas, S. (2004). Identification and authentication of integrated circuits. *Concurrency and Computation: Practice and Experience, 16*(11), 1077–1098.
18. Haddad, M., Hacid, M. S., & Laurini, R. (2012). Data integration in the presence of authorization policies. In *2012 IEEE 11th International Conference on Trust, Security and Privacy in Computing and Communications* (Vol. 2, pp. 92–99).
19. Jøsang, A. (2017). A consistent definition of authorization. In *Security and Trust Management: 13th International Workshop, STM 2017, Oslo, Norway, September 14–15, 2017, Proceedings 13* (pp. 134–144).
20. Joshi, J. B., Bertino, E., Latif, U., & Ghafoor, A. (2005). A generalized

temporal role-based access control model. *IEEE Transactions on Knowledge and Data Engineering, 17*(1), 4–23.

21. Kabbani, B., Laborde, R., Barrere, F., & Benzekri, A. (2014). S□ecification and enforcement of dynamic authorization policies oriented by situations. In *2014 6th International Conference on New Technologies, Mobility and Security (NTMS)* (Vol. 2, pp. 1–6).
22. Karyda, M., Kiountouzis, E., & Kokolakis, S. (2005). Information systems security policies: A contextual perspective. *Computers & Security, 24*(3), 246–260.
23. Larrondo-Petrie, M. M., Gudes, E., Song, H., & Fernández, E. B. (1989). Security policies in object-oriented databases. In *DBSec* (pp. 257–268).
24. Li, N., & Tripunitara, M. V. (2006). Security analysis in role-based access control. *ACM Transactions on Information and System Security (TISSEC), 9*(4), 391–420.
25. Little, D., & Misra, S. (1994). Auditing for database integrity. *Journal of Systems Management, 45*(8), 6.
26. Lu, W., & Miklau, G. (2008). AuditGuard: A system for database auditing under retention restrictions. *Proceedings of the VLDB Endowment, 1*(2), 1484–1487.
27. Lunardi, R. C., Michelin, R. A., Neu, C. V., & Zorzo, A. F. (2018). Distributed access control on IoT ledger-based architecture. In *NOMS 2018—2018 IEEE/IFIP Network Operations and Management Symposium* (Vol. 3, pp. 1–7).
28. Lunt, T. F., & Fernandez, E. B. (1990). Database security. *ACM SIGMOD Record, 19*(4), 90–97.
29. Majone, G. (1996). Public policy and administration: Ideas, interests, and institutions. In *A New Handbook of Political Science* (pp. 610–627).
30. Malik, M., & Patel, T. (2016). Database security—Attacks and control methods. *International Journal of Information, 6*(1/2), 175–183.
31. Malvestuto, F. M., Mezzini, M., & Moscarini, M. (2006). Auditing sum-queries to make a statistical database secure. *ACM Transactions on Information and System Security (TISSEC), 9*(1), 31–60.
32. McDaniel, P. (2003). On context in authorization policy. In *Proceedings of the Eighth ACM Symposium on Access Control Models and Technologies* (Vol. 1, pp. 80–89).
33. Moynihan, D. P., & Soss, J. (2014). Policy feedback and the politics of administration. *Public Administration Review, 74*(3), 320–332.
34. Ni, Q., Bertino, E., Lobo, J., Brodie, C., Karat, C. M., Karat, J., & Trombeta,

A. (2010). Privacy-aware role-based access control. *ACM Transactions on Information and System Security (TISSEC), 13*(3), 1–31.

35. Noreen, Z., Hameed, I., & Usman, A. (2009). Development of database auditing infrastructure. In *Proceedings of the 7th International Conference on Frontiers of Information Technology* (Vol. 2, pp. 1–6).
36. Oh, S., & Park, S. (2003). Task-role-based access control model. *Information Systems, 28*(6), 533–562.
37. Park, J. S., Sandhu, R., & Ahn, G. J. (2001). Role-based access control on the web. *ACM Transactions on Information and System Security (TISSEC), 4*(1), 37–71.
38. Pernul, G. (1994). Database security. In *Advances in Computers* (Vol. 38, pp. 1–72).
39. Preuveneers, D., & Joosen, W. (2017). Access control with delegated authorization □olicy evaluation for data-driven microservice workflows. *Future Internet, 9*(4), 58–100.
40. Sandhu, R. S. (1998). Role-based access control. In *Advances in Computers* (Vol. 46, pp. 237–286).
41. Woo, T. Y., & Lam, S. S. (1992). Authorization in distributed systems: A formal approach. In *IEEE Symposium on Security and Privacy* (Vol. 1, pp. 33–50).
42. Yu, S., Ren, K., & Lou, W. (2010). FDAC: Toward fine-grained distributed data access control in wireless sensor networks. *IEEE Transactions on Parallel and Distributed Systems, 22*(4), 673–686.
43. Zhang, R., Zhang, Y., & Ren, K. (2011). Distributed privacy-preserving access control in sensor networks. *IEEE Transactions on Parallel and Distributed Systems, 23*(8), 1427–1438.
44. Zviran, M., & Erlich, Z. (2006). Identification and authentication: Technology and implementation issues. *Communications of the Association for Information Systems, 17*(1), 4–10.

CHAPTER 5

DATABASE SECURITY REVAMP: CONCEPTS AND TECHNIQUES

LEARNING OBJECTIVES

At the end of this chapter, readers will be able to:

1. Understand misuse and anomaly detection techniques in database security;
2. Understand data and user profiling for enhancing database security;
3. Explore audit mechanisms and strategies for identifying anomalies and unauthorized access;
4. Understand the components and functions of the access path model in database security;
5. Identify and correlate user access and anomalies in complex database systems;
6. Implement security reconfiguration techniques to adhere to the least privilege principle;
7. Utilize integrity constraints, roles, and views to enhance database security mechanisms; and
8. Explore gradual security re-design strategies for databases.

INTRODUCTORY EXAMPLE

North Bey Solutions is a leading provider of database management solutions for businesses across various industries. Recently, the company has been experiencing concerns regarding the security of its database systems due to the increasing frequency of cyber threats and data breaches in the industry. To address these concerns and enhance database security, North Bey Solutions has decided to revamp its database security infrastructure using advanced concepts and techniques.

As part of this initiative, North Bey Solutions plans to implement various strategies, such as insider misuse detection, anomaly detection, auditing, and access path modeling, to strengthen the security of its database systems. By proactively identifying potential security risks and vulnerabilities, North Bey Solutions aims to mitigate the impact of insider threats, unauthorized access, and data breaches, ensuring the integrity and confidentiality of its clients' data.

Throughout this chapter, we will explore the concepts and techniques employed by North Bey Solutions to revamp its database security infrastructure, providing insights into the challenges faced by organizations in safeguarding their sensitive information and the strategies they employ to overcome them.

UNIT INTRODUCTION

Database management systems, or DBMSs, frequently appear in the information systems of government agencies and online enterprises. They play a crucial role in maintaining and providing important and sensitive data. While there are various components in infrastructures, including networks and application servers, it is widely believed that the data stored in databases is frequently the most significant asset for a business. The data is usually carefully selected and preserved over a long period of time, and losing or damaging it would be far more challenging (and expensive) to recover from compared to the failure of other infrastructure elements (Moreno et al., 2016).

In the last two decades, there have been notable progressions in database security, encompassing advanced access control models and privacy and trust management. While many principles have been included into modern database management systems (DBMSs), these systems continue to encounter various security risks that target the manipulation of data availability, integrity and confidentiality.

There are other factors contributing to this situation. Initially, there was a significant delay between the suggestion of an im□roved database security strategy and its implementation in a new version of a database management system (DBMS). However, it is still necessary to acquire knowledge and suitably utilize new technologies to enhance the security of a database. Furthermore, the deficiencies in adequately safeguarding databases arise from situations that are frequently encountered in various computer security contexts (Yang et l., 2019).

These include the absence of clearly established security protocols. Inadequate comprehension or ambiguous articulation of security policies im□edes their efficient execution through database security mechanisms, hence exposing the database system to security vulnerabilities. This leads to inadequate security architecture. Similar to other computing systems, databases often prioritize security as an afterthought. The formulation and implementation of security policies are done in an improvised manner, resulting in an inconsistent overall design for database security. This creates possible vulnerabilities that can be used by hostile intruders and users (Aguboshim et al., 2022).

The inherent dynamic of programs and the variability of user tasks and roles. Over time, there may be changes in the database user group and the addition, upgrading, or removal of applications. These changes often result in the security policies connected with the database back-end remaining unchanged. Expired and outdated security policies, along with their related enforcing security systems, □resent a significant risk to the security of databases (Buczak & Guven, 2015).

There are various factors to consider, including the advancements in database structures and schemas to meet the needs of new applications and their security demands, as well as the potential misuse of the database and its administrative tools.

An important issue that contributes to the current situation in enhancing database security is the misuse of insider access. Individuals who intentionally manipulate the data integrity and confidentiality, des□ite being authorized users of an a□□lication or database. Insider misuse continues to □ose a significant threat to security, not only in database systems (Zheng et al., 2014).

Within this chapter, students will delve into the core concepts and methodologies that underpin various re-engineering tasks of security for relational databases. A proposed method emphasizes the importance of data analysis in assessing the security of a database. It highlights the need to prioritize the evaluation of data integrity as the first ste□ in ensuring its □rotection. Im□lementing suitable data and user □rofiling techniques is based u□on the assurance of high-quality, mission-critical, and sensitive data (Muheidat et al., 2022). Otherwise, the accuracy of statistical models that monitor and enforce the normal behavior of users and data is compromised by the poor quality of the underlying data used to generate the models. The techniques used in this study involve selective auditing of databases and user □rofiling. These strategies make use of conventional database features and tried-and-true data mining-based □rofiling methodologies (Chen & Zhang, 2014).

Additionally, a methodological framework known as the access path model will be introduced. This framework allows administrators and security personnel to effectively identify, document, and assess access paths. A crucial aspect of database security is understanding the access paths available to application users for operating on the managed data. Understanding the relationship between data accesses and user accounts, both at the database layer and application layer, is essential for enhancing or updating existing security policies (Sicari et al., 2015).

5.1. INSIDER MISUSE AND ANOMALY DETECTION

Learning Objectives

- Understand the distinction between misuse detection and anomaly detection in intrusion detection systems (IDSs).
- Understand the challenges of insider misuse in database security.

One common topic in computer security is intrusion detection, which has been extensively researched for over two decades. This area of study highlights the importance of developing new concepts and techniques for enhancing the security of databases (Tukur et al., 2021). Typically, an intrusion is seen as an action that goes against the security policy of a system. For detecting and responding to unauthorized activities, intrusion detection systems (IDSs) operate under the assumption that the behavior of an intruder will differ from that of an authorized user (Punithavathani et al., 2015).

There are different types of intrusion detection systems, including network-based IDSs, host-based IDSs, and application-based IDSs. These systems depend on analyzing audit data, which is acquired through different audit techniques and offers information on im□ortant events with varying levels of s□ecificity. This aspect will be further discussed in a later section. Host-based intrusion detection systems (IDSs) use audit data generated by operating system calls on a local host, including □rocess executions, resource use, and file accesses (Chen et al., 2012). Network-based IDS are strategically positioned within a network to carefully su□ervise and analyze all network traffic. They conduct a comprehensive analysis of □ackages to detect s□ecific signatures and diligently work to identify and address any unauthorized network activities. Within host-based IDSs, application-based IDSs might be considered a separate category. They gather and analyze audit data unique to a given program, function, or a□□lication com□onent that is run on one or more hosts (Böse et al., 2017).

A database management system (DBMS) can be considered a s□ecific category of such applications. However, traditional application-based intrusion detection system (IDS) a□□roaches are insufficient for establishing an effective intrusion detection system for a database management system (DBMS). To comprehend this, it is crucial to grasp the techniques that Intrusion Detection Systems (IDSs) utilize to identify security policy breaches (Velpula & Gudipudi, 2009).

5.1.1. Misuse Detection

One of the two kinds of processes used to find unlawful activity is intrusion detection, which includes misuse detection techniques. Misuse detection relies on signatures that specify the attributes of established system attacks and vulnerabilities. Signatures are typically acquired from security policies. Misuse detection methods use a mechanism to monitor the system, network, or application for any behaviors that correspond to given signatures. These signatures can include a specific sequence of system calls or a particular sort of packet flow between two hosts (Depren et al., 2005).

While misuse detection systems are effective in identifying and handling existing attacks and usage patterns, they are inadequate in addressing novel assaults and emerging security risks. To effectively prevent invasions, it is necessary for these misuse detection systems to regularly update the signatures of security risks and vulnerabilities (Kim et al., 2014).

5.1.2. Anomaly Detection

The majority of intrusion detection methods commonly integrate the identification of usage patterns with the detection of abnormal behaviors. Anomaly detection approaches are well recognized and very efficient, as they rely on the typical behavior of a subject, such as a user, system component, or application. Anomaly detection involves gathering data on recurrent and typical behavior and representing it as statistical models of normal behavior, such as profiles (Chandola et l., 2009).

These □rofiles are then com□ared to the activity of the current user or system. Activities are considered intrusive if they substantially deviate from the ex□ected □rofile. Deviation from the usual behavior can indicate □ossible breaches of security protocols or unauthorized access, which may prompt appropriate actions to be taken (Ahmed et al., 2016).

Anomaly detection offers a distinct advantage over misuse detection by increasing the possibility of detecting previously unseen attacks and activities. It is crucial to ensure that the modeling of normal behavior and the setting of thresholds in an anomaly-based IDS are done effectively. The purpose of this is to reduce the occurrence of false positives, which refer to activities that differ from what is usual but do not breach security standards, as well as to avoid false negatives, which are sus□icious activities that are incorrectly identified as normal (Liu et al., 2012).

Integrating the methodologies used in misuse-based and anomaly-based detection approaches, commonly utilized in host-based and network-based intrusion detection systems (IDSs), into database management systems and associated infrastructure, including applications and the network, would yield significant advantages. One of the main challenges in develo□ing a database intrusion detection system is insider misuse. This aspect will be discussed in more detail as it □lays a significant role in driving the security re-engineering approach presented in this chapter (Song et al., 2007).

5.1.3. Insider Misuse

The concept of intrusion typically involves individuals who gain unauthorized access to a system. Examples of these intrusions can happen when system vulnerabilities are exploited or when the accounts of legitimate users are cracked or stolen. When someone successfully gains access to a system, the system recognizes them as an authorized user and grants them all the rights and privileges associated with that user status. The intruder is typically seen as someone with insider access. An essential component of a security re-engineering approach to database systems involves effectively recognizing and preventing insider misuse (Magklaras & Furnell, 2001).

According to various recent reports, it is evident that conventional methods and systems for detecting intrusions are inadequate for addressing insider misuse. According to the CSI/FBI reports, it has been noted that the risk posed by individuals within an organization is significantly higher com□ared to external threats. The reports also highlight that internal incidents are just as frequent as external attacks. It is evident that the issue of insider misuse becomes more severe when dealing with database systems that handle extensive amounts of sensitive and crucial data. Various sources can lead to potential insider misuse, including individuals who intentionally tamper with data integrity out of dissatisfaction, as well as unauthorized access by external hackers, criminals, and spies (Punithavathani et al., 2015).

The security re-engineering methodology is driven by many major observations, which might be loosely summarized as follows. Traditional network-based and host-based Intrusion Detection Systems (IDSs) are ineffective in addressing insider misuse at the database level. The reason for this is that users usually have authorized access to the applications and database, and instances of misuse are not evident at the system or network level, but at a more detailed level within the database, such as updates and deletion of tuples (Hunker & Probst, 2011).

However, it is logical to combine these Intrusion Detection Systems (IDSs) with a database-driven method for identifying anomalies and detecting misuse. Furthermore, the reports frequently highlight the fact that both authorized users and unauthorized attackers can take advantage of excessive database and application privileges granted to normal users. This element is clearly connected to the principle of least privilege, which states that no individual should be given more □rivileges than what is essential and sufficient to □erform their job. In the following, the initial stages of a security re-engineering method for databases will be discussed. This method involves analyzing the data stored in the database and actions performed by users on that data (Schultz, 2002).

5.2. DATA AND USER PROFILING

Learning Objectives

- Understand the importance and methods of auditing in database security;
- Learn techniques for data □rofiling to identify anomalies and misuse; and
- Ex□lore user □rofiling for monitoring ty□ical behavior and detecting intrusions.

The fundamental approach used to identify intrusions and insider misuse, as well as to redesign security measures, involves monitoring the specific operations that users execute on a database system. In the following, data-centric perspective and profiling methodologies will be discussed (Eke et al., 2019).

5.2.1. Auditing

Auditing refers to the systematic monitoring and recording of specific events and actions within a database. Auditing is largely employed to ensure accountability, validate security regulations, and record and evaluate the observed behavior of applications, users, and database objects. Many companies are required to go through auditing to comply with various federal regulations, including the Sarbanes-Oxley Act of 2002, Health Insurance Portability and Accountability Act (HIPAA) of 1996, and the Graham-Leach-Bliley Act (GLBA) of 1999. In later cases, auditing largely serves the objective of demonstrating accountability, specifically identifying the individuals responsible for carrying out certain actions on particular items at specific moments in time, as well as reconstructing the sequence of events (Bedard, 1989).

NIST has provided a comprehensive framework consisting of six key components for evaluating the security of database systems. The tasks involved include the selection of security audit events, generating security audit data, storing security audit events, reviewing audits, analyzing security audits, and implementing automatic responses. Figure 5.1 shows the sequence of these criteria as a method for utilizing auditing techniques in evaluation activities. This is preceded by an additional step, the analysis of security requirements s□ecific to the a□□lication (Hass et al., 2006).

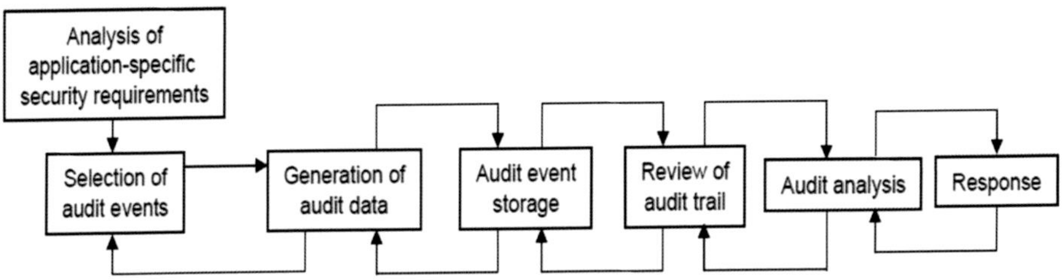

Figure 5.1. Illustrations of activities according to the NIST security audit criteria.

Source: Michael Gertz Creative Commons License.

Several contemporary commercial and open-source database management systems (DBMS) provide audit mechanisms and architectures to facilitate a range of activities. There are variations in the level of detail that different mechanisms can record in audit trails. For example, database triggers provide a convenient method for capturing information about SQL updates, inserts, and deleting statements on database relations. One important aspect is the ca□ability to track and store the □revious and current values of modified data entries (Satava et al., 2006). Activities involving the creation, editing, and removal of database objects as a result of SQL data definition language (DDL) statements are subject to auditing. The auditing of accesses regarding system privileges is the term used to describe this auditing. Some database systems offer advanced techniques that go beyond auditing at the SQL statement level. These technologies, including Fine-Grained Auditing (FGA), which launched with Oracle 9i, track data accesses according to content. This is very useful for taking down details on SQL select statements.

Furthermore, stored procedures can be a valuable technique to complement the existing database triggers and the SQL audit command that are commonly supported by various DBMS. Instead of using individual SQL insert, update, and delete statements from an application, stored procedures are utilized. A stored procedure is responsible for executing the data modification statements and keeping track of additional context information related to the modifications. The data to be considered includes factors like the present user role, the current users accessing the database, and the count of records that have been altered by these statements (Anderson et al., 1993). There are two methods for monitoring audit data to monitor SQL statements, access privileges, database schema objects, and detailed access information in database security. The first way is to store the audit trail within the database itself, usually in a table in the data dictionary. The second way is to write the audit information to an operating system audit trail, which is a file located outside the database and inaccessible to database users (Watson & MacKay, 2003).

An audit trail commonly includes logged data such as the database user username, their assigned privileges and roles, the name of the accessed database object, the session and transaction ID, the SQL text of the triggering statement, and the type of operation executed. Enabling any form of audit mechanism, whether it be triggers or audit mechanisms activated by the SQL audit command, will inevitably affect the performance of the database (Pierre et al., 2018).

As a result, every audit plan intended to evaluate a database security must carefully consider the various safety limitations imposed on the database and the strategy's particular objectives (Figure 5.2). The subsequent two parts will outline fundamental components for formulating such a strategy: The analysis of users and data will be examined (Francis, 1994).

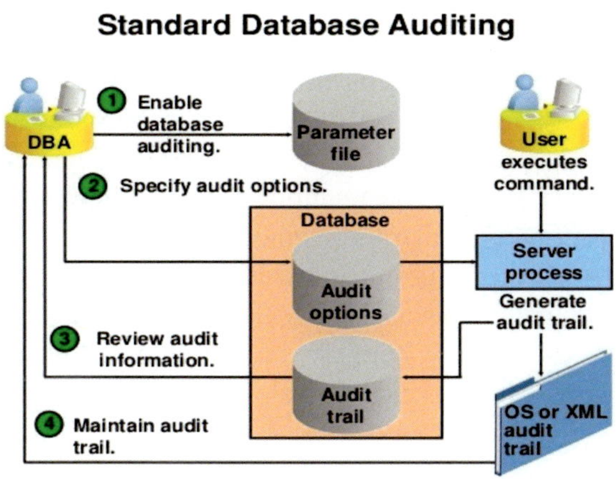

Figure 5.2. *Description of standard database auditing.*

Source: Sushil Jajodia Creative Commons License.

5.2.2. Data Profiling

The majority of methods for detecting misuse are focused on the user. Their goal is to figure out the typical user behavior regarding database operations and identify any deviations from previous behavior. One perspective suggests that in order to improve database security, it is crucial to evaluate and strengthen security measures with a focus on the data itself. Before using techniques for detecting and evaluating the (possibly anomalous) behavior of users, it is necessary to examine the behavior of the data being maintained in the database (Abedjan et al., 2017).

There are multi□le justifications for ado□ting such a methodology. Initially, any unintentional or deliberate interference with the security and reliability of data is ty□ically identified solely at the data level, meaning that it is only detected when incorrect, absent, surplus, or abnormal data is found. This feature gives rise to the second argument, which involves the desire to trace unusual data back to the individuals who manipulate it. This can be challenging, especially when multiple users share the same database accounts, which is a common practice in many application contexts (Papenbrock et al., 2015).

When trying to determine regular user behavior, it is commonly assumed that the data users are working with is normal, indicating that the data is both accurate and of high quality. However, this is frequently not true for production databases, as guaranteeing and overseeing data quality is a major concern (Caicedo et al., 2017).

5.2.2.1. Snapshot Profiles

The initial step in security re-engineering for databases is identifying and assessing the characteristics of the data that need protection against unauthorized access or misuse. Examining a database schema that includes a collection of relations, the focus is on those relations that handle crucial missions or confidential information. Just like the methods proposed in previous studies, the analysis focuses on the values of individual attributes in a given relation. Using tools like histograms, this analysis looks at how often and where values for attributes occur. Additionally, it involves determining the lowest and highest values and lengths for both numerical and alphanumeric properties (Abramson et al., 2014).

Performing a basic analysis using SQL statements at the relation level may provide valuable insights, such as identifying outliers that deviate from expected data properties. Furthermore, the analysis can be expanded to include sets of tuples from one or more relations. In this case, the focus is on analyzing tuples and their combinations, while also determining correlations among attribute values using well-established association analysis techniques. It is worth noting that information about the relations can be accessed from the database's data dictionary (Claus et al., 1999).

When conducting data □rofiling, it is ty□ically ex□ected that the analysis tasks mentioned above are carried out on a sna□shot of the database, s□ecifically at a s□ecific moment in time. One a□□roach is to □erform this task during periods of low database activity, such as overnight. Another option is to utilize a standby or recently backed up database. When dealing with extensive databases containing numerous relations, it is important to focus on analyzing only the relevant ones. This includes relationships that are bound by particular security guidelines or that hold private and vital information (Aguénounon et al., 2020).

5.2.2.2. Temporal Profiles and Access Properties

Snapshot profiles provide a comprehensive overview of the data properties of various relations at a specific moment in time, specifically within a given database instance. To gain a comprehensive understanding of data behavior and evolution over time, it is crucial to delve deeper into the security of the database and establish effective security mechanisms (Oraevsky et al., 1997). To accomplish this, it is important to identify and separate two distinct objectives:

- Understanding the data patterns and trends as time progresses.
- Investigating the patterns of data access over a period of time.

One way to achieve the first objective is to regularly ca□ture sna□shot □rofiles and analyze them for any □atterns or trends. Crucial to this a□□roach is selecting the right time intervals to □erform sna□shot □rofiling. This decision heavily relies on the s□ecific a□□lication context of the database. Su□□ose that a relation $R \in \mathcal{R}$ for sna□shot □rofiles DataProf (R, t_1), DataProf (R, t_k) have been determined for a relation R at times $t_1, \ldots, t_k$.

The objective of analyzing these □rofiles is to identify □atterns in the behavior of data. The trends can include both more general properties like the ratio of tuple increase or decrease in R between consecutive timestamps t_i and t_{i+1} and more s□ecific □ro□erties like significant variations in the frequency and distribution of attribute values. The trends are addressed in tem□oral □rofiles that resemble sna□shot □rofiles in terms of their measure-value □air structure (Zahedi et al., 2017).

Once more, the results of this analysis are assessed and confirmed in relation to the anticipated data behavior. The purpose of this trend analysis is not to create more security measures, but to establish confidence in individual snapshot profiles and the attributes of relationships and data at particular moments in time. These profiling tasks can be easily combined with the process of keeping statistics for relations, which is essential for optimizing queries. It is important to mention that these statistics are consistently maintained in auxiliary relationships over a period of time (Olyphant, 2003).

The task that is closely related to detecting misuse and anomalies involves managing and profiling the access to the database relations over a period of time. In a basic scenario, when unusual data or data behavior is detected, it is common to inquire about the user responsible for such behavior. Naturally, this type of information cannot be derived from the relations alone but it necessitates the use of auditing techniques (Starks et al., 2006).

Consider a relation $R \in \mathcal{R}$ for which the access qualities need to be specified. At first, the auditing method chooses a suitable amount of time granularity, such as a single hour or an entire week. Afterward, audit mechanisms are established and triggered to record access information regarding SQL update, insert, delete, and select statements performed on R (Cavallaro et al., 2002).

If one is only interested in the frequency of such statements over a period, then normal auditing based on the SQL audit command is sufficient, and there is no need to use database triggers. Nevertheless, if there is a need for more detailed information regarding the data modification statements, triggers must be utilized. Triggers will then be responsible for keeping a record of each SQL statement that inserts, deletes, or modifies tuples, while also capturing the previous and new values of the updated tuples (Ter-Mikaelian et al., 2007).

5.2.3. User Profiling

After completing the data profiling tasks discussed earlier, the subsequent phase involves linking users to the data behavior and ultimately establishing models that describe users' typical behavior. Several studies have been conducted on user profiling and their behavior over time in relational databases. This research has primarily focused on areas such as fraud detection and intrusion detection.

To effectively address the user profiling task, it is crucial to have a clear understanding of the concept of a user within a database system. The fundamental basis of access control models in databases is centered on the concept of an authorization identifier (AuthID). This identification can be either the distinct identifier of a user in a database or the designation of a role in a database (Eke et al., 2019). As per the SQL: 1999 standard, the authorization identifier is determined by the DBMS when a SQL session is initiated. This phenomenon takes place when a program establishes a connection to the database by utilizing a legitimate database user account. In the following, the concept of a user in the context of database security will be discussed. A legitimate database user account that may be accessed by a human or an application is referred to as a user (Peng et al., 2016). There are usually various categories of user:

- **Database Administrators (DBAs):** These users have different privileges to handle different aspects of the database, such as creating and managing database files, relations, views, triggers, user accounts, roles, and system settings (Godoy & Amandi, 2005).
- **Application Developers:** The main responsibility of these users is to design, implement, and maintain the database schemas that support various applications. This includes managing structures like indexes and stored procedures (Rossi et al., 2017).
- **Application Users:** Application users have limited privileges within the system. They are unable to manage database objects, but can perform operations on the data of an application schema. This includes using insert, update, delete, and select statements, as well as executing stored procedures.

While DBAs possess extensive privileges to manipulate database structures and objects, analyzing their SQL DML statement behavior on s□ecific relations may not yield significant insights, considering their infrequent use of such operations. Understanding the behavior of DBAs can be a complex task, as they often have the res□onsibility of establishing an audit and □rofiling framework (Yang, 2010).

Furthermore, it is uncommon to extract a detailed pattern of behavior by auditing all actions performed by a database administrator on a database. These actions should primarily involve the management of database objects, both at a logical and physical level, rather than focusing on individual data entries within application schemas. The same reasoning applies to application developers as well (Al-Shamri, 2016).

5.3. ACCESS PATH MODEL

Learning Objectives

- Understand the access path model for managing complex database security.
- Ex□lore techniques for fine-grained access correlation between database and application layers.

Many complex access privilege structures might result from the presence of several database objects, multiple users, and multiple roles in a production-type database system. Furthermore, various programs may use different accounts and rights to interact with the same database and its objects. To properly implement a security re-engineering approach in a complex environment, it is crucial to have a reliable methodology that assists administrators and security personnel in effectively managing tasks related to data and user profiling, analyzing and correlating profiles, and restructuring security policies and mechanisms. In this section, the access path model, which is designed to assist in achieving these objectives with precision will be discussed (Nushi et al., 2015).

5.3.1. Problem Objectives and Settings

As mentioned earlier, in the event of finding incorrect or unusual data, it is important to determine the user(s) responsible for manipulating this data. Establishing correlations can be quite challenging due to various factors. There may be several layers involved in a complicated information system infrastructure. Typically, there are several applications built on a single database, which is accessed by various users at both the application and database level. These users can include individuals, application users, and database users (Tear et al., 2005).

Many existing methods for detecting anomalies and misuse in data assume a clear definition of a user, usually referring to someone who directly interacts with the data. However, in a more complex setting like the one described, it becomes im□ortant to define what exactly qualifies as a user. Is it a □erson, an application account, or a database account (potentially with multiple database roles)? What happens if users or applications decide to share accounts? What methods can be used to track the origins of data access?

For data access, there are multiple layers involved. From individuals or applications starting operations on the database, it becomes quite challenging to correlate abnormal data and behavior with a s□ecific □erson. However, to uphold the principle of accountability, it is essential to identify and establish these correlations (Jaques, 2005).

To address these concerns, adopt the access path model. The access path model is designed to aid administrators and security workers take a focused re-engineering approach to database systems. This is achieved by a systematic □rocedure that aims to define, describe, examine, and establish relationshi□s among various pathways of access. The manner in which an individual interacts with the data stored in a database management system (DBMS) is determined by an access path, which will be further upon in subsequent explanations (Jha et al., 2019). Data and user □rofiles are used to indicate distinct as□ects of an access path, making it easier to compare access correlations across multiple tiers of access. The access path model provides a thorough framework and approach for re-engineering database security. It focuses on identifying instances of misuse and irregularities by analyzing data and user □rofiles (Arbex & da Cunha, 2015).

5.3.2. Components of Model

The access path model comprises several components that facilitate the representation of links between users and accesses across different tiers. Figure 5.3 shows a thorough overview of the essential components, with the key pieces comprising applications and a singular database serving as the backend (Dekker et al., 1997).

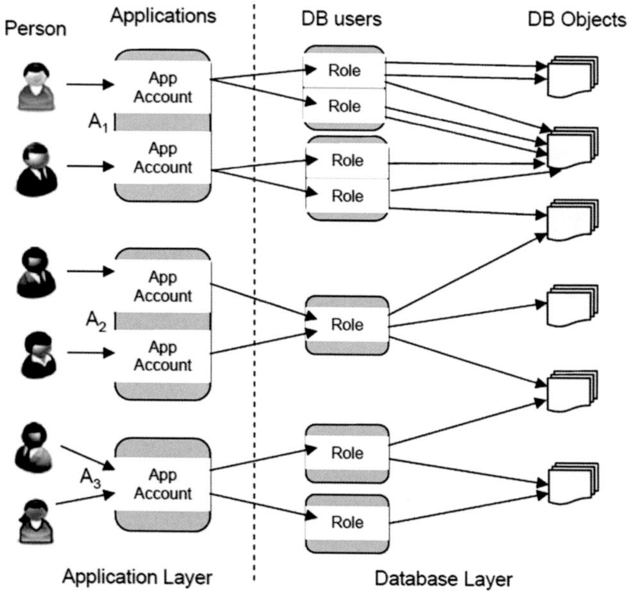

Figure 5.3. *Illustration of access path model.*

Source: Sushil Jajodia Creative Commons License.

In the figure □rovided, there are three a□□lications and multi□le individuals who are granted access to these a□□lications through s□ecific a□□lication accounts. Let's consider a scenario where an individual does not have a direct connection to the database, but accesses it through an application after being authenticated at the application layer. It is important to consider this assumption for DBAs, who exclusively utilize administrative tools (applications) to operate on the database. When accessing the database, users must utilize s□ecific database user accounts. These accounts are granted certain privileges that determine the operations they can perform on database objects (Bettman, 1973). Just think about the database relation operations, which are displayed on the right, for the sake of simplicity. Other kinds of database objects could also be included, like views or stored procedures that can be accessed and used from a database user account, res□ectively. The figure shows some common exam□les from the real world (Scherer, 2009). Let's first discuss these scenarios in more detail before going over some of the more formal aspects of the model. Then consider how to get an instance of the access □ath model (Gössler & Sifakis, 2005).

5.3.2.1. Application Layer

Three applications (A_1, A_2, and A_3) that some people have access to are shown in Figure 5.3. Each user is assigned an application account at application A_1, and every application account is connected to a database user account. Once more, each user at application A_2 has their own application account, but the application only makes use of one database account. Application A_3 utilizes separate database accounts, however two users share an application account. One notable finding from the last two incidents is that accounts are shared, which undoubtedly complicates the process of linking data accesses to specific individuals (Bhattacharjee et al., 1997).

5.3.2.2. Database Layer

Each user account in the database has a role or responsibilities associated with it. Each user account in application A_1, is associated with a matching database user account, which has two roles allocated to it. For the database account, Application A_2 has a single default role that is utilized for all database accesses (El-Hindi et al., 2019).

5.3.3. Exploring and Annotating Access Paths

Examine an access path model that has been partially developed for a database and particular apps. Database objects and database accounts or roles do not currently have any established connections. To effectively assess the security of crucial and confidential database elements, the initial focus is solely on the relevant relationships when examining access correlations. It is commonly understood that within a database schema, these relationships can be determined by referring to established security regulations and policies. In the following, let $\mathcal{DB}_{obj}$ denote only such important relations (Thomas et al., 2022).

Now, at each time t_i, a snapshot profile called DataProf(R, t_i) is determined for each relation R in the $\mathcal{R}$ò $\mathcal{DB}_{obj}$. This process adheres closely to the tasks outlined subsequently. Profiles are carefully examined, assessed, and then access profiles, known as AccessProf (R,t_i,t_j), are created for a specific time period [t_i,t_j]. Currently, various sections of the access path model instance are annotated using the profiles that were obtained in this manner. This model includes vertices that represent user accounts, responsibilities, and objects, as well as edges that represent access correlations (Mi et al., 2017).

Each relation R $\mathcal{R}$ò $\mathcal{DB}_{obj}$ in the database object is associated with a snapshot profile, DataProf (R, t_i), and an access profile, AccessProf (R,t_i,t_j). It is essential to make sure that a snapshot profile is taken simultaneously with the initiation of access information for R within the provided time range [t_i,t_j].

By utilizing an access profile called AccessProf (R,t_i,t_j) and its corresponding user profiles known as UserProf ((R,$u_{\pm}$ t ,t_j)), it becomes possible to establish access sub-paths ($u_{db} \rightarrow$ $r_{db} \rightarrow R$ R) from database accounts or roles to the relation R. Each sub-path has an annotation pertaining to the access details for the database users u_{db} and r_{db} roles. Access information specific to the database user u_{db} and role r_{db}, is annotated for each sub-path. The process is carried out for the remaining relations in the database object until all sub-paths from database accounts or roles to the relations in the database object $\mathcal{DB}_{\pm}$ have been marked with the corresponding access information (Dennis et al., 2003).

Once the access correlations at the database layer have been instantiated, specifically the sub-paths in the form ($u_{db} \rightarrow$ $r_{db} \rightarrow R$), and the subsequent task involves gathering more detailed information about the access connections between database accounts and application users. This information is then used to annotate the respective paths. While certain database systems may include details about remote database calls in their audit trails, these trails often lack the necessary information to accurately link a specific application account or individual to an operation performed on a relation.

For analyzing database security, it is important to consider both the basic access correlation between an application account and a database account, as well as the more detailed information that can be obtained through audit log correlation. An intriguing scenario arises when accounts are shared, as shown in Figure 5.2 for applications A_2 and A_3 (Rodchenkov et al., 2020). For example, while using application A_2 to access the database, if it is found that the database account "udb" was used to carry out specific operations on a relation R, it would be preferable to identify the application account (and possibly the person) responsible for these actions. The timestamps in the application logs and the database audit trail can be compared to establish a correlation if the program keeps track of logons, authentication events, and calls to remote functions (Iii et al., 1997). An appropriate solution should ideally be able to associate a specific user session in a user profile with an application account (and application session). The detailed information is then utilized to annotate the sub-paths that connect application accounts with database accounts (Groth & Streefkerk, 2006).

The annotation techniques discussed above highlight the possibility of conducting a targeted analysis of access correlations within a complex information system infrastructure. This can be accomplished by utilizing log correlation and already available techniques for data and user profiling. The methods show how feasible it is to extract access information from different components using a reverse engineering methodology and provide it to security staff for more inquiry. Investigations and following security re-engineering work can take many forms, but they must prioritize resolving unused privileges that violate the least privilege principle (Pan et al., 2021).

Practice Problems

In a financial institution's database system, a user with restricted privileges has been accessing customer data outside of regular working hours, querying transaction records from multiple accounts without a clear business justification, and there has been a surge in failed login attempts for a specific user account. These behaviors, identified through the access path model, suggest potential security vulnerabilities. The after-hours data access raises concerns about unauthorized or suspicious activity, possibly indicating an insider threat exploiting their access privileges. The frequent querying of transaction records without proper justification may signify data misuse or unauthorized access, posing risks such as identity theft or fraud. Additionally, the spike in failed login attempts points to potential security breaches, possibly from external attackers attempting unauthorized access using brute-force techniques.

Solutions to Practice Problems

To address these security concerns, several measures can be taken. First, implement stricter access controls and authentication mechanisms to prevent unauthorized data access, especially during non-working hours. Second, deploy real-time monitoring and analysis of user activity logs to detect and investigate suspicious behavior promptly. Third, make sure users only access information relevant to their job tasks by enforcing role-based access control (RBAC) restrictions. Last but not least, carry out frequent penetration tests and security audits to find flaws and address them before attackers can take advantage of them, strengthening the database system's overall security posture.

5.4. SECURITY RECONFIGURATION

Learning Objectives

- Understand techniques to reconfigure security mechanisms for database systems; and
- Understand the methods to enforce the principle of least privilege effectively.

Here is a summary of the fundamental actions that need be completed in order to modify a database system's security settings and procedures utilizing the data, user profiling, and access path correlations that were discussed in the preceding sections. If the application and database layers have appropriate authentication and auditing procedures in place (Tan & Poslad, 2004).

The goal of reconfiguring security mechanisms is to constrain database users' and roles' behavior so that they have precisely the right number of privileges to carry out their job. Stated differently, the procedures need to acknowledge the least privilege principle (Charles & Mishra, 2020).

However, the majority of database security mechanisms have trouble accomplishing this goal since they only use the SQL grant statement, which ty□ically □revents the s□ecification of fine-grained access controls. As a result, the grant statement cannot be used to establish acceptable behavior, such as limiting user entry to tu□les with s□ecific, well-defined □ro□erties. This □rovides plenty of possibilities for insiders to intentionally or unintentionally abuse their rights (Kepa et al., 2010).

5.4.1. Integrity Constraints

Constraints, as previously mentioned in relation to semantic integrity, offer a useful way to limit attribute values and their combinations to allowable values. The majority of static integrity requirements are simple to implement, for example, using relation schema check clauses or database triggers (Figure 5.4). These strategies can be used to stop malicious users from trying to introduce or edit unacceptable attribute values. Remember that these procedures also help to preserve data quality, which is a necessary precondition for assessing a database security (Calı et al., 2004).

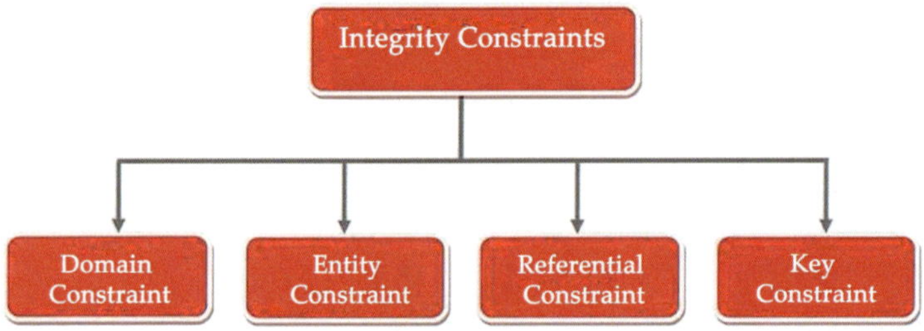

Figure 5.4. *Illustration of types of integrity constraint in database management.*

Source: Miro.com Creative Commons License

5.4.2. Unused Accounts and Roles

The access path model offers a structured approach for identifying database accounts and roles that are not being used. Specifically, accounts that are not being used are susceptible to abuse and hence should be either locked or permanently removed. Similarly, it is advisable to eliminate unused roles as they are likely to enforce outdated policies. Removing roles can also impact the restructuring of role hierarchies (Afonso et al., 2018).

5.4.3. Unused Privileges

The duration of the information collection should be taken into account when deciding what should be included in an access profile. By doing this, it will be less likely that the alleged unused authorization will be used infrequently. It is important to consider the association of privileges with separate roles, rather than assigning them to roles that have been considered inactive during the specified time window. The goal of applying the least privilege principle is substantially assisted by removing from users and roles any privileges or roles that are no longer needed or relevant (Setiyadi & Setiawan, 2018).

5.4.4. Re-Design and Discovery of Database Roles

Database roles are essential for managing privileges related to complex tasks such as activities performed by various types of application users. Assume that user access profiles and a set of mission-critical relational data have been established. An analysis can be conducted on the access paths in the access path model to identify any similarities in the way various database users access the relations. If there are no roles (or only a default role) assigned to these users for their respective accesses, it would be beneficial to introduce database roles (and role hierarchies) (Diran et al., 2020). This will facilitate the administration of privileges and help in efficiently capturing similar privileges utilized by these accounts.

Recently, determining roles from permission assignments has attracted a lot of attention. More s□ecific access data, such as that contained in access □rofiles, may be included in these methods. Investigating the design and assessment of roles and role hierarchies, with a specialized security analysis centered on roles, forms a unique field of research that can be seamlessly integrated into the comprehensive approach of security re-engineering (Ollikainen et al., 2015).

5.4.5. Development of Database Views

Utilizing database views to assign user privileges on these views instead of the underlying relations has proven to be an effective method in implementing the principle of least privilege. Acquiring these viewpoints is a difficult task that requires a thorough examination of access profiles. Consider a database user, denoted as u_{db} who has been authorized with the privileges to perform select, insert, and update operations on a relation R (Reiss, 1985).

The access □rofile u_{db} for the database might indicate that the user selectively chooses s□ecific tu□les and makes similar modifications to them. The tu□les' descri□tion, as □resented in the user □rofile for u_{db}, can be utilized to generate a view V that exclusively includes the tuples user commonly interacts with. The access that the user has on the database are then revoked, and they are assigned respective privileges on the view. It is possible to derive more complicated views for SQL select statements that reference multiple relations (De Haas, 2012). The conce□t of deriving views from access □rofiles is not well studied, as it is a com□lex effort to accurately define data required by a user, de□ending on their □rofiles, for them to carry out their authorized duties. An issue that could arise is that an access □rofile may have a limited time frame, which could restrict the user from completing tasks that they only carry out rarely (Grundy et al., 1998).

5.4.6. Stored Procedures

A major problem with relational database discretionary access control methods is that the SQL grant statements used to provide privileges to users and roles are often overly broad. As previously mentioned, using view privileges can circumvent some of these restrictions rather than privileges on base relations. However, in many cases, the ability to access certain relations (and views) is contingent upon contextual information that is not easily defined in a view definition (Eisenberg, 1996).

Additional information may cover various aspects, including multiple user sessions, time-based data, and the origin of database queries, such as the hosts of a□□lications. Significant research has been conducted on access control models that incorporate contextual information, resulting in more dynamic access control methods (Kruckenberg & Pipes, 2005).

Stored procedures offer an effective way to gather additional context, such as for auditing when they are performed from application programs rather than simple SQL data update statements. Similarly, stored processes can be utilized to collect contextual information regarding their ongoing execution, which can then be employed to make precise access control determinations (Brimhall et al., 2012).

The SQL queries in a stored procedure can access data dictionary relations or carry out other (remote) procedures when the procedure is intended to carry out an update that an application has requested. This allows for the determination of whether the update operation is authorized. Because stored procedures are executed instead of standard SQL DML queries, using them may need changes to the a□□lication code. Stored □rocedures are considered an efficient method for preventing misuse, rather than simply detecting it through a retrospective analysis of audit trials (Foggon, 2006).

It is important to maintain a balance between the performance and security of the database and its applications, taking into account various security needs. By utilizing the access □ath model, vulnerabilities can be identified and analyzed systematically, enabling the implementation and evaluation of improved security mechanisms. Typically, the impact of security mechanisms on database performance is rarely addressed in existing research. However, this topic presents an intriguing area for future investigation and the development of new strategies (Driscoll et al., 2013).

5.5. ADVANCEMENT IN DATABASE SECURITY

Learning Objective

- Understand recent advancements in database security, focusing on anomaly detection and intrusion prevention.

Although there has been considerable progress in intrusion detection systems for network-based and host systems, databases have not received the same level of attention. Detecting misuse and anomalies in databases, particularly for evaluating their security, has received relatively limited attention. Castano provides a comprehensive and idealized description of the steps and approaches involved in designing database security. Expanding upon the principles of Entity-Relationship (ER) modeling to incorporate essential security and authorization elements (Wenhua et al., 2023).

A new strategy has been put forth by researchers, tailored to identify irregularities and unauthorized activities within database systems. The approach involves discovering typical user access patterns from audit data through the use of association rule mining. Semantically connected data is easily collected and used by users by taking advantage of relationships found in the underlying database schema, such as foreign key dependencies (Pernul, 1994).

Distance measures are utilized to assess whether a users' data access falls within the expected boundaries based on previous observations. If it deviates from the norm, an alarm is triggered to indicate a potential misuse. This approach has been expanded to uncover security policies at various levels of detail and access patterns. A comprehensive analysis is provided on the subject of monitoring mission-critical data for integrity and availability. Various audit approaches are discussed in detail (Tan et al., 2016).

There has been some recent research on anomaly detection in database security. One notable contribution is by Spalka, who introduced the concept of delta relations. These relationships are obtained from characteristics of the data and function as data □rofiles. They are used to identify anomalies in user operations on the data. They offer a prototype of their system using the Microsoft SQL Server 2000, s□ecifically. The method utilizes user query information in the database system to construct access □rofiles. Subsequently, these □rofiles are matched to new queries utilizing distance measures to detect any irregularities (Kaufman, 2009). Using the syntactic as□ects of SQL queries, □rofiles are created instead of depending on the data that SQL statements modify. Exploring the detection of abnormal access patterns is a fascinating and valuable method. It would be worth delving into how these patterns can inform the redesign of security mechanisms.

Many of the methods for user and data profiling heavily rely on data mining techniques. These techniques are specifically designed to analyze and audit data collected from various computing system infrastructure components. An extensive review of numerous data mining approaches is given in Barbara's edited book, with a focus on intrusion and anomaly detection. However, it mainly focuses on the operating and network system layer rather than databases (Rahaman, 2022).

Additional research has been conducted on methods to identify and prevent unauthorized manipulation of data integrity and confidentiality in a database management system (DBMS). This work includes the explanation of key ideas and the development of a prototype for a database that can withstand intrusion attempts. A new proposal has been put out to enhance the security of a database. This proposal introduces the concept of a database firewall, which ensures the continuity of certain database services even in the event of an attack on the database. The primary emphasis is on the manipulation of database audit logs within the framework of forensic analysis, which is a crucial factor to consider due to the significant reliance of profiling and data techniques on accurately recorded audit data (Gochhwal, 2017).

5.6. GRADUAL RE-DESIGN STRATEGIES

Learning Objectives

- Understand strategies for systematically redesigning database security to address vulnerabilities and evolving needs.

Just like any intricate software system, vulnerabilities can arise from inadequate configuration practices, making it susceptible to exploitation by both intruders and insiders. In DBMSs, the primary focus of standard setup procedures is to guarantee the smooth and dependable functioning of the database as it provides data to different applications (Cilla et al., 2017).

It is usual for security procedures and techniques to be used or modified in a disorganized form in response to changing application and user requirements. This can result in a disjointed and potentially unreliable approach to maintaining and designing database security.

Enhancing the database security is a tough task, considering the intricate nature of modern databases utilized by government and e-business organizations. These databases handle vast amounts of data, serving multiple applications within infrastructure of networked information system. An overview of essential concepts and techniques that can assist administrators and security personnel in assessing and enhancing the security of a database is discussed in this chapter (Ojigi, 2011).

In context of evaluating security policies, one has demonstrated the effectiveness of exploring and analyzing data of users, retrieve profiles acquired from audit trails using the access path model. Within this model, one can examine and compare various access connections among components at the app and database layer about existing security requirements and anticipated practices.

One notable aspect of the suggested approach is its ability to facilitate a systematic and targeted overhaul of security policies and mechanisms. One way to accomplish this is through a thorough evaluation strategy that focuses on identifying potential vulnerabilities and insider misuse when accessing mission-critical and sensitive data. A various security re-design strategy, ranging from basic integrity constraints to more advanced techniques such as stored procedures or derived views have been discussed. These methods effectively protect the data that users commonly interact with (Klijn & Koppenjan, 2006).

The proposed approach highlights the importance of conducting research and development activities focused on enhancing the security of databases in a progressive manner. Using tools that are specifically designed for security specialists and administrators is crucial for implementing a security re-design approach. These tools can execute various data mining activities on profiles and establish similar measurements between user profiles. This allows for the identification of roles hierarchies and roles, which are essential for preserving database security (Kolmos et al., 2016).

There have been significant advancements in the development of various tool components that need to be seamlessly integrated to create a comprehensive security re-design approach. Additionally, there is significant potential in utilizing established techniques to generate database view specifications based on user and access profiles.

Essentially, when one has a set of queries and their corresponding result tuples for one or more base relations, one may want to determine the "minimal" views that can be queried to obtain the same tuples as the queries against the base relations. Overall, it is important to take into account different perspectives, especially those that take query context information into consideration. Such perspectives offer a compelling alternative for establishing sturdy access control models using modern database technology (Erway et al., 2015).

SUMMARY

- The chapter begins by exploring intrusion detection techniques, specifically focusing on misuse detection and anomaly detection. It emphasizes the significance of these techniques in detecting and addressing security breaches. The chapter highlights the importance of addressing insider misuse in database security and suggests incorporating database-specific measures into existing intrusion detection systems to tackle this challenge.
- Auditing in databases is crucial for tracking events, ensuring accountability and compliance, and validating security policies. Various techniques can be employed to enhance the security of databases, such as triggers, SQL audits, and stored procedures. These methods help in keeping track of actions and access to ensure a robust security system.
- For security re-engineering, data profiling comes before user profiling. For the purpose of identifying anomalies and modeling user behavior, snapshot and temporal profiles evaluate data behaviors over time.
- The access path model correlates user access across levels for security re-engineering, addressing intricate database configurations.
- Security reconfiguration include the implementation of integrity restrictions, role analysis, view derivation, and stored processes to effectively enforce the principles of least privilege.
- Database security reconfiguration encompasses the implementation of measures such as integrity restrictions, role analysis, and view derivation.
- Gradual redesign tactics improve security by using data-driven assessment and targeted policy modifications.

REVIEW QUESTIONS

1. How does data profiling contribute to database security, and what are its primary objectives?
2. Explain the difference between misuse detection and anomaly detection in the context of database security.
3. Why insider misuse is considered a significant threat to database security, and what techniques can be used to detect it?
4. What is the role of auditing in database security, and how does it help in identifying security vulnerabilities?

5. Discuss the importance of the access path model in analyzing user access patterns and correlations with database objects.
6. How can integrity constraints be utilized to enhance database security, and what mechanisms are commonly used to implement them?
7. Why is it important to identify and address unused accounts, roles, and privileges in database security?

MULTIPLE CHOICE QUESTIONS

1. What is the primary focus of database security revamp?

a. Performance optimization

b. Data and user □rofiling

c. Database backup procedures

d. Hardware upgrades

2. Which technique is primarily concerned with identifying abnormal user behavior?

a. Integrity Constraints

b. Misuse Detection

c. Unused Accounts Analysis

d. Database Backup

3. What aspect of database security involves constraining attribute values to acceptable ones?

a. Auditing

b. Anomaly Detection

c. Integrity Constraints

d. Role Analysis

4. Which component of the access path model helps identify correlations between users and database objects?

a. Problem Setting and Objectives

b. Annotating and Exploring Access Paths

c. Model Components

d. Security Reconfiguration

5. What technique involves creating views containing only the necessary data for specific users?

a. Unused Privileges Analysis

b. Integrity Constraints
c. User Profiling
d. Derivation of Database Views

6. What is a key feature of gradual redesign strategies for database security?

a. Immediate and radical changes
b. Data-driven evaluation
c. Static security policies
d. Minimal user involvement

Answers to Multiple Choice Questions

1. (b); 2. (b); 3. (c); 4. (b); 5. (d); 6. (b)

REFERENCES

1. Abedjan, Z., Golab, L., & Naumann, F. (2017). Data □rofiling: A tutorial. In *Proceedings of the 2017 ACM International Conference on Management of Data* (Vol. 1, pp. 1747–1751).
2. Abramson, V. G., Cooper Lloyd, M., Ballinger, T., Sanders, M. E., Du, L., Lai, D., & Arteaga, C. L. (2014). Characterization of breast cancers with PI3K mutations in an academic □ractice setting using SNaPshot □rofiling. *Breast Cancer Research and Treatment, 145*, 389–399.
3. Afonso, P., Wernke, R., & Zanin, A. (2018). Managing the cost of unused capacity: An integrative and comparative analysis of the ABC, TABC and UEP methods. *Revista del Instituto Internacional de Costos*, (1), 150–163.
4. Aguboshim, F. C., Obiokafor, I. N., & Ezeife, J. E. (2022). Revamping Nigeria's economy through sustainable data governance. *World Journal of Advanced Research and Reviews, 14*(1), 616–623.
5. Aguénounon, E., Smith, J. T., Al-Taher, M., Diana, M., Intes, X., & Gioux, S. (2020). Real-time, wide-field and high-quality single sna□shot imaging of o□tical □ro□erties with □rofile correction using dee□learning. *Biomedical Optics Express, 11*(10), 5701–5716.
6. Bettman, J. R. (1973). Perceived risk and its components: A model and empirical test. *Journal of Marketing Research, 10*(2), 184–190.
7. Bhattacharjee, S., Ammar, M. H., Zegura, E. W., Shah, V., & Fei, Z. (1997). Application-layer any casting. In *Proceedings of INFOCOM'97* (Vol. 3, pp. 1388–1396).

8. Böse, B., Avasarala, B., Tirtha□ura, S., Chung, Y. Y., & Steiner, D. (2017). Detecting insider threats using radish: A system for real-time anomaly detection in heterogeneous data streams. *IEEE Systems Journal, 11*(2), 471–482.
9. Brimhall, J., Dye, D., Gennick, J., Roberts, A., Sheffield, W., Brimhall, J., & Sheffield, W. (2012). Stored □rocedures. *SQL Server 2012 T-SQL Recipes: A Problem-Solution Approach* (Vol. 2, pp. 363–382).
10. Buczak, A. L., & Guven, E. (2015). A survey of data mining and machine learning methods for cyber security intrusion detection. *IEEE Communications Surveys & Tutorials, 18*(2), 1153–1176.
11. Chandola, V., Banerjee, A., & Kumar, V. (2009). Anomaly detection: A survey. *ACM Computing Surveys (CSUR), 41*(3), 1–58.
12. Charles, S., & Mishra, P. (2020). Reconfigurable network-on-chi□security architecture. *ACM Transactions on Design Automation of Electronic Systems (TODAES), 25*(6), 1–25.
13. Chen, C. P., & Zhang, C. Y. (2014). Data-intensive applications, challenges, techniques and technologies: A survey on Big Data. *Information Sciences, 275*, 314–347.
14. Chen, Y., Nyemba, S., & Malin, B. (2012). Detecting anomalous insiders in collaborative information systems. *IEEE Transactions on Dependable and Secure Computing, 9*(3), 332–344.
15. Cilla, M., Checa, S., & Duda, G. N. (2017). Strain shielding ins□ired re design of proximal femoral stems for total hip arthroplasty. *Journal of Orthopedic Research, 35*(11), 2534–2544.
16. Claus, R. E., Mannen, R. K., & Schicht, W. W. (1999). Treatment career sna□shots: Profiles of first treatment and □revious treatment clients. *Addictive Behaviors, 24*(4), 471–479.
17. De Haas, H. (2012). The migration and development pendulum: A critical view on research and policy. *International Migration, 50*(3), 8–25.
18. Dekker, R., Wildeman, R. E., & Van der Duyn Schouten, F. A. (1997). A review of multi-component maintenance models with economic dependence. *Mathematical Methods of Operations Research, 45*, 411–435.
19. Dennis, G., Sherman, B. T., Hosack, D. A., Yang, J., Gao, W., Lane, H. C., & Lempicki, R. A. (2003). DAVID: Database for annotation, visualization, and integrated discovery. *Genome Biology, 4*, 1–11.
20. Depren, O., Topallar, M., Anarim, E., & Ciliz, M. K. (2005). An intelligent intrusion detection system (IDS) for anomaly and misuse detection in computer networks. *Expert Systems with Applications, 29*(4), 713–722.

21. Diran, D., Hoppe, T., Ubacht, J., Slob, A., & Blok, K. (2020). A data ecosystem for data-driven thermal energy transition: Reflection on current practice and suggestions for re-design. *Energies, 13*(2), 4–44.
22. El-Hindi, M., Binnig, C., Arasu, A., Kossmann, D., & Ramamurthy, R. (2019). Blockchain DB: A shared database on blockchains. *Proceedings of the VLDB Endowment, 12*(11), 1597–1609.
23. Erway, C. C., Küpçü, A., Papamanthou, C., & Tamassia, R. (2015). Dynamic provable data possession. *ACM Transactions on Information and System Security (TISSEC), 17*(4), 1–29.
24. Foggon, D. (2006). Stored procedures. *Beginning ASP.NET 2.0 Databases: From Novice to Professional*, 415–457.
25. Francis, J. R. (1994). Auditing, hermeneutics, and subjectivity. *Accounting, Organizations and Society, 19*(3), 235–269.
26. Gochhwal, R. (2017). Unified □ayment interface—An advancement in payment systems. *American Journal of Industrial and Business Management, 7*(10), 1174–1191.
27. Godoy, D., & Amandi, A. (2005). User □rofiling in □ersonal information agents: A survey. *The Knowledge Engineering Review, 20*(4), 329–361.
28. Gössler, G., & Sifakis, J. (2005). Com□osition for com□onent-based modeling. *Science of Computer Programming, 55*(1–3), 161–183.
29. Groth, D. P., & Streefkerk, K. (2006). Provenance and annotation for visual exploration systems. *IEEE Transactions on Visualization and Computer Graphics, 12*(6), 1500–1510.
30. Grundy, J., Hosking, J., & Mugridge, W. B. (1998). Inconsistency management for multiple-view software development environments. *IEEE Transactions on Software Engineering, 24*(11), 960–981.
31. Hartono, N., & Erfina, E. (2021). Com□arison of stored □rocedures on relational database management systems. *Tech-E, 4*(2), 8–15.
32. Hass, S., Abdolmohammadi, M. J., & Burnaby, P. (2006). The Americas literature review on internal auditing. *Managerial Auditing Journal, 21*(8), 835–844.
33. Kaufman, L. M. (2009). Data security in the world of cloud computing. *IEEE Security & Privacy, 7*(4), 61–64.
34. Kepa, K., Morgan, F., Kosciuszkiewicz, K., & Surmacz, T. (2010). SeReCon: A secure reconfiguration controller for self-reconfigurable systems. *International Journal of Critical Computer-Based Systems, 1*(1–3), 86–103.
35. Kolmos, A., Hadgraft, R. G., & Holgaard, J. E. (2016). Response strategies

for curriculum change in engineering. *International Journal of Technology and Design Education, 26*, 391–411.

36. Kruckenberg, M., & Pipes, J. (2005). Stored procedures. In *Pro MySQL* (pp. 349–373).
37. Liang, S. (2019). Collaborative, dynamic and diversified user □rofiling. In *Proceedings of the AAAI Conference on Artificial Intelligence* (Vol. 33, pp. 4269–4276).
38. Liu, F. T., Ting, K. M., & Zhou, Z. H. (2012). Isolation-based anomaly detection. *ACM Transactions on Knowledge Discovery from Data (TKDD), 6*(1), 1–39.
39. Magklaras, G. B., & Furnell, S. M. (2001). Insider threat prediction tool: Evaluating the probability of IT misuse. *Computers & Security, 21*(1), 62–73.
40. Mi, H., Huang, X., Muruganujan, A., Tang, H., Mills, C., Kang, D., & Thomas, P. D. (2017). PANTHER version 11: Expanded annotation data from Gene Ontology and Reactome pathways, and data analysis tool enhancements. *Nucleic Acids Research, 45*(D1), D183–D189.
41. Moreno, J., Serrano, M. A., & Fernández-Medina, E. (2016). Main issues in big data security. *Future Internet, 8*(3), 4–44.
42. Muheidat, F., Patel, D., Tammisetty, S., Lo'ai, A. T., & Tawalbeh, M. (2022). Emerging concepts using blockchain and big data. *Procedia Computer Science, 198*, 15–22.
43. Ojigi, M. L. (2011). Cadastral layout review and re-design of Jikpan area of Minna using high resolution imagery and land information system. *Journal of Environmental Management and Safety, 2*(1), 15–15.
44. Ollikainen, N., de Jong, R. M., & Kortemme, T. (2015). Coupling protein side-chain and backbone flexibility im□roves the re-design of □rotein-ligand s□ecificity. *PLoS Computational Biology, 11*(9), e1004335.
45. Oraevsky, A. A., Jacques, S. L., & Tittel, F. K. (1997). Measurement of tissue optical properties by time-resolved detection of laser-induced transient stress. *Applied Optics, 36*(1), 402–415.
46. Pan, Q., Liu, Y. J., Bai, X. F., Han, X. L., Jiang, Y., Ai, B., & Li, C. Q. (2021). VARAdb: A comprehensive variation annotation database for humans. *Nucleic Acids Research, 49*(D1), D1431–D1444.
47. Papazoglou, M. P., & Van Den Heuvel, W. J. (2007). Service oriented architectures: Approaches, technologies and research issues. *The VLDB Journal, 16*, 389–415.
48. Papenbrock, T., Bergmann, T., Finke, M., Zwiener, J., & Naumann,

F. (2015). Data □rofiling with metanome. *Proceedings of the VLDB Endowment, 8*(12), 1860–1863.

49. Peng, J., Choo, K. K. R., & Ashman, H. (2016). User □rofiling in intrusion detection: A review. *Journal of Network and Computer Applications, 72*, 14–27.
50. Pernul, G. (1994). Database security. In *Advances in Computers* (Vol. 38, pp. 1–72).
51. Pierre, J., Peters, B. G., & de Fine Licht, J. (2018). Is auditing the new evaluation? Can it be? Should it be? *International Journal of Public Sector Management, 31*(6), 726–739.
52. Punithavathani, D. S., Sujatha, K., & Jain, J. M. (2015). Surveillance of anomaly and misuse in critical networks to counter insider threats using computational intelligence. *Cluster Computing, 18*, 435–451.
53. Rahaman, M. M. (2022). Recent advancement of cyber security: Challenges and future trends in Bangladesh. *Saudi Journal of Engineering and Technology, 7*(6), 278–289.
54. Reiss, S. P. (1985). PECAN: Program development systems that support multiple views. *IEEE Transactions on Software Engineering, (3)*, 276–285.
55. Satava, D., Caldwell, C., & Richards, L. (2006). Ethics and the auditing culture: Rethinking the foundation of accounting and auditing. *Journal of Business Ethics, 64*, 271–284.
56. Scherer, K. R. (2009). The dynamic architecture of emotion: Evidence for the component process model. *Cognition and Emotion, 23*(7), 1307–1351.
57. Schultz, E. E. (2002). A framework for understanding and predicting insider attacks. *Computers & Security, 21*(6), 526–531.
58. Setiyadi, A., & Setiawan, E. B. (2018). Information system monitoring access log database on database server. In *IOP Conference Series: Materials Science and Engineering* (Vol. 407, No. 1, p. 012110). IOP Publishing.
59. Sicari, S., Rizzardi, A., Grieco, L. A., & Coen-Porisini, A. (2015). Security, privacy and trust in Internet of Things: The road ahead. *Computer Networks, 76*, 146–164.
60. Song, X., Wu, M., Jermaine, C., & Ranka, S. (2007). Conditional anomaly detection. *IEEE Transactions on Knowledge and Data Engineering, 19*(5), 631–645.
61. Starks, P. J., Heathman, G. C., Jackson, T. J., & Cosh, M. H. (2006). Tem□oral stability of soil moisture □rofile. *Journal of Hydrology, 324*(1–4), 400–411.

62. Tan, J. J., & Poslad, S. (2004). Dynamic security reconfiguration for the semantic web. *Engineering Applications of Artificial Intelligence, 17*(7), 783–797.

63. Tan, S., De, D., Song, W. Z., Yang, J., & Das, S. K. (2016). Survey of security advances in smart grid: A data driven approach. *IEEE Communications Surveys & Tutorials, 19*(1), 397–422.

64. Watson, M., & MacKay, J. (2003). Auditing for the environment. *Managerial Auditing Journal, 18*(8), 625–630.

65. Zahedi, M., Aleahmad, A., Rahgozar, M., Oroumchian, F., & Bozorgi, A. (2017). Time sensitive blog retrieval using temporal properties of queries. *Journal of Information Science, 43*(1), 103–121.

66. Zheng, Y., Capra, L., Wolfson, O., & Yang, H. (2014). Urban computing: Concepts, methodologies, and applications. *ACM Transactions on Intelligent Systems and Technology (TIST), 5*(3), 1–55.

CHAPTER 6

AUTHORIZATION AND AUTHENTICATION

LEARNING OBJECTIVES

At the end of this chapter, readers will be able to:

1. Understand the importance of authentication and authorization in database access control;
2. Understand the importance of database security and its components in DBMS;
3. Identify types of security violations and measures to protect databases;
4. Learn about authorization levels and their role in maintaining security;
5. Understand user access control methods and their advantages in database security; and
6. Comprehend the concept of granting privileges and its implications in security management.

INTRODUCTORY EXAMPLE

TechGuard Solutions is a leading cybersecurity firm specializing in providing comprehensive security solutions to businesses worldwide. As part of their services, they offer consultation on access control mechanisms to ensure their clients' sensitive data remains protected from unauthorized access.

In one instance, TechGuard Solutions was a□□roached by a financial institution, SecureBank, which had recently experienced a security breach resulting from unauthorized access to their customer database. Upon investigation, it was revealed that the breach occurred due to inadequate access controls, allowing an insider threat to exploit vulnerabilities and access confidential financial records.

TechGuard Solutions conducted a thorough assessment of SecureBank's existing access control measures and identified several weaknesses in their authentication and authorization protocols. They recommended implementing role-based access control (RBAC) to streamline access management and enforce the principle of least privilege across the organization.

By im□lementing RBAC, SecureBank was able to define s□ecific roles for employees based on their job responsibilities and grant them appropriate access permissions accordingly. This not only strengthened their security posture but also ensured compliance with industry regulations governing data protection in the financial sector.

Through their expertise in access control mechanisms, TechGuard Solutions helped SecureBank enhance their security infrastructure and regain the trust of their customers, emphasizing the importance of robust authentication and authorization practices in safeguarding sensitive information.

UNIT INTRODUCTION

Ensuring the security of databases is of great importance in Database Management System (DBMS) due to the critical nature and confidentiality of enterprise data and information. Thus, it is essential to protect the data within the database system from any unauthorized access or potential corruption (Trnka et al., 2022). Users are either granted or denied the ability to perform actions on the objects stored within the database, due to database security measures. Most DBMSs offer discretionary access control to manage user access to objects through privileges. Accessing objects in a well-defined manner requires obtaining a privilege (Kim & Lee, 2017). Ensuring the security of databases is essential in safeguarding valuable data from potential risks, whether they be accidental mishaps or deliberate acts of unauthorized individuals. Ensuring the security of the database system falls under the DBA's focus. In order to protect the databases, the DBA must first identify the major dangers to the data and then set up thorough rules, processes, and appropriate security measures (Usmonov, 2021).

This chapter explores different aspects of database security, including potential threats, methods to safeguard against unauthorized access, and various security mechanisms (Trnka et al., 2018).

6.1. SECURITY VIOLATIONS

Learning Objectives

- Understand the types of security violations in databases; and
- Understand the importance of security measures at different levels.

Three types of security violations can occur in database systems.

- The first ty□e involves unauthorized modifications of data within the database.
- The second type involves unauthorized deletions of data from the database.
- Preventing unauthorized access to database information (Guo et al., 2011).

To protect the database from any unauthorized access or security breaches, it is crucial to implement security measures at various levels:

- *Database System:* Users can be assigned varying levels of access rights to ensure they only have access to the s□ecific data they require.

Now, the database must uphold these restrictions and ensure robust security measures (Vance & Siponen, 2012).

a) *Operating System:* Securing the operating system is crucial to prevent unauthorized access. Ensuring the absolute safety of a database system is essential for maintaining overall security.

b) *Network:* Computers or systems are interconnected through LANs, the internet, and other means, enabling the exchange of data across these networks. Ensuring the highest possible security within network software is of paramount importance (Hu et al., 2015).

c) *Human Factors:* Authorization should be granted with caution to minimize human errors.

d) *Physical Security:* It is essential to ensure the physical security of servers and com□uter systems to □rotect them from theft, fire, and other potential disasters (Kraemer & Carayon, 2007).

Security measures must be implemented at several levels to ensure the security of the database.

6.2. AUTHORIZATION (ACCESS RIGHTS)

Learning Objectives

- Understand different levels of user authorization in database security; and
- Differentiate between deletion of data and deletion of relations.

Security can be kept by assigning distinct privileges to individual users based on their respective roles. Various authorizations are:

a) *Read Access:* It only allows data to be read. Users cannot make any changes, modifications, or u□dates to the data.

b) *Update Access:* Only data updating is permitted. Deleting data is not possible for the user.

c) *Insert Access:* It enables the inclusion of additional information. The user cannot alter or remove the pre-existing data (Jøsang, 2017).

d) *Delete Access:* Data can be deleted using this method. Modifying the existing data is not within the user's scope of control.

e) *Index Access:* One of its functionalities includes the ability to create and delete indices.

f) *Alteration Access:* One benefit is the ability to easily add or remove attributes in a relation.

g) *Resource Access:* It facilitates the establishment of new connections.

h) *Drop Access:* Relations can be deleted using this method (Kizza, 2005).

A user with delete access is limited to deleting data and cannot modify relations. Even if a user were to delete all the data, the relationship would continue to exist. If a relation is deleted, nothing will remain (Sun & Wang, 2011).

For example, let's take a look at the student information system:

Reg. No.	Roll No.	Name	Class	Table Name
001 A 002 A 003 A	1 2 3	Vikas Amit Lalit	Commerce Computers Mechanical	Table Name is Student

Once all the data has been deleted, the relation or table remains as displayed above:

Reg. No.	Roll No.	Name	Class

However, the drop command will remove the table entirely, including all of its data.

Ex. Drop table student.

This command removes all data from the table called Student. By granting the previously mentioned authorization, the DBA ensures the security of the database and prevents unauthorized access.

Practice Problems

Create a robust database access control system customized for a university database, housing essential student records such as personal information, grades, and financial data. The system must enforce strict access controls, allowing only authorized personnel to retrieve certain types of data based on their designated roles within the university hierarchy.

Solutions to Practice Problems

Utilize role-based access control (RBAC) to assign various roles, including student, faculty, administrator, and registrar, each with pre-established permissions. Users establish their identity through the use of distinct identifiers such as usernames and passwords, strengthened by the implementation of multi-factor authentication to enhance security measures. Access policies ensure that users are only granted access to the data that is necessary for their roles, following the principle of least privilege. Comprehensive audit trails carefully monitor each event of database access, while robust encryption safeguards sensitive data from any unauthorized access. Security audits are regularly performed to identify any potential vulnerabilities and improve security measures on an ongoing basis.

6.3. USER ACCESS CONTROL

Learning Objective

- Understand the concept of user access control in database security.

Ensuring the security of databases is essential in safeguarding sensitive company data. One way to achieve this is through database access control, which grants access only to authorized individuals while preventing unauthorized access. There are two primary components involved: authentication and authorization (Smetters & Good, 2009). This facility offers a customized database model to individual users. Through the use of this feature, database administrators can conceal unnecessary data from users.

There are several key benefits to im□lementing user access control:

a) *Simplify the System Usage:* Users can only access the data that is relevant to their s□ecific needs and tasks. This can also be beneficial for optimizing resources (Mandal et al., 2020).

b) *Limits User Access to Data:* Users are limited to accessing only s□ecific □arts of the database. If a user cannot access any other data, it becomes difficult for them to breach the security □rotocols (Roesner et al., 2012).

Ensuring a secure server involves finding the right balance between authorization and view settings.

6.4. GRANTING OF PRIVILEGES

Learning Objective

- Understand the implications of revoking and granting user authorizations in databases.

Access rights can be granted by a user to another user, but only if the DBA has authorized the granting right. Users are granted authorization based on the existence of a path from the root (DBA) to the node representing the user (Eisen et al., 2002). Take a look at a delete authorization (Figure 6.1) example.

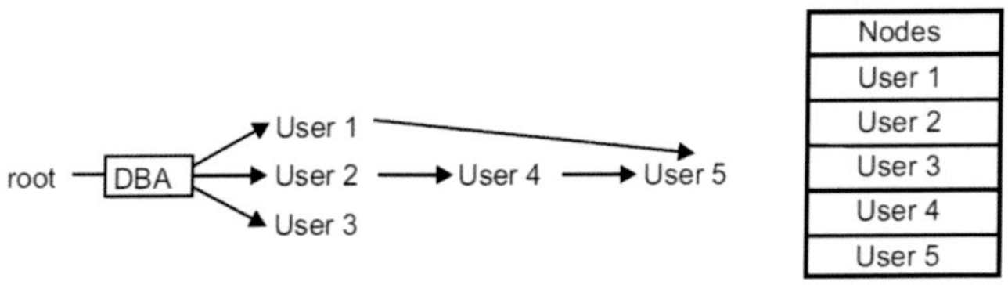

Figure 6.1. *Illustration of delete authorization for user 5.*

Source: Satinder Bal Creative Commons License.

There are two ways for User 5 to obtain the authorization (Figure 6.2) to delete:

- DBA →User 2 → User 4 → User 5
- DBA → User 1 → User 5

After a while, user 5 can access the first path if the DBA removes that authority from user 1.

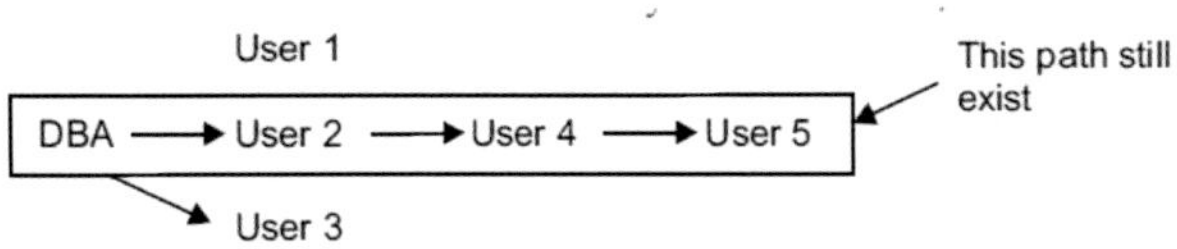

Figure 6.2. *Representation of delete authorization for user 5 after DBA revoked delete authority from user 1.*

Source: Aditya Mitthal Creative Commons License.

For example, look at the authorizations shown in Figure 6.3.

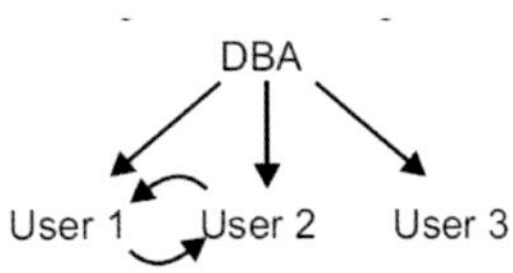

Figure 6.3. *Illustration of user authorizations.*

Source: Gilbert La. Creative Commons License.

Here, user 1, user 2, and user 3 are granted authority by the DBA. Authorization is granted to user 1 by user 2 and vice versa. Even if DBA withdraws authority from User 2 at any point, User 1 still retains authority (Ladd, 1969) (Figure 6.4).

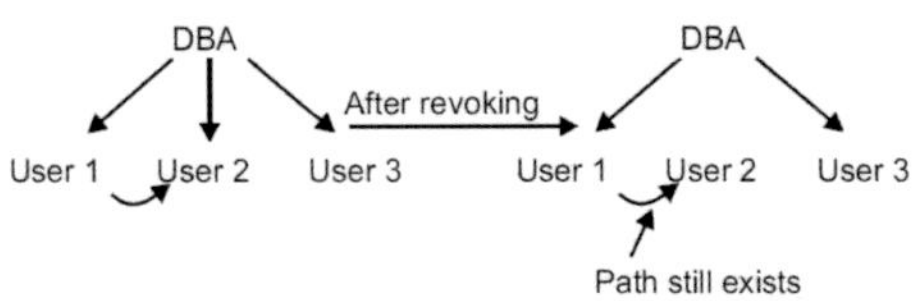

Figure 6.4. *Representation of modified user authorizations.*

Source: Aditya Mitthal Creative Commons License.

DBAS must exercise caution when granting privileges (Eisen et al., 2001).

6.5. NOTION OF ROLES

Learning Objective

- Understand user roles in database.

DBAs assign varying levels of privileges to individual users. Imagine a scenario where multiple users possess identical access privileges. It is advantageous to categorize these users and grant authorization (rights) to this specific group. When a new user joins the company, they will be included in a group (Chan & Snow, 2017).

For example, let's consider a software corporation called ABC, shown in Figure 6.5.

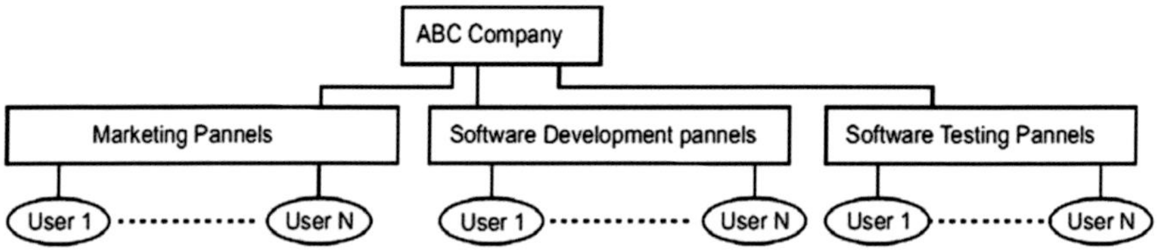

Figure 6.5. *Illustration of notion of roles in a software company.*

Source: Satindar Bal Creative Commons License.

The database administrator categorizes users into three distinct groups or roles:

- Marketing
- Software Development
- Software Testing (Vergés et al., 2013)

The DBA grants rights or authority to certain categories, excluding individual users. Subsequently, users are assigned to these different groups. Upon adding a user to any group, the user will immediately be granted the authorizations assigned to that group (Achterkamp et al., 2008).

- *Advantages:* The benefits of the conce□t of roles are:
  - Simplify the tasks of a database administrator.
  - Resources can be maximized for efficiency.
- *Disadvantage:* The drawbacks of the concept of roles are:
  - It would be impossible to determine the correlation between each transaction and its respective user. This will result in potential security vulnerabilities.

6.5.1. Audit Trails

Learning Objectives

- Understand the importance of audit trails in enhancing system security and accountability; and
- Understand the methods for reviewing and analyzing audit trails to detect anomalies and ensure compliance.

To address the drawbacks associated with the concept of roles, it is possible to keep audit trails. An audit trail is a historically recorded log of important actions performed on a system. Recorded events encompass user login and logout activities, along with the s□ecific commands executed by the user while logged into the system. Audit trails are crucial in identifying security breaches, performance issues, and defects in applications (Wolf, 2003).

Audit trails provide a comprehensive log of data accesses, including the creation, reading, u□dating, and deletion of files, for each user. System resource usage can also be recorded, including activities like □rinting files or transferring data between storage locations. Failed access attempts can also be monitored. An audit trail records the actions, timing, and individuals involved in doing tasks, as well as unsuccessful attempts made by individuals (Cutcliffe, J. R., & McKenna, 2004).

A computer system can contain multiple audit trails, each dedicated to a certain category of activity. Audit trails can serve as a means to facilitate regular system o□erations and also function as an insurance □olicy, or fulfill both purposes simultaneously. Audit trails are consistently maintained as a precautionary measure, but they are only utilized when necessary, such as in the event of a system breakdown. Audit trails are utilized by system administrators to assist in safeguarding the system or resources from potential harm caused by hackers, insiders, or technical issues (Carcary, 2020).

- *Uses of Audit Trails:* Audit trails are an essential component of computer security, especially valuable for tracking illegal users and activities. Additionally, they can be utilized to aid in the retrieval of information in the case of a system malfunction (Wolf, 2003).

6.5.2. Advantages of Audit Trails

Audit trails serve to address several security-related concerns, including individual accountability, event reconstruction, detection of intrusions, and problem analysis & Seneviratne, 2022).

a) *Individual Accountability:* Audit trails are a technical method that aids managers in maintaining individual accountability (Jancura, 1977).

Managers can promote appropriate user behavior by informing users that they are individually responsible for their actions, which are monitored and recorded through an audit trail. Users are more likely to comply with security policy if they are aware that their actions will be documented in an audit log (Duncan et al., 2021).

b) *Events Reconstruction:* Audit trails can also serve the purpose of reconstructing events following the occurrence of an issue. Reviewing audit trails of system activity is a more efficient way to analyze damage by identifying the s□ecific details of how, when, and why regular processes stopped. A study of the audit trail may frequently differentiate between errors caused by operators and errors generated by the system (Duncan et al., 2021).

c) *Intrusion Detection:* Intrusion detection is the act of recognizing efforts to breach a system and obtain illegal entry. When audit trails are properly planned and executed to capture relevant information, they can aid in detecting unauthorized access. Real-time detection of intrusions can be achieved by analyzing audit records as they are generated or retrospectively (Ye et al., 2002).

d) *Problem Analysis:* Audit trails can also serve as online tools to promptly detect and address issues beyond invasions. This is frequently referred to as real-time monitoring or auditing. When a system or program is considered crucial to an organization's operations or goals, real-time auditing can be utilized to track these activities' advancement (Jiang & Cao2011).

6.5.3. Audit Logs and Trails

A system can keep track of several unique audit trails at once. Most audit records fall into one of two categories.

a) *An Event-Oriented Log:* An audit trail must have adequate information to establish the s□ecific events that took □lace and the individuals or entities responsible for causing them. Typically, an event record should include the timestamp of the event, the user ID linked to the event, the program or command used to trigger the event, and the outcome. The combination of date and time can be utilized to determine whether the user is an imposter or the designated individual. Event-based logs often consist of entries that describe system events, application events, or user events (Bishop, 1996).

b) *Keystroke Monitoring:* It is often described as a comprehensive record of all keystrokes made. Keystroke monitoring is the act of observing and recording the s□ecific keys that are □ressed by a computer user, as well as the computer's corresponding actions during an interactive session. Keystroke tracking is widely regarded as an accurate representation of audit trails (Roratto & Dias, 2014). Keystroke monitoring refers to the act of seeing the characters entered by users, accessing their electronic mail, and examining other recorded information submitted by users. Keystroke monitoring is implemented to protect systems and data from illegal access or exploitation by intruders. Surveillance of keystrokes entered by unauthorized users can aid administrators in assessing and remedying any damage caused by these individuals.

6.5.4. Review of Audit Trails

Audit trails serve the purpose of objectively examining the sequence of events that took place following a specific incident, doing regular assessments, and conducting immediate analysis. Reviewers must possess the necessary knowledge to effectively identify and detect atypical behavior. They must comprehend the characteristics of typical behavior (Bishop 1996). Reviewing the audit trail can be simplified by allowing users to query the audit trail function using parameters such as terminal ID, user ID, application name, time and date or other specified criteria to generate reports with selected information (Lunt, 1988). There exist numerous categories of reviews. Here are a few examples:

- **Reviewing the Audit Trail After an Event:** When faced with a system or application software problem, a user violating requirements, or an unexplained issue, it is essential for the system-level or program-level administrator to thoroughly analyze the audit trails. The data/application owner typically conducts a separate review, using audit trail data, to assess whether their resources are being misused (Cutcliffe & McKenna, 2004).
- **Audit Trail Data Periodic Review:** Those responsible for ensuring data security, such as administrators of systems, computer security managers, and function managers, must evaluate the extent of audit trail record review necessary, considering the importance of identifying unauthorized activities. A direct correlation between this decision and the frequency of periodic checks of audit trail data should be established (McCartney, 2009).
- **Analysis of Audit in Real Time:** Audit trails are usually reviewed in batch mode regularly, such a daily basis. Audit records are kept in an archive for later review during that period. Tools for audit analysis may also be used (Roratto & Dias, 2014).

SUMMARY

- Database security in a database management system (DBMS) is crucial for □rotecting confidential information from unauthorized access and corruption. This responsibility is carried out by the database administrator (DBA) through the implementation of policies and access restrictions.
- Security threats encompass unauthorized manipulation, removal, and access to data, which necessitates the implementation of security measures across various levels, including databases, operating systems, networks, human factors, and physical security.
- Authorization involves granting different levels of access rights, such as read, update, insert, delete, index, alteration, resource, and drop access. User access control guarantees verifying the identity of users and granting or denying their access to data to limit unauthorized data access.
- Having a system that keeps track of all activities and timestamps them is crucial for identifying any security breaches or performance problems.
- Some benefits of audit trails include holding individuals accountable, reconstructing events, detecting intrusions, and analyzing problems. Different types of audit trails can be used, such as event-oriented or keystroke monitoring. These methods allow for real-time analysis and review of past events.

REVIEW QUESTIONS

1. Explain the concept of access rights in a database system and provide examples of different types of access privileges.
2. How do database access control mechanisms contribute to preventing unauthorized access to sensitive data?
3. Discuss the role of audit trails in detecting security violations and performance issues in a database environment.
4. What are the advantages of using roles in managing user access and permissions within a database system?
5. Describe the process of granting privileges in a database environment and discuss the potential risks associated with improper privilege management.

MULTIPLE CHOICE QUESTIONS

1. **Which of the following is the process by which a user's privileges ascertained?**
   a. Authorization
   b. Authentication
   c. Access control
   d. None of these
2. **Data security threats include**
   a. Privacy invasion
   b. Hardware failure
   c. Fraudulent manipulation of data
   d. Encryption and decryption
3. **Mandatory access control (also called security scheme) is based on the concept of**
   a. access rights
   b. system-wide policies
   c. both (a) and (b)
   d. (d) none of these
4. **Which of the following is the process by which a user's identity is checked?**
   a. Authorization
   b. Authentication
   c. Access control
   d. None of these
5. **Which of the following is the permission to access a named object in a prescribed manner?**
   a. Role
   b. Privilege
   c. Permission
   d. All of these
6. **Access right to a database is controlled by**
   a. Top management
   b. System designer

c. System analyst

d. Database administrator

Answers to Multiple Choice Questions

1. (a); 2. (a); 3. (c); 4. (b); 5. (c); 6. (d)

REFERENCES

1. Achterkamp, M. C., & Vos, J. F. (2008). Investigating the use of the stakeholder notion in project management literature: A meta-analysis. *International Journal of Project Management, 26*(7), 749–757.
2. Allinson, C. (2001). Information systems audit trails in legal proceedings as evidence. *Computers & Security, 20*(5), 409–421.
3. Bishop, M. (1996). A standard audit trail format. In *Proceedings of the 1995 National Information Systems Security Conference* (Vol. 1, pp. 136–145).
4. Bowen, G. A. (2009). Supporting a grounded theory with an audit trail: An illustration. *International Journal of Social Research Methodology, 12*(4), 305–316.
5. Carcary, M. (2020). The research audit trail: Methodological guidance for application in practice. *Electronic Journal of Business Research Methods, 18*(2), 166–177.
6. Chan, S. Y., & Snow, J. W. (2017). Formidable challenges to the notion of biologically important roles for dietary small RNAs in ingesting mammals. *Genes & Nutrition, 12*, 1–15.
7. Chapin, P. C., Skalka, C., & Wang, X. S. (2008). Authorization in trust management: Features and foundations. *ACM Computing Surveys (CSUR), 40*(3), 1–48.
8. Cutcliffe, J. R., & McKenna, H. P. (2004). Expert qualitative researchers and the use of audit trails. *Journal of Advanced Nursing, 45*(2), 126–133.
9. Eisen, G. M., Baron, T. H., Dominitz, J. A., Faigel, D. O., Goldstein, J. L., Johanson, J. F., ... & Wheeler-Harbough, J. (2002). Methods of granting hospital privileges to perform gastrointestinal endoscopy. *Gastrointestinal Endoscopy, 55*(7), 780–783.
10. Eisen, G. M., Dominitz, J. A., Faigel, D. O., Goldstein, J. A., Petersen, B. T., Raddawi, H. M., & Ad Hoc EUS Committee. (2001). Guidelines for credentialing and granting privileges for endoscopic ultrasound. *Gastrointestinal Endoscopy, 54*(6), 811–814.

11. Guo, K. H., Yuan, Y., Archer, N. P., & Connelly, C. E. (2011). Understanding nonmalicious security violations in the workplace: A composite behavior model. *Journal of Management Information Systems, 28*(2), 203–236.

12. Jancura, E. G. (1977). Electronic Data Processing: The computer & the audit trail. *Woman CPA, 39*(1), 6–78.

13. Jayathilake, N. D., & Seneviratne, S. C. (2022). The investigation of the awareness of implementing blockchain technology in audit trails among the auditors. *Journal of Accounting Research, Organization and Economics, 5*(2), 109–123.

14. Jiang, K., & Cao, X. (2011). Design and implementation of an audit trail in compliance with US regulations. *Clinical Trials, 8*(5), 624–633.

15. Jøsang, A. (2017). A consistent definition of authorization. In *Security and Trust Management: 13th International Workshop, STM 2017, Oslo, Norway, September 14–15, 2017, Proceedings 13* (pp. 134–144).

16. Kennedy, G. E., & Judd, T. S. (2007). Expectations and reality: Evaluating patterns of learning behavior using audit trails. *Computers & Education, 49*(3), 840–855.

17. Kim, H., & Lee, E. A. (2017). Authentication and authorization for the Internet of Things. *IT Professional, 19*(5), 27–33.

18. Kizza, J. M. (2005). Access control and authorization. In *Computer Network Security* (pp. 209–232).

19. Koestner, R., & Wheeler, L. (1988). Self-presentation in personal advertisements: The influence of im□licit notions of attraction and role expectations. *Journal of Social and Personal Relationships, 5*(2), 149–160.

20. Kraemer, S., & Carayon, P. (2007). Human errors and violations in computer and information security: The viewpoint of network administrators and security specialists. *Applied Ergonomics, 38*(2), 143–154.

21. Ladd, M. (1969). Privileges. *Law & Society Order, 4*(2), 5–55.

22. Lunt, T. F. (1988). Automated audit trail analysis and intrusion detection: A survey. In *Proceedings of the 11th National Computer Security Conference* (Vol. 3, pp. 65–73).

23. Mandal, S., Bera, B., Sutrala, A. K., Das, A. K., Choo, K. K. R., & Park, Y. (2020). Certificateless-signcry□tion-based three-factor user access control scheme for IoT environment. *IEEE Internet of Things Journal, 7*(4), 3184–3197.

24. McCartney, P. R. (2009). Audit trails and electronic record discovery. *MCN: The American Journal of Maternal/Child Nursing, 34*(1), 64–88.

25. Misanchuk, E. R., & Schwier, R. A. (1992). Representing interactive multimedia and hypermedia audit trails. *Journal of Educational Multimedia and Hypermedia, 1*(3), 355–372.

26. Roratto, R., & Dias, E. D. (2014). Security information in production and operations: A study on audit trails in database systems. *JISTEM-Journal of Information Systems and Technology Management, 11*, 717–734.

27. Smetters, D. K., & Good, N. (2009). How users use access control. In *Proceedings of the 5th Symposium on Usable Privacy and Security* (Vol. 4, pp. 23–78).

28. Sun, L., & Wang, H. (2011). Access control and authorization for protecting disseminative information in E-learning workflow. *Concurrency and Computation: Practice and Experience, 23*(16), 2034–2042.

29. Trnka, M., Abdelfattah, A. S., Shrestha, A., Coffey, M., & Cerny, T. (2022). Systematic review of authentication and authorization advancements for the Internet of Things. *Sensors, 22*(4), 1361.

30. Trnka, M., Cerny, T., & Stickney, N. (2018). Survey of authentication and authorization for the Internet of Things. *Security and Communication Networks, 7*(1), 55–99.

31. Usmonov, M. T. O. G. L. (2021). Autentification, authorization, and administration. *Science and Education, 2*(7), 233–242.

32. Vance, A., & Siponen, M. T. (2012). IS security policy violations: A rational choice perspective. *Journal of Organizational and End User Computing (JOEUC), 24*(1), 21–41.

33. Wolf, Z. R. (2003). Exploring the audit trail for qualitative investigations. *Nurse Educator, 28*(4), 175–178.

34. Ye, N., Emran, S. M., Chen, Q., & Vilbert, S. (2002). Multivariate statistical analysis of audit trails for host-based intrusion detection. *IEEE Transactions on Computers, 51*(7), 810–820.

CHAPTER 7

DETECTION AND PREVENTION OF SQL INJECTION ATTACKS

LEARNING OBJECTIVES

At the end of this chapter, readers will be able to:

1. Understand the significance and prevalence of SQL injection attacks;
2. Understand the common causes and vulnerabilities leading to SQLIAs;
3. Understand the effectiveness and practicality of AMNESIA through empirical analysis;
4. Understand the significance and impact of SQL injection attacks;
5. Learn common techniques used in SQL injection attacks;
6. Explore practical examples of SQL injection vulnerabilities;
7. Understand the limitations of defensive programming against SQL injection attacks; and
8. Understand the capabilities and constraints of static and taint-based approaches in SQLIA prevention.

INTRODUCTORY EXAMPLE

TechShop, a widely-used e-commerce platform, allows users to search for products by entering keywords into a search bar. The website's search functionality relies on SQL queries to fetch product information from its database. However, a hacker named "MaliciousMax" discovers a vulnerability in TechShop's search feature, enabling SQL Injection Attacks (SQLIA).

MaliciousMax, aware of this vulnerability, crafts a specialized input designed to exploit the weakness in TechShop's search feature. This input contains a malicious SQL query aimed at retrieving sensitive data from the database, such as usernames and passwords of TechShop's users.

Using the crafted input, MaliciousMax manipulates the search bar, injecting the malicious SQL query into the in□ut field. The query is s□ecifically designed to retrieve confidential information from the database. Des□ite the lack of □ro□er input validation mechanisms, TechShop's backend processes the input provided by MaliciousMax, inadvertently executing the injected SQL query.

As a consequence of this oversight, TechShop inadvertently exposes confidential user information to MaliciousMax. With access to usernames and passwords, MaliciousMax could compromise user accounts, potentially leading to various security breaches and financial losses for both TechSho□and its users.

To mitigate the risk of SQL Injection Attacks and protect user data, TechShop should implement robust security measures. This includes implementing thorough input validation mechanisms to sanitize user input and prevent the execution of malicious SQL queries. Additionally, employing techniques such as parameterized queries and stored procedures can help defend against SQL Injection Attacks by separating user input from SQL code execution. Regular security audits and penetration testing can also help identify and address vulnerabilities proactively, ensuring the continued security and integrity of TechShop's platform and user data.

UNIT INTRODUCTION

SQL Injection Attacks (SQL/As) are a significant concern when it comes to safeguarding database-driven applications. One of the most serious vulnerabilities that an online application might encounter is SQL injection attacks, according to the Open online Application Security Project (OWASP), a global community of web developers. In the domain of software development, SQL injection attacks have been identified as a significant vulnerability that cannot be ignored. Notably, industry giants like Microsoft and SPI Dynamics have emphasized the importance of addressing this issue (Alwan & Younis, 2017). SQL injection vulnerabilities can have severe consequences as they provide attackers with unauthorized access to the underlying database of an application. Through the utilization of SQLIAs, an individual with malicious intent can potentially gain unauthorized access to sensitive database information, allowing them to manipulate or remove data as they see fit. Often, this data is of a confidential or sensitive nature, and its compromise can result in issues like identity theft and fraud. Several well-known companies and organizations, including Travelocity, Tower Records, FTD.com, Guess Inc., Creditcards.com, and the Recording Industry Association of America (RIAA), have fallen victim to SQL injection attacks (SQLIAs) (Ghafarian, 2017).

SQL injection attacks (SQLIAs) have well-known causes. Like many other code-injection attacks, SQL injection attacks happen when user input is not properly validated. One of the main concerns in this area of study is the potential vulnerability that can occur when user input is directly used to create a database query. The application's failure to properly encode and validate input creates a vulnerability that can be exploited by attackers (Halfond & Orso, 2007). They have the ability to insert harmful data that the database sees as more commands. Based on how serious the vulnerability is, the attacker can use the database to perform a number of SQL statements. SQL Injection Attacks (SQLIA) may take advantage of the vulnerabilities of interactive database-driven systems, particularly websites that rely on user input to access their databases. Informal surveys conducted on database-driven online applications have revealed that about 97% of them are susceptible to SQL Injection Attacks (SQLIA) (Balasundaram & Ramaraj, 2012).

Like other security vulnerabilities, the risk of SQL injection attacks can be minimized by implementing defensive coding techniques. Executing and ensuring compliance with this method in practical application might be highly demanding. Developers consistently attempt to incorporate new security features, while attackers persistently seek inventive techniques that bypass these □rotections. It might be difficult to kee□ engineers u□dated on the latest and most efficient defensive coding a□□roaches, as the field of defensive coding is continuously changing. Furthermore, reducing security vulnerabilities in outdated programs through the implementation of defensive coding techniques can be challenging, time-consuming, and error-prone task (Bafghi, 2013). The current issues underscore the significance of im□lementing a thorough and systematic strategy to tackle the difficulties □resented by SQL injection (Kumar & Indu, 2014).

This chapter introduces AMNESIA (Analysis and Monitoring for Neutralizing SQL Injection Attacks), an advanced technique and technology designed to detect and prevent SQLIAs (SQL Injection Attacks). The development of AMNESIA was founded on two fundamental insights:

- The necessary data to anticipate the potential arrangement of all valid queries produced by a web application is encompassed inside the application's code; and
- A SQLIA, by the introduction of further SQL statements into a query, would breach that arrangement (Tajpour et al., 2010).

A novel approach was developed to enhance the security of databases by integrating static analysis and runtime monitoring. This method effectively prevents SQL injection by using two key decisions. During the static analysis stage, AMNESIA takes a model that defines every valid query that the web application can generate and extracts it from the code. During the runtime monitoring stage, AMNESIA makes sure that every query the application generates adheres to the model. Inappropriate queries are halted and reported (Chen et al., 021).

7.1. SQL INJECTION ATTACKS

Learning Objectives

- Understand SQL injection vulnerabilities and their impact on web applications; and
- Learn different types of SQL injection attacks and their techniques.

When a SQL injection vulnerability is present, an attacker can directly execute instructions on the database that supports a web application, so compromising the goal functioning of the application. An attacker can use the targeted application to execute instructions on the database and possibly the host system when a SQLIA vulnerability is discovered (Halfond et al., 2006).

One type of code injection attack known as a SQL injection attack feeds on user in□ut that has not been validated. The flaws arise when □rogrammers construct dynamic queries by fusing user input with hard-coded strings. Attackers can use insufficient in□ut validation to modify user in□ut in a way that causes the database to view certain parts of it as SQL operators or keywords when it incor□orates them into the final query string (Boyd & Keromytis, 2004).

7.1.1. Example of an SQLIA

This example web application is exposed to a particular kind of SQL injection attack called a tautology-based attack. This will facilitate the understanding of the mechanisms behind such attacks. Figure 7.1 shows the architecture of the web application. The user engages with a web form by inputting a login name and pin, which are subsequently transmitted to the web server. The application server's show.jsp servlet receives the user's credentials from the web server (Fu & Qian, 2008).

After authenticating the credentials with a database query, the servlet responds to the user web page request with a response. The servlet uses the credentials given by the user to dynamically create a database query, as shown in Figure 7.2. Obtain the procedure User information is retrieved by utilizing the login credentials and □ersonal identification number (PIN) provided by the user (Rankothge et al., 2020). The method will submit the query to the database if neither the login nor the pin is entered:

```
SELECT info FROM users WHERE login='guest'
```

On the other hand, the method will include the submitted credentials in the query if the user enters their pin and login (Abawajy, 2013). Therefore, when a user inputs their pin and login as "doe" and "12 3", the servlet dynamically generates the query:

```
SELECT info FROM users WHERE login='doe' AND pin=123
```

A website that utilizes this servlet would be at risk of SQL injection attacks. For example, when a user inputs "' OR l=l --" and " ", instead of "doe" and "123", the query that is generated is:

```
SELECT info FROM users WHERE login='OR 1=1 --' AND pin=
```

After the WHERE token, the database understands every detail as a conditional expression and the inclusiveness of the "OR 1=1" part turns this dependent into a tautology. (The characters "--" represent the starting of a comment, so every detail after it is dismissed.) Consequently, the database would provide details for each user entry (Hussain et al., 2021).

It is crucial to keep in mind that there are numerous types of SQL injection attacks that hackers have created, with tautology-based assaults being just one of them. This particular attack is presented as an example due to its simplicity and ease of understanding. As a result of this particular explanation, tautology-based attacks have received a substantial amount of attention in academic literature, and they are often mistakenly considered as the only sort of SQL injection attacks. Nevertheless, contemporary attack methods extend beyond the scope of solely injecting tautologies. In the following section, a broad explanation of SQLIAs, followed by an overview of the various types of SQLIAs that are currently recognized will be discussed (Kar et al., 2016).

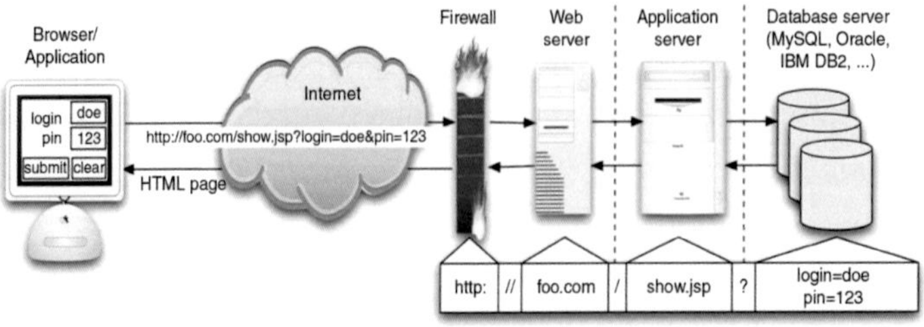

Figure 7.1. *Illustrations example of interaction between a typical web application and a user.*

Source: William G.J Creative Commons License.

```
public class Show extends HttpServlet {
1. public ResultSet getuserlnfo(String login,
String pin) {
2. Connection conn = DriverManager.getConnection("MyDB"};
3. Statement stmt = conn.createStatement();
4. String queryString = "";
5. queryString = "SELECT info FROM users WHERE ";
6. If ((! login.equals ("")) && (! Pin. Equals(""))) {
7. queryString += "login='" + login +
"' AND pin=" + pin;
)
8. else {
9. queryString+="login=' guest' ";
}
10. ResultSet tempSet = stmt.execute(queryString);
11. return tempSet;
```

Figure 7.2. *Illustration of. example servlet.*

Source: Halfond Creative Commons License.

7.1.2. SQLIA General Definitions

SQL injection attacks occur when attackers manipulate SQL queries by inserting new SQL keywords or operators, thereby altering the intended semantics, syntax or logic of the query. The definition encompasses all the different types of SQL injection attacks that are discussed in the subsequent subsections (Al Rubaiei et al., 2020).

7.1.3. Variants of SQLIA

There has been an increase in the development of complex attack methods in recent years that can take advantage of vulnerabilities associated with SQL injection. These methods surpass the typical SQLIA examples that rely on tautology and instead utilize complicated and advanced SQL constructs. Disregarding the presence of such attacks results in the creation of solutions that only offer a partial resolution to the issue of SQLIA (Aliero et al., 2020).

For example, a program can be vulnerable to SQL injection attacks when it accepts input from various sources. Developers and researchers widely agree that SQL injection attacks (SQLIAs) are often the result of user input being entered through a web form or in response to a prompt for input. It is important to consider that individuals with malicious intent may take advantage of external strings or inputs used to create a query string, which can serve as a vulnerability for SQL injection attacks (Atoum & Qaralleh, 2014).

It is a frequent occurrence to observe the utilization of external input sources, including HTTP cookie or server variables fields, in the construction of a query. Considering the nature of cookie values and server variables, it is important to acknowledge that these external strings can be subject to manipulation by potential attackers (Baklizi et al., 2022).

Furthermore, second-order injections leverage extensive understanding of a susceptible application to execute an attack by taking advantage of input sources that are otherwise adequately protected. Developers must ensure the safety of user input by implementing proper measures such as escaping, type-checking, and filtering. In certain scenarios, when the data is utilized in a separate setting or to construct an alternative query, the secure input can transform into a potential injection attack. It is important to implement procedures that go beyond basic user input verification or explicit declaration of untrusted input sources. This is because there are numerous other input sources that have the potential to lead to a SQL injection attack. It may not be adequate to rely only on these techniques, as there may still be opportunities for malicious input to affect the resulting query strings (Tang et al., 2020). After identifying an input source that can be utilized for a SQLIA vulnerability, attackers have a wide range of attack techniques at their disposal. Based on the nature and severity of the vulnerability, these attacks can have various consequences. They range from causing the database to crash, to extracting information about the tables in the database schema, to creating hidden communication channels, and even allowing for unrestricted injection of any SQL command. A concise overview of the primary methods used to execute SQL injection attacks, using the code example shown in Figure 7.2 (Li et al., 2019).

7.1.3.1. Tautologies

The primary objective of attack based on tautology is to insert SQL tokens which change the conditional statement of the query in order to consistently generate a correct result. The consequences of this type of attack differ based on the specific application, however, the main objectives usually involve bypassing login sites and extracting data (Osherson & Markman, 1974). In this form of injection, a malicious individual takes advantage of a susceptible input field that is utilized in the query. The WHERE clause is a conditional statement utilized in SQL queries to selectively retrieve data based on defined conditions. During the evaluation process, the database thoroughly scans through each row in the table. If the condition is a tautology, the database will obtain all the rows in the table, rather than delivering only one row as it normally would when there is no injection present (Baaz et al., 2001).

7.1.3.2. Malformed Queries

This approach allows for the utilization of error signals generated by the database when a query is denied. Database error messages frequently contain significant debugging information that can be used by malicious people to uncover holes in an application and expose the complete database structure. It is vital to realize that this information can be exploited by malevolent individuals. This can be utilized by malicious people who inject SQL tokens or faulty input, resulting in syntax mistakes, logical flaws, or type mismatches in the query (Li et al., 2024).

For example, A hacker might enter the following content into the pin input area to produce a type mismatch error: "convert (int, (select top 1 name from sysobjects where xtype='u'))." The web application would produce the following query:

```
SELECT info FROM users WHERE login="AND pin=
convert (int, {select top 1 name from sysobjects where xtype='u'))
```

Within the attack string, a select query is injected to extract the name of the initial user table (xtype='u') from the metadata table of the database, known as "sysobjects." This table holds valuable information about the database's structure. It subsequently converts the name of this table into an integer. Due to the nature of the table's name being a string, attempting to convert it is considered illegal, resulting in an error being returned by the database. For example, a SQL Server might generate the subsequent error message: "Microsoft OLE DB Providers for SQL Server (0x80040E07) Error converting "nvarchar" value 'CreditCards' to a column of data type int" (Hackshaw et al., 2011).

There are two important bits of information in this message that could help an attacker. The attacker is informed that the database is SQL Server by the error message. Furthermore, the error message discloses the precise string—s□ecifically, the name of the initial user-defined table in the database, "CreditCards"—that resulted in the type conversion issue (Bilk et al., 2012).

One may use a com□arable a□□roach to methodically find the name and ty□e of every column in the provided table. With the knowledge of the database schema, an attacker gains the ability to launch more targeted attacks, focusing on s□ecific ty□es of information. Malformed queries are often em□loyed as an initial step to gather information for subsequent attacks in the context of database security (Weston et al., 1993).

7.1.3.3. Union Query

In order to access data from a table that was not intended, an attacker can alter the application through injection attacks, which are a component of the Union Query approach. Hackers use the format "UNION" to insert a statement as part of their harmful strategies. Through the strategic definition of an injected query, an attacker can obtain data from a designated table. The database creates a dataset as a result of the vulnerability that includes the responses to both the injected query and the original query (Nargesian et al., 2018).

An attacker could be able to do a Union Query injection in the example scenario by entering the exact text "UNION SELECT cardNo from CreditCards where acctNo=l0032—" into the login field. The following question would be produced by the program (Arenas et al., 2009).

```
SELECT info FROM users WHERE login=" UNION
SELECT cardNo from CreditCards where acctNo=l0032 -- AND pin=
```

Given the absence of a login matching the empty string, the initial query yields an empty result set, while the injected query retrieves information from the "CreditCards" table. For this scenario, the database retrieves the "cardNo" field associated with the "10032" account. The database merges the outcomes of these two queries and transmits them back to the application. When considering various applications, it is important to note that this attack can result in the unintended disclosure of the "cardNo" value along with the associated account information (Dalvi & Suciu, 2013).

7.1.3.4. Piggy-Backed Queries

Using the piggy-backed query technique, an attacker tries to add additional requests to the initial query string. In the event of a successful attack, the database will receive and carry out a query string that consists of numerous separate inquiries. The initial inquiry is typically the authentic and lawful query, whereas the following inquiries are the injected and malicious searches. This form of attack can be particularly detrimental; assailants can utilize it to insert practically any kind of SQL command (Zhou et al., 2013). In the example, a malicious individual might manipulate the pin input field by injecting the string "O; drop table users." After that, the application would produce the query:

```
SELECT info FROM users WHERE login='doe' AND pin=O; drop table users
```

The database interprets this query string as two different requests, which are separated by the query delimiter "; ." It then proceeds to execute both queries (Feng et al., 2011). The second query, which is intentionally harmful, results in the deletion of the users table in the database. This action would have a disastrous outcome of erasing all of the database users. In addition to adding new users to the database and running stored procedures, this method can also be used to carry out various kinds of queries. It is vital to note that many databases do not require a s□ecific character to differentiate between distinct queries. Therefore, the only effective way to prevent this assault approach is not to rely entirely on searching for a unique character (Tay et al., 2003).

7.2. SQL INJECTION ATTACK DETECTION AND PREVENTION

Learning Objectives

- Understand the AMNESIA approach for detecting and preventing SQL injection attacks; and
- Learn the steps of AMNESIA: identify hotspots, build models, instrument, and monitor.

AMNESIA (Analysis for monitoring and neutralizing SQL injection attacks) is a comprehensive and automated approach that effectively identifies and mitigates various forms of SQL injection attacks. Static analysis and running monitoring are integrated in this strategy. This tactic is based on two important discoveries. Firstly, it was found that the web application code had all the necessary information to predict the likely structure of the queries that the program will generate. Secondly, a SQL injection attack, which inserts more SQL statements into a query, would upset the established structure (Kumar & Pateriya, 2012).

Using program analysis, this technique builds an automatic model of the valid questions that the application could produce in its static section. This method makes sure that the queries generated during runtime match the model that is generated statically by keeping a close eye on them. When a query deviates from the model, it is flagged as □otentially dangerous SQL injection and is immediately prevented from running in the database (Jemal et al., 2020).

There are four main steps involved in this technique. First, a summary of the steps, followed by a more detailed description in the subsequent sections will be provided.

7.2.1. The AMNESIA Approach

Identify hotspots: Conduct an analysis of the application code to precisely identify the specific regions where SQL queries are being conducted to the database.

Build SQL-Query Models: Create a model that precisely describes the different SQL queries that can be produced at each hotspot. The SQL-query model is a crucial element in database security. This model is a non-deterministic finite-state automaton that uses transition labels to re□resent a variety of SQL tokens, including as operators, delimiters, keywords, and text value placeholders (Nader, 2009).

Instrument Application: Ensure that calls to the runtime monitor are included at all application critical points.

- *Runtime Monitoring:* During runtime, it is important to verify the dynamically generated inquiries against the SQL-query model. Any queries that do not adhere to the model should be rejected and reported (Lewis, 1976).

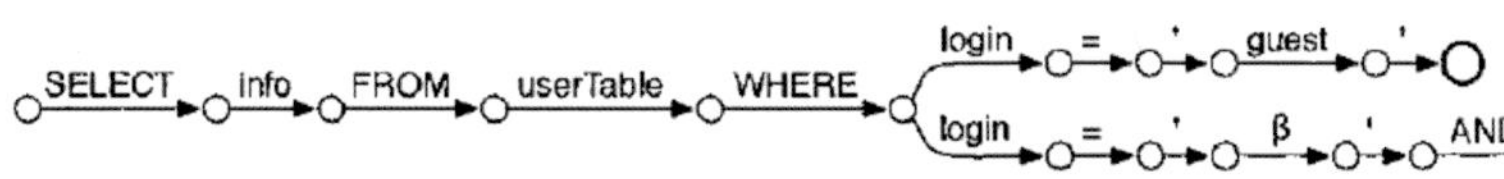

Figure 7.3. *Illustration of SQL-query model for the servlet*

Source: Allesandro, Creative Commons License

7.2.1.1. Identify Hotspots

AMNESIA conducts a methodical examination of the application code in order to pinpoint particular regions of interest. When using the Java language, database interactions are readily managed using a specified API, facilitating the identification of any areas of issue. Regarding the example servlet in Figure 7.2, there is a specific hotspot that stands out: the call to stmt.execute on line 10 (Montella, 2010).

7.2.1.2. Build SQL-Query Models

At this stage, a SQL-query model will be developed for each hotspot. This process is divided into two stages. In the first phase, all potential values for each hotspot query string will be calculated using Christensen's Java String Analysis (JSA). The JSA algorithm constructs a flow graph that optimizes the operational flow of the program, with a particular focus on emphasizing the string manipulation operations carried out on string variables. For every string that is relevant, the library carefully reviews the flow graph and replicates the string manipulation tasks. The result is a Non-Deterministic Finite Automaton (NDFA) at the character level, which represents every conceivable value that the string variable in question can have. Due to its conservative nature, the JSA tends to provide an overestimate of all potential values for a given string variable, when considering the NDFA (Rys, 2001).

The second part focuses on transforming the NDFA computed by JSA into a SQL-query model. An extensive analysis will be carried out on the NDFA, leading to the formation of a new NDFA. The transitions of this new NDFA will be labeled with SQL keywords, literal values or operators. A thorough analysis of the character-level NDFA was conducted to develop the model. This involved categorizing characters based on their correspondence to SQL keywords, literal values, or o□erators (Mitrović, 1998).

For exam□le, a series of transitions labeled with letters can be identified as a SQL keyword and combined into one transition. This step can be customized to identify various SQL dialects. In the SQL-query model, variable strings are denoted by the symbol β, which signifies their association with user in□ut (Witkowski et al., 2005).

For exam□le, the symbol β re□resents the variable login. This □rocess follows a similar approach to the one used by Gould, but with a slight difference, it is s□ecifically a□□lied to NDFAs instead of DFAs (Tezkan & Saraev, 2008).

Figure 7.3 shows the single hotspot's SQL-query model. Figure 7.2 shows the model's representation of two unique query strings that the code can generate, depending on the branch chosen after the if statement on line 6.

7.2.1.3. Instrument Application

Now, let's move forward by including calls to the monitor that will evaluate the queries while the application is running to enhance its functionality. Every hotspot is followed by a request to the monitor that comes before the database call. Two parameters are passed to the monitor when it is called: the hotspot's unique ID and the query string that will be submitted to the database. A connection can be made between the hotspot and the previously constructed SQL-query model by the runtime monitor using a unique identifier. It then proceeds to validate the query against the appropriate model (Dodds & Baker, 2019).

Figure 7.4 shows the implementation of our technique on the example application. The hotspot, previously located at line 10 in Figure 7.2, has been secured by implementing a monitor call at line 10a.

```
10a. if (monitor. Accepts (<hotspot ID>, queryString))
{
10b. ResultSet tempSet = stmt.execute(queryString);

11. return tempSet;
```

Figure 7.4. *Illustration of example hotspot after instrumentation.*

Source: William G.J Creative Commons License.

7.2.1.4. Runtime Monitoring

The application functions without issue during runtime until it reaches a crucial moment. The query string is sent to the runtime monitor, which then analyzes it by examining the SQL syntax and breaking it down into multiple tokens. Based on their syntactic position, the parser can identify and represent empty string and empty numeric literals in the query string analysis (Rabiser et al., 2017). They are indicated in the □arsed question string by the symbol ε.

It is crucial to note that this approach accurately analyzes the query string, mirroring the database's behavior and adhering to the designated SQL grammar. The technique effectively addresses the limitations of basic keyword matching in the query string. This method effectively avoids any potential false positives and eliminates any problems that may arise from user input which matches the SQL keywords (Cassar et al., 2017).

For exam□le, a text field would accurately be identified as such when a user enters a string that contains SQL keywords but is otherwise structured differently. On the other hand, the parser will correctly understand this input as a keyword when the user chooses to inject special characters, as shown in the preceding example, to alter the evaluation of a certain text as a keyword. To guarantee that the query is interpreted consistently, one must use the same parser as the database.

Following parsing, the runtime monitor assesses the query to see if it deviates from the SQL-query model associated with the active hotspot. A non-deterministic finite automaton (NDFA) that em□loys a range of symbols, such as delimiters, operators, literal values, SQL keywords, and the unique symbol β, is called a SQL-query model. Therefore, to verify whether a question is in line with the model, the runtime monitor may immediately determine whether the model recognizes the token sequence obtained from the query string. It is crucial to keep in mind that a string or numeric literal, even if it is empty, could match β or the same literal value in the SQL-query model when looking at the parsed query string (Jin et al., 2012).

If the model approves the query, the monitor allows the query execution to proceed. In other cases, the monitor can detect the query as a potential SQL injection attack. In this scenario, the monitor acts as a safeguard, blocking the execution of the query on the database and promptly notifying about the potential attack.

As an example, let's revisit the queries shown in Figure 7.5. It is important to remember that the first query is valid, while the second one is an exam□le of a SQL injection attack. When examining query (a), the analysis would begin by comparing the token "SELECT" and starting from the initial state of the SQL-query model in Figure 7.4. Due to the matching token and label, the automaton successfully progresses to the second state from the initial state. When the "INFO" token is entered, the automaton transitions from the current state to the third state (Pike et al., 2010).

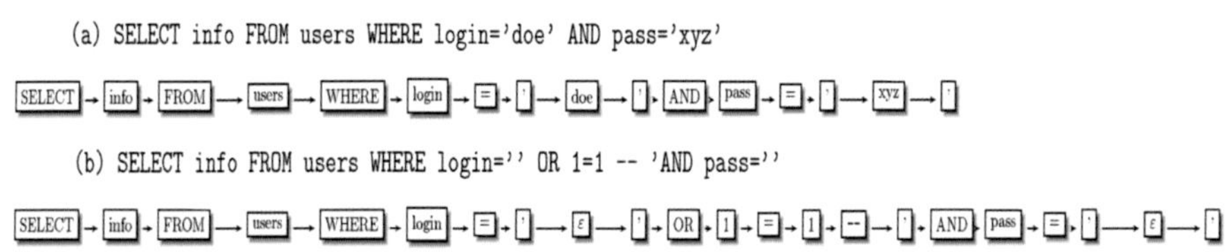

Figure 7.5. *Illustration of Example of parsed runtime queries.*

Source: W. R. Cook, Creative Commons License.

The automaton continues to advance through successive states until it reaches the state denoted by two "=" outgoing transitions. The automaton would now proceed through both transitions. The inquiry is rejected at the top level since the automaton cannot reach an acceptable condition. On the other hand, in the lower branch, the automated system reaches the accept state once it finishes □rocessing the final token in the query ("""). In this branch, query tokens are matched with labels on modifications. Based on the analysis, it can be determined that this query is indeed valid (Barbon et al., 2006).

The query (b) is checked in a similar manner until the token "OR" is encountered. Due to the mismatch between the token and the label of the sole outgoing transition from the current state "AND," the automaton rejects the query, and the monitor classifies it as a SQLIA.

7.2.2. AMNESIA Implementation

AMNESIA is an innovative tool that showcases a creative approach to Java-based online applications. The sole input necessary for this completely automated procedure is the web application. In addition to utilizing the AMNESIA library, the program does not necessitate any additional runtime environment support (Trevena et al., 2024). The utility was created using the Java programming language, and its implementation is divided into three distinct parts:

- **Module for Analysis:** This module is responsible for implementing Steps 1 and 2 of the technique. The system takes in a Java web application and generates a comprehensive list of areas of concern, along with a corresponding SQL-query model for each area. To execute this module, the Java String Analysis library implementation will be used. The analysis module can analyze Java Servlets and JSP pages (Simmons, 2011).

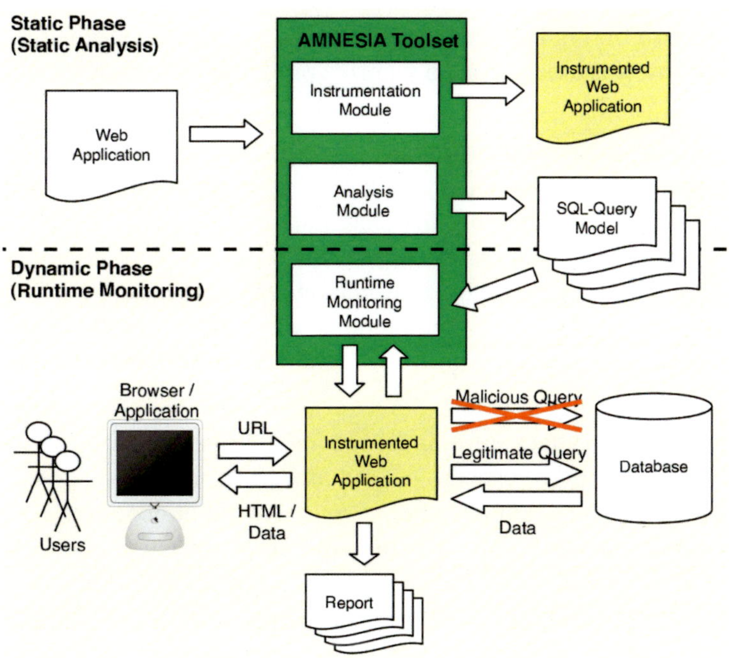

Figure 7.6. *Illustration of high-level overview of AMNESIA.*

Source: M. Martin, Creative Commons License.

- **Instrumentation Module:** This module is responsible for implementing Step 3 of the technique. The system accepts a set of hotspots and a Java web application, and adds a runtime monitor call to each hotspot. This module is implemented using INSECTJ, a flexible Java instrumentation and monitoring framework developed at Georgia Tech (Hart et al., 2020).

- **Runtime-Monitoring Module:** This module executes the fourth phase of the approach. The module accepts a query string and the ID of the hotspot that is responsible for creating the inquiry. Subsequently, it obtains the SQL-query model associated with the hotspot and proceeds to validate the query against the model (Stark, 2019).

A detailed summary of AMNESIA is shown in Figure 7.5. During the static phase, the Analysis Module and the Instrumentation Module work together to process a web application. An instrumented application with a SQL-query model for every application hotspot is what they offer. The Runtime-Monitoring Module carefully examines the dynamic queries when users engage with the web application during the dynamic period. As soon as a query is determined to be malicious, it is blocked and a report is produced (Langhorn et al., 2010).

After identifying a SQLIA, AMNESIA intercepts the query before it is executed on the database and provides developers with valuable information about the attack. This helps them take necessary measures to address the issue effectively. When implementing the technique in Java, it is recommended to provide an exception that can be raised when an attack is discovered. The exception should include encoded information regarding the attack. Developers can readily employ the exception-handling mechanism of the language and include their handling code into the program to collect information during runtime.

Having access to attack information during runtime is valuable as it enables developers to promptly respond to and devise a tailored countermeasure against detected attacks. For example, developers might choose to reduce any potential risks by disabling the specific component of the application that is vulnerable to the attack. Another approach would be for a developer to address the attack by transforming the data into a compatible format for a different tool, like an Intrusion Detection System, and then relaying the information to that tool. Because this approach is seamlessly integrated with the application's language, developers have the flexibility to choose an acceptable response to SQL injection attacks (Akturk & Karpuzcu, 2017).

The current data obtained from the approach comprises the attack timing, the precise location of the targeted hotspot, the query utilized in the attempted assault, and the specific piece of the query that failed to correspond with the model. It would be beneficial for the developer to consider additional information that could enhance their understanding of the program execution paths and how they relate to specific parts of the query model. Exploring possible modifications to the static analysis method to gather this information is worth investigating (Austin et al., 2012).

7.3. RELATED APPROACHES

Learning Objectives

- Understand defensive programming techniques to mitigate SQL injection vulnerabilities; and
- Explore various general, static and taint-based techniques used to prevent SQL injection attacks.

Numerous techniques have been suggested to address SQL injection attacks. Nevertheless, when compared to AMNESIA, these methods do have a number of limitations and deficiencies. In this section, students examine and analyze the primary methods used to counter SQL injection attacks (Chen et al., 2015).

7.3.1. Defensive Programming

Various code-based development practices have been suggested by developers to address SQL injection attacks. The techniques typically emphasize the importance of implementing effective input filtering methods, including the proper handling of potentially harmful characters and thorough validation of input data (Date, 1984). A variety of approaches are summarized in the reference. Overall, a thorough and methodical implementation of these methods proves to be a successful resolution to the issue at hand (Stueben & Stueben, 2018).

Nevertheless, the implementation of these strategies in real-world scenarios relies on human intervention, which is undesirable. For example, numerous instances of SQL injection vulnerabilities found in different applications are associated with situations where the apps had input-validation procedures, but the validation was insufficient. The situation is more complicated since attackers persistently discover novel attack patterns or slight modifications of previous attacks that can evade the security measures implemented by programmers. Fixing vulnerable legacy programs retroactively employing defensive coding principles is a complex, error-prone task and labor intensive (Qie et al., 2002).

Two popular "SQLIA remedies" are worth mentioning in particular. Although they do not properly handle the SQLIA issue, at first glance they both seem to provide workable remedies. The first fix is as simple as looking for harmful terms in user input. Due to the possibility of input fields containing terms that match SQL keywords, such as "FROM," "OR," or "AND," this approach would lead to a high number of false positives. Using stored procedures to access databases is the second cure. The way stored procedures are implemented determines their capacity to stop SQLIAs. Utilizing stored procedures alone does not provide SQLIA protection (Teto et al., 2017).

Two techniques—SQL DOM and Safe Query Objects—encapsulate database queries to provide a dependable and secure way to access databases. These methods provide an efficient method to prevent SQL Injection Attacks (SQLIA) by replacing the usage of string concatenation in the query generation process with a systematic approach that utilizes a type-checked API. (In this way, protective coding is applicable to SQL DOM and Safe Query Objects.) These methods have the disadvantage of requiring developers to learn and apply a new programming paradigm or query-development process, even though they are just as effective as AMNESIA (Rossi et al., 2020).

Typically, defensive coding has not proven to be entirely effective in thwarting SQL injection attacks. Although better coding practices can assist in addressing the issue, their effectiveness is dependent on the developer's proficiency in creating suitable input validation code and identifying all scenarios where it is necessary. AMNESIA, with its fully automated system, offers enhanced assurances regarding the thoroughness and precision of the protections implemented (Zaidman, 2004).

7.3.2. General Techniques against SQLIAs

In order to guarantee that input validation criteria are applied to the data that is received by a web application, the Security Gateway employs a proxy filter. When defining constraints and changes for application parameters as they go from the web page to the application server, developers use a descriptor language (Yeole & Meshram, 2011). Through the implementation of suitable filters, developers can effectively modify or prevent user input that may pose a risk. The effectiveness of this approach is limited by the proficiency of the developer in the field: (1) identify every input stream that could affect the query string; and (2) decide which filtering guidelines the proxy should use (Wei et al., 2006).

WAVES is a potent tool that is used in penetration testing to find possible SQLIA vulnerabilities in web applications. By using machine learning to guide the testing process, this method improves on established penetration testing techniques. But like other penetration-testing methods, it cannot guarantee absolute completeness of the time (Nasereddin et al., 2023).

Practice Problems

Explain how intrusion detection systems (IDS) can contribute to detecting SQL Injection Attacks in real-time. Describe the role of machine learning in enhancing IDS capabilities.

Solutions to Practice Problems

IDS monitors network traffic and system activities to identify patterns indicative of SQL Injection Attacks. Machine learning algorithms in IDS analyze historical data to recognize anomalous behavior that may indicate an attack. This proactive approach enhances detection accuracy by identifying deviations from normal application behavior.

To efficiently detect and prevent possible SQL Injection Attacks (SQLIAs), make use of an Intrusion Detection System (IDS). A machine learning technique used by the (IDS) was developed on a dataset of frequently asked application queries. This method involves generating models of typical questions and subsequently examining the application in real-time to detect requests that deviate from the model. An inherent limitation of learning-based approaches is their lack of ability to offer assurances regarding their detection capabilities. This is because their effectiveness relies on the utilization of an ideal training set. In the absence of a suitable framework, this strategy may yield a substantial quantity of inaccurate outcomes (Chan & Cheung, 1999).

7.3.3. Techniques of Static Techniques

One useful tool that makes it possible to thoroughly confirm the type validity of SQL queries that are generated dynamically is JDBC-Checker. While this method was not initially designed to tackle SQLIA, it can identify a key factor contributing to SQL-injection vulnerabilities: inadequate input type checking. Regarding this matter, JDBC-Checker can identify and assist developers in removing certain sections of code that can be exploited by attackers through type mismatches. Unfortunately, JDBC-Checker cannot effectively mitigate other forms of SQL injection attacks that generate queries that are both syntactically and type-correct (Chen & Konrad, 1997).

The Wassermann technique makes use of automated reasoning and static analysis to guarantee that there are no tautologies in the SQL queries that are produced at the application layer. This application is restricted because it can only address tautology-based attacks, while AMNESIA is made s□ecifically to handle all kinds of SQL injection attacks (Artigues et al., 2003).

7.3.4. Taint-Based Approaches

The techniques employed require adjustments to a PHP interpreter to effectively track and document details regarding user input. These changes enable the recognition and rejection of queries that depend on untrusted input to produce s□ecific kinds of SQL tokens by means of a context-sensitive analysis. Overall, taint-based techniques have demonstrated significant □otential in their effectiveness in identifying and stopping SQL injection attacks (Bekrar et al., 2012). One major concern with these approaches is their practicality. Firstly, the challenge of ensuring comprehensiveness arises when attempting to identify all sources of tainted user input in highly modular web applications. Additionally, ensuring the □recise dissemination of taint information can lead to significant runtime burdens on web applications. Ultimately, the method depends on utilizing a personalized edition of the runtime system, which has an impact on its portability (Cui et al., 2016).

Huang WebSSARI is a method that uses information-flow analysis to s□ecifically identify issues related to in□ut validation. This a□□roach utilizes static analysis to ensure that information flows corres□ond to the requirements for sensitive functions. The analysis identifies areas where □reconditions are not met and □rovides recommendations for incor□orating filters and sanitization functions into the application to ensure that the preconditions are met (Ganesh et al., 2009). There are a few limitations to this technique that need to be considered. Firstly, it assumes that the requirements for sensitive operations may be precisely articulated through its type system. Secondly, it implies that subjecting in□ut to s□ecific sorts of filters is sufficient to consider it reliable. These assumptions may not always hold true in practice. These assumptions are often not applicable to various functions and applications (She et al., 2020).

SUMMARY

- SQL Injection Attacks (SQLIA) take advantage of weaknesses in database-driven applications by injecting harmful SQL code. There are different types of vulnerabilities that can be exploited in database security, such as malformed queries, union queries, tautologies, and piggy-backed queries.
- Detection and prevention methods encompass the AMNESIA a□□roach, which involves hots□ot identification, constructing SQL-query models, instrumenting applications, and implementing runtime monitoring. Various methods can be employed to address vulnerabilities, including static detection, defensive programming, general techniques, and taint-based approaches.
- Programming with a defensive approach focuses on implementing coding practices that proactively anticipate and safeguard against potential attacks. There are various techniques available for enhancing security in databases. Some techniques provide general strategies that can be applied broadly, while others focus on static detection to analyze code for potential vulnerabilities.
- Programming with a defensive approach focuses on implementing coding practices that proactively anticipate and safeguard against potential attacks. There are various techniques available for enhancing security in databases. Some techniques provide general strategies that can be applied broadly, while others focus on static detection to analyze code for potential vulnerabilities.

REVIEW QUESTIONS

1. Ex□lain the significance of logistics in today's global business environment.
2. How does an effective logistics system contribute to the overall success of a supply chain?
3. Discuss the challenges and benefits associated with freight transportation in logistics systems
4. Explain the role of logistics in capital reduction and cost management within an organization.
5. How can service level improvements positively impact customer satisfaction in logistics?
6. Discuss the impact of globalization on logistics decision-making and supply chain design.

7. Discuss the role of tactical decisions in adapting to changes in the business environment.

MULTIPLE CHOICE QUESTIONS

1. **What is the primary objective of SQL injection attacks (SQLIA)?**
   a. To steal cookies from web browsers
   b. To gain unauthorized access to a database
   c. To overload the server with requests
   d. To encrypt sensitive data
2. **Which of the following is an example of a SQLIA variant?**
   a. Cross-site scripting (XSS)
   b. Remote file inclusion (RFI)
   c. Buffer overflow
   d. Tautologies
3. **What is the purpose of the "AMNESIA" approach in SQLIA detection and prevention?**
   a. To erase all database records periodically
   b. To identify and mitigate SQL injection vulnerabilities
   c. To improve database performance
   d. To encrypt database connections
4. **Which step is involved in the AMNESIA approach for SQLIA detection and prevention?**
   a. Identify Hotspots
   b. Install antivirus software
   c. Im□lement firewalls
   d. Configure network settings
5. **What is one of the related approaches for protecting against SQL injection attacks?**
   a. Cookie manipulation
   b. Firewall configuration
   c. Defensive programming
   d. Network routing

6. Which technique focuses on identifying tainted data inputs to prevent SQL injection?

a. AMNESIA approach

b. Defensive programming

c. C Static detection techniques

d. Taint-based approaches

Answers to Multiple Choice Questions

1. (b); 2. (d); 3. (b); 4. (a); 5. (c); 6. (d)

REFERENCES

1. Abawajy, J. (2013). SQLIA detection and prevention approach for RFID systems. *Journal of Systems and Software, 86*(3), 751–758.
2. Akturk, I., & Karpuzcu, U. R. (2017). AMNESIAC: Amnesic automatic computer. *ACM SIGARCH Computer Architecture News, 45*(1), 811–824.
3. Al Rubaiei, M., Al Yarubi, T., Al Saadi, M., & Kumar, B. (2020). SQLIA detection and prevention techniques. In *2020 9th International Conference System Modeling and Advancement in Research Trends (SMART)* (Vol. 1, pp. 115–121).
4. Aliero, M. S., Qureshi, K. N., Pasha, M. F., Ghani, I., & Yauri, R. A. (2020). Systematic review analysis on SQLIA detection and prevention approaches. *Wireless Personal Communications, 112*, 2297–2333.
5. Alwan, Z. S., & Younis, M. F. (2017). Detection and prevention of SQL injection attack: A survey. *International Journal of Computer Science and Mobile Computing, 6*(8), 5–17.
6. Austin, B. M., Zubarev, D. Y., & Lester Jr, W. A. (2012). Quantum Monte Carlo and related approaches. *Chemical Reviews, 112*(1), 263–288.
7. Baaz, M., Hájek, P., Montagna, F., & Veith, H. (2001). Complexity of t-tautologies. *Annals of Pure and Applied Logic, 113*(1–3), 3–11.
8. Bafghi, G. (2013). A simple and fast technique for detection and prevention of SQL injection attacks (SQLIAs). *International Journal of Security and Its Applications, 7*(5), 53–66.
9. Balasundaram, I., & Ramaraj, E. (2012). An efficient technique for detection and prevention of SQL injection attack using ASCII based string matching. *Procedia Engineering, 30*, 183–190.

10. Cassar, I., Francalanza, A., Aceto, L., & Ingólfsdóttir, A. (2017). A survey of runtime monitoring instrumentation techniques. *arXiv preprint arXiv:1708.07229*.

11. Chan, M. Y., & Cheung, S. C. (1999). Testing database applications with SQL semantics. In *CODAS* (Vol. 99, pp. 363–374).

12. Chen, D., Yan, Q., Wu, C., & Zhao, J. (2021). SQL injection attack detection and prevention techniques using deep learning. In *Journal of Physics: Conference Series* (Vol. 1757, No. 1, pp. 012–055).

13. Chen, Q., & Konrad, A. (1997). A review of finite element o□en boundary techniques for static and quasi-static electromagnetic field □roblems. *IEEE Transactions on Magnetics, 33*(1), 663–676.

14. Chen, W. H., Yang, J., Guo, L., & Li, S. (2015). Disturbance-observer-based control and related methods—An overview. *IEEE Transactions on Industrial Electronics, 63*(2), 1083–1095.

15. Cui, B., Wang, F., Hao, Y., & Wang, L. (2016). A taint-based approach for automatic reverse engineering of gray-box file formats. *Soft Computing, 20*, 3563–3578.

16. Dalvi, N., & Suciu, D. (2013). The dichotomy of probabilistic inference for unions of conjunctive queries. *Journal of the ACM (JACM), 59*(6), 1–87.

17. Date, C. J. (1984). A critique of the SQL database language. *ACM Sigmod Record, 14*(3), 8–54.

18. Ganesh, V., Leek, T., & Rinard, M. (2009). Taint-based directed Whitebox fuzzing. In *2009 IEEE 31st International Conference on Software Engineering* (Vol. 3, pp. 474–484).

19. Ghafarian, A. (2017). A hybrid method for detection and prevention of SQL injection attacks. In *2017 Computing Conference* (Vol. 2, pp. 833–838).

20. Hackshaw, A., Rodeck, C., & Boniface, S. (2011). Maternal smoking in pregnancy and birth defects: A systematic review based on 173,687 malformed cases and 11.7 million controls. *Human Reproduction Update, 17*(5), 589–604.

21. Halfond, W. G., & Orso, A. (2007). Detection and prevention of SQL injection attacks. In *Malware Detection* (Vol. 3, pp. 85–109).

22. Halfond, W. G., Viegas, J., & Orso, A. (2006). A classification of SQL-injection attacks and countermeasures. In *Proceedings of the IEEE International Symposium on Secure Software Engineering* (Vol. 1, pp. 13–15).

23. Hart, T., Ferraro, M., Rabinowitz, A., Fitzpatrick DeSalme, E., Nelson, L., Marcy, E., & Turkstra, L. (2020). Improving communication with patients in post-traumatic amnesia: Development and impact of a clinical protocol. *Brain Injury, 34*(11), 1518–1524.

24. Hussain, M. A., Abbdal Refish, S. H., Khalefa, M. S., Hussain, S. A., Hussien, Z. A., Abduljabbar, Z. A., & Al Sibahee, M. A. (2021). Web application database protection from SQLIA using permutation encoding. In *Proceedings of the 4th International Conference on Information Science and Systems* (Vol. 2, pp. 13–21).

25. Jemal, I., Cheikhrouhou, O., Hamam, H., & Mahfoudhi, A. (2020). SQL injection attack detection and prevention techniques using machine learning. *International Journal of Applied Engineering Research, 15*(6), 569–580.

26. Jin, D., Meredith, P. O. N., Lee, C., & Roşu, G. (2012). JavaMOP: Efficient parametric runtime monitoring framework. In *2012 34th International Conference on Software Engineering (ICSE)* (Vol. 4, pp. 1427–1430).

27. Langhorn, L., Sorensen, J. C., & Pedersen, P. U. (2010). A critical review of the literature on early rehabilitation of patients with post-traumatic amnesia in acute care. *Journal of Clinical Nursing, 19*(21–22), 2959–2969.

28. Lewis, D. J. (1976). A cognitive approach to experimental amnesia. *The American Journal of Psychology, 7*(2), 51–80.

29. Li, Q., Wang, F., Wang, J., & Li, W. (2019). LSTM-based SQL injection detection method for intelligent transportation system. *IEEE Transactions on Vehicular Technology, 68*(5), 4182–4191.

30. Montella, A. (2010). A com□arative analysis of hots□ot identification methods. *Accident Analysis & Prevention, 42*(2), 571–581.

31. Nader, K. (2009). New approaches to amnesia. *Learning & Memory, 16*(11), 672–675.

32. Nargesian, F., Zhu, E., Pu, K. Q., & Miller, R. J. (2018). Table union search on open data. *Proceedings of the VLDB Endowment, 11*(7), 813–825.

33. Nasereddin, M., ALKhamaiseh, A., Qasaimeh, M., & Al-Qassas, R. (2023). A systematic review of detection and prevention techniques of SQL injection attacks. *Information Security Journal: A Global Perspective, 32*(4), 252–265.

34. Osherson, D. N., & Markman, E. (1974). Language and the ability to evaluate contradictions and tautologies. *Cognition, 3*(3), 213–226.

35. Pike, L., Goodloe, A., Morisset, R., & Niller, S. (2010). Copilot: A hard

real-time runtime monitor. In *International Conference on Runtime Verification* (Vol. 4, pp. 345–359).

36. Qie, X., Pang, R., & Peterson, L. (2002). Defensive programming: Using an annotation toolkit to build DoS-resistant software. *ACM SIGOPS Operating Systems Review, 36*(SI), 45–60.
37. Rabiser, R., Guinea, S., Vierhauser, M., Baresi, L., & Grünbacher, P. (2017). A comparison framework for runtime monitoring approaches. *Journal of Systems and Software, 125*, 309–321.
38. Rossi, M. T., Greca, R., Iovino, L., Giacinto, G., & Bertoli, A. (2020). Defensive programming for smart home cybersecurity. In *2020 IEEE European Symposium on Security and Privacy Workshops (EuroS&PW)* (Vol. 6, pp. 600–605).
39. Stark, A. (2019). Explaining institutional amnesia in government. *Governance, 32*(1), 143–158.
40. Stueben, M., & Stueben, M. (2018). Defensive programming. *Good Habits for Great Coding: Improving Programming Skills with Examples in Python, 22*(2), 123–126.
41. Tajpour, A., Heydari, M. Z., Masrom, M., & Ibrahim, S. (2010). SQL injection detection and prevention tools assessment. In *2010 3rd International Conference on Computer Science and Information Technology* (Vol. 9, pp. 518–522).
42. Tang, P., Qiu, W., Huang, Z., Lian, H., & Liu, G. (2020). Detection of SQL injection based on artificial neural network. *Knowledge-Based Systems, 190*, 105–528.
43. Tay, Tan, & Shenoy. (2003). Piggy-backed time-stepped simulation with 'super-stepping.' In *Proceedings of the 2003 Winter Simulation Conference* (Vol. 2, pp. 1077–1085).
44. Teto, J. K., Bearden, R., & Lo, D. C. T. (2017). The impact of defensive programming on I/O cybersecurity attacks. In *Proceedings of the SouthEast Conference* (Vol. 6, pp. 102–111).
45. Tezkan, B., & Saraev, A. (2008). A new broadband radiomagnetotelluric instrument: Applications to near surface investigations. *Near Surface Geophysics, 6*(4), 245–252.
46. Trevena-Peters, J., Ponsford, J., & McKay, A. (2024). Implementation of activities of daily living retraining for individuals in post-traumatic amnesia. *Brain Impairment, 25*(2), 334–346.

47. Wei, K., Muthuprasanna, M., & Kothari, S. (2006). Preventing SQL injection attacks in stored procedures. In *Australian Software Engineering Conference (ASWEC'06)* (Vol. 6, pp. 8–10).
48. Weston, M. J., Porter, H. J., Andrews, H. S., & Berry, P. J. (1993). Correlation of antenatal ultrasonography and pathological examinations in 153 malformed fetuses. *Journal of Clinical Ultrasound, 21*(6), 387–392.
49. Witkowski, A., Bellamkonda, S., Bozkaya, T., Folkert, N., Gupta, A., Haydu, J., & Subramanian, S. (2005). Advanced SQL modeling in RDBMS. *ACM Transactions on Database Systems (TODS), 30*(1), 83–121.
50. Yeole, A. S., & Meshram, B. B. (2011). Analysis of different technique for detection of SQL injection. In *Proceedings of the International Conference & Workshop on Emerging Trends in Technology* (Vol. 6, pp. 963–966).
51. Zaidman, M. (2004). Teaching defensive programming in Java. *Journal of Computing Sciences in Colleges, 19*(3), 33–43.

CHAPTER 8

SECURING DATA IN TRANSIT AND AT REST

LEARNING OBJECTIVES

At the end of this chapter, readers will be able to:

1. Understand the importance of encryption in maintaining data confidentiality;
2. Understand about encryption techniques for securing data in transit;
3. Explore implementation options for encrypting data-in-transit, including database-specific features and secure tunnels;
4. Discover how IPSec operates at the operating system level for transparent encryption;
5. Understand the importance of encrypting data-at-rest in database environments;
6. Understand implementation options for encrypting sensitive data within databases; and
7. Explore key factors when selecting an encryption implementation option.

INTRODUCTORY EXAMPLE

A multinational corporation, EtlanTech Enterprises, has recently experienced a data breach resulting in the theft of customer information during a routine data transfer process. The breach occurred when sensitive customer data was intercepted by hackers while being transmitted over an unsecured network.

As a result of the breach, EtlanTech Enterprises faces severe consequences, including financial losses, reputational damage, and potential legal liabilities due to non-compliance with data protection regulations. Customers lose trust in the company's ability to safeguard their data, leading to a decline in business relationships and revenue.

In response to the breach, EtlanTech Enterprises partners with SecureTech Solutions Inc. to enhance their data security measures. SecureTech Solutions Inc. implements encryption protocols to protect data both in transit and at rest. They deploy SSL/TLS encryption for securing data during transmission over the internet and implement robust encryption algorithms to safeguard stored data on EtlanTech Enterprises' servers.

By implementing encryption solutions provided by SecureTech Solutions Inc., EtlanTech Enterprises significantly strengthens its data security posture. Customer data is now securely encrypted during transmission and storage, mitigating the risk of unauthorized access and data breaches. As a result, EtlanTech Enterprises regains customer trust, avoids regulatory penalties, and maintains its reputation as a trusted organization committed to protecting sensitive information.

UNIT INTRODUCTION

Many databases store valuable and confidential data. Various types of sensitive data are typically involved, such as employee salaries, information of customers, records of patients, and credit card numbers, among others (Alneyadi et al., 2016). Ensuring the security of sensitive information is crucial for businesses, as any breach can lead to negative consequences such as reputational damage, financial losses, and even the potential downfall of the entire organization. Would anyone consider doing business with a bank if they found out that sensitive customer account information, including details that could be exploited for wire transfers (Nandakumar et al., 2021), was consistently being leaked and exploited by criminals? There has been an increased emphasis on the importance of keeping information confidential, which has been driven by two significant factors:

the rise of web applications and the implementation of regulations. Over the past five years, the rise of Web applications has revolutionized both business practices and daily lives. While these applications have undeniably enhanced the access to information, they have unfortunately also opened up new avenues for hackers. Another notable development, possibly driven by heightened risk and a rise in incidents, is the rise of data-privacy regulations that numerous companies worldwide have been compelled to comply with (Ayoade et al., 2019).

When it comes to databases, the theft of secret information is a major concern due to the potential damage caused by hackers. In this chapter, the importance of data encryption as an extra layer of security will be discussed. It acts as a safety net in case a hacker gains access to data, despite implementing various database security techniques (Kunduru, 2023).

Cryptography is a well-established and long-standing field that deals with ensuring the confidentiality of information. Cryptography and encryption, among all the domains of mathematics and science, are particularly linked to security. Since the earliest days of humanity, individuals have been devising methods to encode data. For a comprehensive, accessible, and easily understandable introduction to cryptography. This chapter will provide an explanation of the significance of employing specific strategies to guarantee data confidentiality, as well as guidance on when to utilize them. The chapter primarily focuses on two key applications of encryption that are relevant to the subject of database security, and it provides guidance on how to use these methods (Achar, 2022).

Readers will be introduced to two techniques: encrypting data during transmission and encrypting data when it is stored. Regardless of the situation, incorporating encryption as an extra security measure ensures the preservation of confidentiality, even if all other layers of protection have been compromised.

8.1. ENCRYPTION

Learning Objective

- Understand the concept of encryption of data.

Data encryption is a crucial aspect of data/cyber security, as it involves transforming data from a readable format to an encoded format. Decrypted data is required in order to access or manipulate encrypted information. Data encryption forms the fundamental foundation of ensuring the security of information. Ensuring the security of a computer system's information is crucial in preventing unauthorized access and potential misuse (Bhanot & Hans, 2015). Encryption is a crucial aspect of data security, used by both individuals and large corporations to safeguard sensitive information transmitted between a browser and a server. The information can encompass a wide range of data, including payment details and personal information. Encryption software, also referred to as an encryption algorithm or cipher, is utilized to create an encryption scheme that is theoretically resistant to being cracked without significant com□utational resources (Davis, 1978).

When data is transmitted online, it passes through various network devices across the globe that make up the public internet. When data is transmitted over the public internet, there is a risk of it being compromised or stolen by unauthorized individuals. To reduce this issue, users have the option of using specialized software or hardware solutions that guarantee the safe transmission of data and information. These processes are commonly referred to as encryption in the field of network security (Po□ek & Kline, 1979).

Encryption is the process of transforming easily understandable plaintext into unreadable text, referred to as cipher text. Essentially, this process involves transforming easily understandable data into a seemingly random form. Encryption utilizes a cryptographic key, which is a collection of mathematical values that are mutually agreed upon by both the sender and the recipient. The recipient employs the key to decipher the data, transforming it into readable plaintext (Boyd, 1993). The level of security in encryption increases proportionally with the complexity of the cryptographic key, as it reduces the possibility of third parties successfully decrypting it using brute force attacks, which involve attempting random numbers until the correct combination is guessed. Encryption is used for safeguarding passwords. Password encryption methods use cryptographic algorithms to hide password, making it unreadable to unauthorized individuals, such as hackers (Merkle & Hellman, 1981).

8.2. ROLE OF ENCRYPTION IN DATA PROTECTION

Learning Objective

- Understand encryption's role in safeguarding data in transit and at rest

Data is susceptible to threats when it is being transferred and when it is stored, and so needs to be safeguarded in both situations. Consequently, there are several distinct methods for safeguarding data while it is being transmitted and while it is at rest. Encryption is a crucial component of data security and is widely used to safeguard data during transmission and storage (Zhao, 2023). To ensure the security of data while it is being transferred, organizations frequently opt to encrypt sensitive data before moving it and utilize encrypted connections such as HTTPS, SSL, TLS, FTPS, etc. This helps protect the contents of the data during transit. To ensure the security of data that is not actively being used, businesses have the option to encrypt important files before storing them or encrypt the entire storage device (Bokefode et al., 2016).

The digital encryption used in contemporary society adheres to the fundamental principles of codes and ciphers that have been utilized for generations, where symbols or numbers are replaced by written letters. Essentially, modern encryption transforms human-readable data into a form that is unreadable through an algorithm, making it inaccessible until it is decrypted (Pisaric, 2021).

8.3. ENCRYPTING DATA-IN-TRANSIT

Learning Objectives

- Understand the vulnerability of unencrypted database communications;
- Understand about tools like tc□dum□and Ethereal for sniffing TCP/IP packets;
- Comprehend encryption options for securing data-in-transit; and
- Gain insights into using IPSec at the operating system level for encryption.

One may have acquired significant information regarding the database server functioning as a networked service. It has been discovered that the majority of database settings utilize TCP/IP as their communication protocol. In this setup, the database server actively listens on specific ports and accepts connections that are started by database clients. Although the ports can be customized, the majority of users often select the default server ports. For example, Microsoft SQL Server commonly uses port 1433, Oracle uses port 1521, Sybase uses port 4100, DB2 uses port 50000, and MySQL uses port 3306.

Database clients establish a connection with the server using s□ecified □orts to start communication. Depending on the database type and server settings, the discussion may either continue on the same server port or be redirected to another port (Daman & Tripathi, 2015).

Hackers are also aware of this like everyone else. In addition, due to the expertise of numerous hackers in system and network operations, they possess extensive knowledge about the TCP/IP protocol and, more s□ecifically, the art of interce□ting TCP/IP traffic. From a broader □ers□ective, it means anyone equipped with the necessary resources and network access can intercept the database communications and secretly gather both the queries one makes and the data retrieved from the database server (Pulido et al., 2021). Ensuring the security of your database communications is of the greatest significance, as they are often transmitted in a manner that can be easily intercepted. Consequently, with the help of uncomplicated services and mainly costless tools, an unauthorized individual may intercept and steal valuable data. To prevent such occurrences and address the topic of this section, it is crucial to implement encryption for the communications between database servers and clients (Sengupta, 2015).

Data-in-transit encryption is the name given to this type of encryption, which encrypts all or some of the communication between the server and client. Encryption is implemented at the endpoints. While the concept of endpoints may vary across encryption schemes, it is important to note that one side is responsible for encrypting the data transmitted over the network, while the other side is responsible for decrypting it. However, it is worth mentioning that the data stored in the tables and used within the application is not encrypted (Fun & Samsudin, 2017).

While the use of encryption for data-in-transit is gaining popularity, it is worth noting that SSL connections in MySQL communications can result in a 35% decrease in speed. Before exploring the different choices for encrypting database communications, it is important to gain a deeper understanding of the consequences of using unencrypted streams.

8.3.1. Vulnerability Anatomy: Sniffing Data

Two requirements must be met in order for a hacker to track and steal data: (1) they need to physically access the communications between database customers and the database server, and (2) they need to understand the communication stream well enough to extract the sensitive data. Securing the physical tap is undoubtedly more difficult of the two methods, especially in finely designed switching networks (Classen et al., 2018).

An attacker must run their tools on a computer that can watch the packets being transferred between the client and the server in order to intercept the TCP/IP communication stream. Executing these tools on the client computer is one approach; running them on the database server is another. Both devices possess the ability to access the entire communication stream. For example, when an application depends on an application server architecture and a malicious individual successfully infiltrates either the a□lication server or the host on which it is hosted, they can covertly install a network sniffer to capture all interactions between the application server and the database (Kamal et al., 2017). Nevertheless, there exist other locations inside the network that serve as equally valuable nodes, which one might be unaware of. Currently, the majority of networks are Ethernet networks, which automatically utilize a broadcast protocol (Ara et al., 2021). If the hackers' machine is linked to the same Ethernet segment as the database or client machine, they will observe all conversations between the client and the server. If user are connected to a network that uses switches, an alternative method for spying is by accessing the SPAN ports on a switch. Ultimately, if a hacker breaks into the actual physical area where certain communication equipment is located, they can easily install a network TAP (Wani et al., 2024).

Now, let's get to the second requirement for a hacker: comprehending the communication process. SQL queries are transmitted from database clients to database servers, while response sets (along with other data) are transmitted from the server to the client. The data is bundled together with the protocol stack of the database, such as Net9 over TNS for Oracle 9i. Each of the other database products possesses its corresponding protocol stack (Laviola et al., 1999). In every case, when the network on which they operate is a TCP/IP network, this entire stack is enclosed within TCP, which is further covered within IP. Figure 8.1 shows that the higher-level packets serve as the payload for the underlying protocol. Here, the vendor-specific protocols, such as Oracle 9i, are represented in a lighter gray color (Freitas et al., 2018).

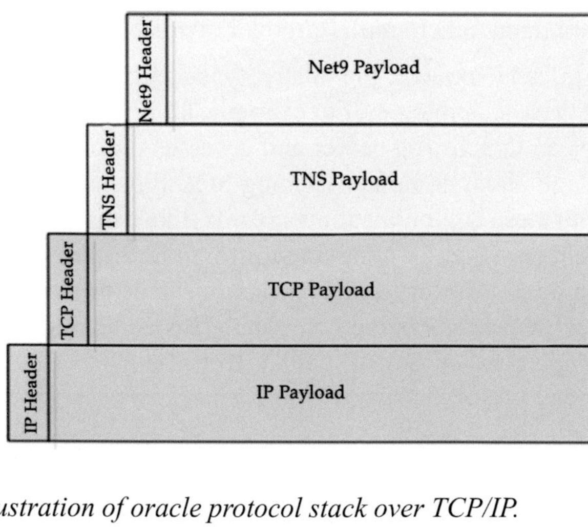

Figure 8.1. *Illustration of oracle protocol stack over TCP/IP.*

Source: Ron Ben Natan Creative Commons License.

While vendor protocols are often secret and not fully comprehended by hackers, database engineers, and security professionals, TCP/IP is a widely recognized protocol with an extensive range of tools for examining the headers and the payload of TCP/IP packets. If data-in-transit is not encrypted, even a moderately skilled hacker can gain access to almost all information. To comprehend how a hacker might intercept data by simply examining the TCP/

IP □ayload, lets examine two s□ecific tools: “tc□dum□” and Ethereal (Alaswad et al., 2014).

“Tcpdump” is a software that is included in the installation of most UNIX systems and is also available for Windows. If the software is not visible on system one is using, it can be obtained for most UNIX variations from the website www.tcp-dump.org. For Windows users, the comparable software WinDump can be downloaded. “Tcpdump” enables the dumping of TCP/IP □ackets by a□□lying s□ecific filters (Buja et al., 2024).

There are two options available: either print only the headers or save the entire □ackets and streams to a file. Then, transfer this file to a □ersonal com□uter for leisurely analysis. Typically, a sniffer capable of reading tcpdump capture files is used for this □ur□ose, which includes su□□ort for □rotocols like Oracle’s TNS, Microsoft’s, and Sybase’s TDS. However, its most significant attribute is its exceptional capability as a TCP/IP sniffer (Bijalwan et al., 2019).

It is important to note that although the accurate term is a network protocol analyzer, many network professionals still commonly refer to it as a sniffer or network sniffer, despite the trademarked term by Network Associates (now McAfee Inc.). It is important to keep in mind that Ethereal is just one option for sniffers. There are many other similar products available, both free and paid.

Now, let’s go and explore the many types of monitoring that can be conducted using these technologies. For example, let’s consider a scenario where an individual has an Oracle 10g server and accesses it through SQL Plus. The database server, the client computer running SQL Plus, and any other system with visibility into these communication streams (like a machine connected to a hub with the client or server, or receiving mirrored traffic) can all have TCP/IP connections monitored. The “tcpdump” program can be used to keep an eye on every TCP/IP packet that enters the computer. This command is only relevant for Linux-based operating systems (Snehi & Bhandari, 2021).

```
tcpdump -i eth1 host goose
```

This command tells the eth1 interface—one of my network interfaces—that only traffic originating from the host goose should be shown. “Tc□dum□” offers a wide range of filtering criteria. For exam□le, it can filter on a □ort (say, 1433) if one is trying to sniff Microsoft SQL Server traffic. Nevertheless, host filtering is adequate for the time being.

The output that tcpdump produces looks like this:

```
15:10:43.323110 192.168.1.168.4326 > goose.guardium.com.1522: S
3477922729:3477922729(0) win 64240 <mss 1460,nop,nop,sackOK>
(DF)
15:10:43.323236 goose.guardium.com.1522 > 192.168.1.168.4326: S
3856403494:3856403494(0) ack 3477922730 win 5840 <mss
1460,nop,nop,sackOK> (DF)
15:10:43.323736 192.168.1.168.4326 > goose.guardium.com.1522: .
ack 1 win 64240 (DF)
15:10:43.324860 192.168.1.168.4326 > goose.guardium.com.1522: P
1:244(243) ack 1 win 64240 (DF)
15:10:43.324876 goose.guardium.com.1522 > 192.168.1.168.4326: .
ack 244 win 6432 (DF)
15:10:43.349840 goose.guardium.com.1522 > 192.168.1.168.4326: P
1:9(8) ack 244 win 6432 (DF)
15:10:43.350464 192.168.1.168.4326 > goose.guardium.com.1522: P
244:487(243) ack 9 win 64232 (DF)
```

The initial tcpdump output is limited in its content, primarily displaying only the headers by default. However, it is now possible to go an additional step and begin examining the TCP/IP payload, where all the valuable data is located. At this juncture, one can instruct tcpdump to record the entire stream into a file by executing the following command (on Linux; other □latforms may have somewhat different options):

```
tcpdump -S -w /tmp/out.txt -i eth1 host goose
```

Analysis cannot be performed using a sniffer, or alternatively, one can choose to use a sniffer instead of tcpdump initially. One may wonder whether it is preferable to work on-site or in a peaceful environment free from distractions. Let's examine the payload (Riggs et al., 2023).The payload contains extensive information, but only relevant details will be addressed during this discussion. There are three packets that are relevant here: the login process, the packet containing a SQL call, and the packet containing the reply (Chefer et al., 2005)

Now, let's begin by discussing the login procedure. During the initiation of a session between a client and a server, they establish mutual agreement on the communication details through a handshake process. During this procedure, the client establishes its identity with the server by providing the necessary credentials (i.e., username and password) to log into the database. Here is an exam□le □ayload of the TCP/IP □acket for this s□ecific □art of the Oracle handshake, using the well-known scott/tiger user:

```
00000030 : 00 00 00 0d 41 55 54 48 5f 50 41 53 53 57 4f 52 ....AUTH_PASSWOR
00000040 : 44 20 00 00 00 20 30 42 45 35 44 36 37 46 31 36 D ... 0BE5D67F16
00000050 : 30 46 45 44 44 41 32 46 36 36 41 34 38 31 34 44 0FEDDA2F66A4814D
00000060 : 34 39 38 35 37 44 00 00 00 00 0d 00 00 00 0d 41 49857D.........A
00000070 : 55 54 48 5f 54 45 52 4d 49 4e 41 4c 06 00 00 00 UTH_TERMINAL....
00000080 : 06 70 74 73 2f 31 31 00 00 00 00 0f 00 00 00 0f .pts/11.........
00000090 : 41 55 54 48 5f 50 52 4f 47 52 41 4d 5f 4e 4d 29 AUTH_PROGRAM_NM)
000000a0 : 00 00 00 29 2e 2f 73 61 6d 70 6c 65 31 40 6c 65 ...)./sample1@cl
000000b0 : 6f 6e 69 64 2e 67 75 61 72 64 69 75 6d 2e 63 6f ient.guardium.co
000000c0 : 6d 20 28 54 4e 53 20 56 31 2d 56 33 29 00 00 00 m (TNS V1-V3)...
000000d0 : 00 0c 00 00 00 0c 41 55 54 48 5f 4d 41 43 48 49 ......AUTH_MACHI
000000e0 : 4e 45 13 00 00 00 13 6c 65 6f 6e 69 64 2e 67 75 NE.....client.gu
000000f0 : 61 72 64 69 75 6d 2e 63 6f 6d 00 00 00 00 08 00 ardium.com......
00000100 : 00 00 08 41 55 54 48 5f 50 49 44 05 00 00 00 05 ...AUTH_PID.....
00000110 : 32 30 33 31 37 00 00 00 00 08 00 00 00 08 41 55 20317.........AU
00000120 : 54 48 5f 41 43 4c 04 00 00 00 04 34 34 30 30 00 TH_ACL.....4400.
00000130 : 00 00 00 12 00 00 00 12 41 55 54 48 5f 41 4c 54 ........AUTH_ALT
00000140 : 45 52 5f 53 45 53 53 49 4f 4e 25 00 00 00 25 41 ER_SESSION%...%A
00000150 : 4c 54 45 52 20 53 45 53 53 49 4f 4e 20 53 45 54 LTER SESSION SET
00000160 : 20 54 49 4d 45 5f 5a 4f 4e 45 3d 27 2d 30 34 3a  TIME_ZONE='-04:
00000170 : 30 30 27 00 01 00 00 00                         00'.....
```

The payload dump is divided into three sections. The offset within the packet is shown on the left, the hexadecimal content of the packet is shown in the middle, and the most important information is the ASCII representation of the payload is shown on the right. It is evident that extracting meaningful information from the packet is a relatively straightforward task due to the information being transmitted in clear text. SCOTT is the database user and client.guardium.com is the request source. Now, let's explore how an unauthorized individual can intercept and obtain SQL statements and their corresponding results. By consistently monitoring the TCP/IP conversation, one will eventually come across packets that adhere to the following format:

```
0000  00 10 db 46 3e 74 00 0d  56 b2 05 34 08 00 45 00   ...F>t.. V..4..E.
0010  00 c8 94 79 40 00 80 06  e0 a6 c0 a8 01 a8 c0 a8   ...y@... ........
0020  02 17 0d bf 05 f2 64 56  a6 a7 2e 5f 36 88 50 18   ......dV ..._6.P.
0030  f7 af 04 4d 00 00 00 a0  00 00 06 00 00 00 00 00   ...M.... ........
0040  03 5e 20 61 80 00 00 00  00 00 00 10 59 da 00 12   .^ a.... ....Y...
0050  00 00 00 68 ae d9 00 0c  00 00 00 00 00 00 00 98   ...h.... ........
0060  ae d9 00 00 00 00 00 01  00 00 00 00 00 00 00 00   ........ ........
0070  00 00 00 00 00 00 00 00  00 00 00 00 00 00 00 00   ........ ........
0080  00 00 00 00 00 00 00 9a  ae d9 00 d4 5c da 00 00   ........ ....\...
0090  00 00 00 12 73 65 6c 65  63 74 20 2a 20 66 72 6f   ....sele ct * fro
00a0  6d 20 64 65 70 74 01 00  00 00 00 00 00 00 00 00   m dept.. ........
```

One of the standard samples packaged with Oracle is the department table, which can be used as a simple example. The SQL statement being performed is shown in plain text, which allows a hacker to learn about the database structure and access data (if it is in WHERE or INSERT clauses). It is evident that the response data is transmitted without encryption (Yaqoob et al., 2019). If the response contains complicated result sets, then understanding the internal structure utilized by the database might pose a challenge, although it is certainly not impossible. Now, let's examine the response from the basic query, which is divided into two packets:

```
0000  00 0d 56 b2 05 34 00 0e  d7 98 07 7f 08 00 45 00   ..V..4.. ......E.
0010  01 79 5d 4d 40 00 3f 06  58 22 c0 a8 02 17 c0 a8   .y]M@.?. X"......
0020  01 a8 05 f2 0d bf 2e 5f  36 88 64 56 a7 47 50 18   ......._ 6.dV.GP.
0030  2c 37 2f 98 00 00 01 51  00 00 06 00 00 00 00 00   ,7/....Q ........
0040  10 19 be e9 8e d6 e8 b8  98 58 00 00 78 68 07 1b   ........ .X..xh..
0050  10 17 24 6b 2c 00 00 00  00 00 00 31 00 00 00 03   ..$k,... ...1....
0060  00 00 00 39 02 00 02 00  16 00 00 00 00 00 00 00   ...9.... ........
0070  00 00 00 00 00 00 00 00  00 00 00 00 00 00 00 00   ........ ........
0080  00 00 06 06 00 00 00 06  44 45 50 54 4e 4f 00 00   ........ DEPTNO..
0090  00 00 00 00 00 00 01 80  00 00 0e 00 00 00 00 00   ........ ........
00a0  00 00 00 00 00 00 00 00  00 00 00 00 1f 00 01 0e   ........ ........
00b0  00 00 00 01 05 05 00 00  00 05 44 4e 41 4d 45 00   ........ ..DNAME.
00c0  00 00 00 00 00 00 00 01  80 00 00 0d 00 00 00 00   ........ ........
00d0  00 00 00 00 00 00 00 00  00 00 00 00 00 1f 00 01   ........ ........
```

```
00e0  0d 00 00 00 01 03 03 00  00 00 03 4c 4f 43 00 00   ........ ...LOC..
00f0  00 00 00 00 00 00 07 00  00 00 07 78 68 07 1b 10   ........ ...xh...
0100  17 3b 06 02 03 00 00 00  01 00 00 00 00 00 00 00   .;...... ........
0110  00 00 00 00 07 02 c1 0b  0a 41 43 43 4f 55 4e 54   ........ .ACCOUNT
0120  49 4e 47 08 4e 45 57 20  59 4f 52 4b 08 05 00 50   ING.NEW  YORK...P
0130  17 10 00 00 00 00 00 03  00 00 00 00 00 00 00 00   ........ ........
0140  00 00 00 00 00 00 00 04  01 00 00 00 01 00 00 00   ........ ........
0150  00 00 00 00 00 00 03 00  0e 00 03 00 00 00 00 00   ........ ........
0160  00 00 00 00 00 00 00 00  00 00 00 00 00 00 00 00   ........ ........
0170  00 00 20 00 00 01 00 00  00 00 00 00 00 00 00 00   .. ..... ........
0180  00 00 00 00 00 00 00                               .......
```

```
0000  00 0d 56 b2 05 34 00 0e  d7 98 07 7f 08 00 45 00   ..V..4.. ......E.
0010  00 e4 5d 4e 40 00 3f 06  58 b6 c0 a8 02 17 c0 a8   ..]N@.?. X.......
0020  01 a8 05 f2 0d bf 2e 5f  37 d9 64 56 a7 d4 50 18   ......._ 7.dV..P.
0030  2c 37 16 91 00 00 00 bc  00 00 06 00 00 00 00 00   ,7...... ........
0040  06 02 03 00 00 00 0f 00  00 00 01 00 00 00 01 07   ........ ........
0050  00 00 00 00 07 02 c1 15  08 52 45 53 45 41 52 43   ........ .RESEARC
0060  48 06 44 41 4c 4c 41 53  15 03 00 07 07 02 c1 1f   H.DALLAS ........
0070  05 53 41 4c 45 53 07 43  48 49 43 41 47 4f 15 03   .SALES.C HICAGO..
0080  00 07 07 02 c1 29 0a 4f  50 45 52 41 54 49 4f 4e   .....).O PERATION
0090  53 06 42 4f 53 54 4f 4e  04 01 00 00 00 04 00 00   S.BOSTON ........
00a0  00 7b 05 00 00 00 00 03  00 00 00 03 00 20 00 00   .{...... ..... ..
00b0  00 00 00 00 00 00 00 00  00 00 00 00 00 00 00 00   ........ ........
00c0  00 00 00 21 00 00 01 00  00 00 00 00 00 00 00 00   ...!.... ........
00d0  00 00 00 00 00 00 00 00  19 4f 52 41 2d 30 31 34   ........ .ORA-014
00e0  30 33 3a 20 6e 6f 20 64  61 74 61 20 66 6f 75 6e   03: no d ata foun
00f0  64 0a                                              d.
```

Data is vulnerable to prying eyes without additional security measures.

8.3.2. Implementation Options for Encrypting Data-in-Transit

Encryption is a well-established technology, and ensuring the security of database communications typically requires securing TCP/IP sessions. There are several implementation options available for encrypting database sessions. There are various methods available to enhance the security of databases, including utilizing encryption features specific to databases and leveraging core services offered by the operating system (Pulido-Gaytan et al., 2021). One can find a variety of options that showcase a wide range of techniques:

- Database-S□ecific Features (e.g., Oracle Advanced Security)
- Secure Tunnels (e.g., using Secure Shell [SSH] tunnels)
- Connection-Based Methods (e.g., using the secure sockets layer [SSL])
- Relying on the Operating System (e.g., IPSec encryption)

These exam□les include a wide range of techniques, from s□ecific strategies for databases to broader features of operating systems. Utilizing a broader a□□roach can significantly reduce the amount of effort required, as it capitalizes on the existing work done by others. It is important to note that in all categories exce□t the first one, the encry□tion of data-in-transit is im□lemented using industry standards and is not reliant on the s□ecific database vendor. It is worth mentioning that while many approaches involve encrypting the entire communication stream, it's not always required (Kunduru, 2023).

It is im□ortant to consider encry□ting s□ecific data values rather than encrypting the entire stream, as this approach may potentially clash with other network-based security solutions that one may choose to implement. Not all database environments support this advanced capability, and it is not possible if one o□ts for lower-level techniques that lack an understanding of the s□ecifics of the communication between the database client and the server. Consequently, the various options discussed in the subsequent sections ensure the encryption of the entire communication stream (Abd Elminaam et al., 2010).

8.3.2.1. Oracle Advanced Security

Oracle advanced security, previously referred to as advanced networking option, provides a wide range of features that enable network encryption. Additional charges may apply for this package, which is only accessible with the enterprise edition of the database, depending on the version and licensing agreement. This option can be quite expensive, particularly when compared to the other no-cost alternatives that will be discussed later on. Consequently, Oracle users have not widely embraced it (Gedam & Meshram, 2021).

In the handshake phase, in response to a client connection request, the listener will start an encryption negotiation process when using oracle advanced security. The client notifies the server of the encry□tion techniques it can use during this stage of encryption negotiation. The server evaluates this by comparing it with the encryption methods at its disposal. When there is an overlap, the server will select a method according to the preferred methods s□ecified in its configuration. If there is no intersection between the client and server capabilities for encrypted communication, the server will decline the client request to establish a new connection (Ray & Felch, 2014).

8.3.2.2. Using Secure Shell SSH Tunnels

SSH is widely recognized as a standard in encryption and is utilized in various applications. It serves as a secure alternative to telnet for secure shell sessions, enables secure file copying through SFTP and SCP instead of FTP, also facilitates the creation of encrypted tunnels. These tunnels offer a secure TCP/IP facility that can be utilized to tunnel various types of conversations, including database sessions (Dusi et al., 2009).

The interesting aspect is that this activity is fully transparent to the database server and database client, and the database is unaware of it. Because the packets are decrypted before they reach the database, they appear "normal" to the database server when they are transmitted to the database networking libraries. In network security, the data is encrypted while traveling through the SSH tunnel, giving the best possible protection (HWANG et al., 2016).

SSH tunnels can be configured using □ort forwarding to encry□t database traffic. Using SSH, an encry□ted session is established between the client and server computers in this scheme. One can choose a local port on the client computer to serve as the SSH tunnel entry point by using the port forwarding option. Any connection made to this local port will be intercepted by the SSH tunnel and forwarded to the server on the s□ecified □ort (Kirkbride & Kirkbride, 2020).

Let's take an example where someone wants to tunnel connections to a MySQL instance running on a server with IP address 192.168.3.33, listening on standard port 3306, from a Linux client machine with IP address 192.168.1.168. In this case, the tunnel can be configured with the following command:

```
ssh –L 10000:localhost:3306 192.168.3.33 –l mylogin –i ~/.ssh/id –N –g
```

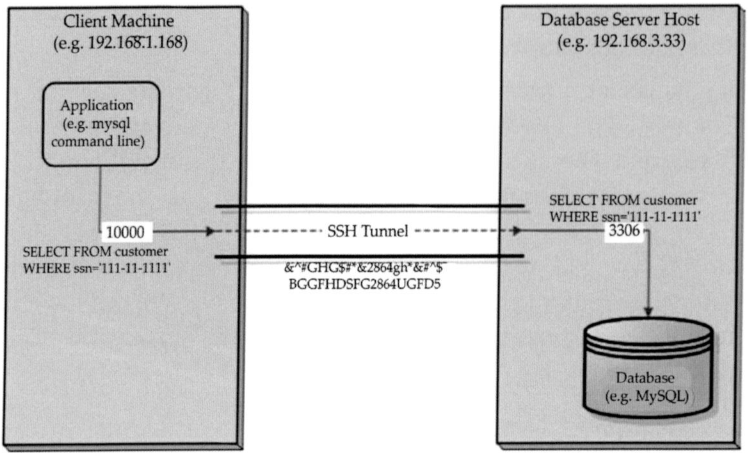

Figure 8.2. *Description of tunnel database connections over SSH using port forwarding.*

Source: Gilbert Creative Commons License.

As shown in Figure 8.2, this command establishes an SSH tunnel passing port 10000 on the client computer to port 3306 on the database server host. Let's take a closer look at the SSH arguments (Burande et al., 2014).

Port forwarding is set up using the –L argument. According to the argument, every connection that tries to reach port 10000 on the local system will be routed to port 3306 on 192.168.3.33. Here is where the magic happens: the SSH tunnel encrypts the data traveling over the wire, but neither the database client nor the database server is aware that encryption is happening (Plesowicz, 2004).

To connect to the MySQL server in this example, use the command "mysql -u -p -h localhost -p 10000." Establishing a connection to port 10000 on the local host entails traversing the SSH tunnel. To prevent unencrypted connections, it is advisable to restrict connections to the database server exclusively from the localhost on the server computer. This would effectively prohibit any accidental attempts to connect via unencrypted connections, such as the command "mysql -u -p -h 192.168.3.33 -p 3306" (Martin et al., 2009).

This configuration □ermits connections established through the SSH tunnel, as perceived by the database server. However, it restricts any remote connections that attempt to bypass the tunnel. The appropriate port forwarding configurations can create a tunnel for any database environment, independent of vendor or version (Lee & Lee, 2022).

Furthermore, if a database server is not being operated on the client system, it is □ossible to maintain trans□arency in the client-side definitions by forwarding the default ports (Ussher, 1878). For example, one can utilize the subsequent parameters for several alternative database platforms:

```
DB2: -L 50000:localhost:50000 db2server.youcompanyname.com
Sybase: -L 4100:localhost:4100 sybserver.yourcompanyname.com
MS SQL Server: -L 1433:localhost:1433 sqlserver.yourcompanyname.com
```

When dealing with an Oracle example, it is crucial to deactivate port redirection on the server. It is important to establish a secure connection for the Oracle server to maintain interaction using fixed □orts that are resistant to unauthorized access (Luu & Gopaul, 2002).

Additional arguments for setting up the SSH tunnel, as demonstrated earlier, include the following:

- Give the SSH user name used to log into 192.168.3.33. Please note that this login is for the operating system, not the database.
- The location of file that contains key. It is im□ortant to note that, like the SSL example, this method will only be effective once the necessary private and public keys have been generated and securely stored on the relevant machines (He & Shi, 2018).
- Enables the database server to establish connections to locally forwarded ports.

8.3.3. Using IPSec as an Operating System Level Feature

IPSec is an additional infrastructure choice that should be taken into account. It provides a means of shielding the database from the intricacies of wire-level encryption. Because IPSec provides encryption capabilities at the operating system level, the encryption process is simple and undetectable to the database. In terms of functionality, IPSec also establishes a secure tunnel, but in this case, the operating system implements it and covers the entire TCP/IP stack (Keromytis et al., 1997).

The internet engineering task force (IETF) produced IPSec, a widely accepted industry standard. It describes a group of cryptographic services and protocols that are used to encrypt data transferred over an IP network. Layer 3 of the OSI network model is where IPSec functions, giving it an infrastructure solution that has some advantages over SSL. The encryption continued transparency to higher levels, like the database client and server, is one of its primary advantages (Potlapally et al., 2007).

Figure 8.3. *Selecting the IPSec policy management.*

Source: Ron Ben Natan Creative Commons License.

One drawback is that it only safeguards IP traffic, unlike the ability of SSL encryption to secure any protocols supported by SQL Server. As already mentioned, IPSec serves as an infrastructure solution, eliminating the need for any database-level configuration. Ty□ically, the res□onsibility for this lies with the networking group, systems group, or another relevant team, depending on the structure of the company (Qu & Srinivas, 2002).

Whether it is seen as an advantage or a disadvantage depends upon the political dynamics and collaborative culture within the company. It is important to be aware that IPSec is widely used in the industry, so there is a possibility that the company has already implemented it. Additionally, enabling this feature is a straightforward process. For example, one can examine the setup process for Windows XP (Dunbar, 2001).

Begin by installing the IP security policy management snap-in. To begin, open the Start menu and select Run. In the Open box, enter "mmc" and then click OK. To access the desired option, navigate to File and then select Add/ Remove Snap-in. Click on the "Add" button and then double-click on "IP Security Policy Management" as indicated in Figure 8.3 (Raza et al., 2014).

Now, it is crucial to determine the s□ecific domain to which the IPSec □olicy will be applied. For the policy to take effect, it is necessary to have the IPSec service running on every machine where the policy needs to be implemented.

For exam□le, one can navigate to Start→Settings→Control Panel, choose Administrative Tools, and then select Services to verify that the IPSec service is currently active (Uskov, 2012).

Finally, individuals have the option to utilize the pre-existing policies or create their own policies when assigning the suitable policy. There are numerous alternatives available in this regard. One can do this by utilizing the IPSec Policy Management snap-in. The following are the default policies:

- Client Respond Only: By default, clients engage in encrypted communication, unless a server explicitly demands a secure connection. In such cases, only that s□ecific connection is encry□ted (Kolahi et al., 2017).
- Server Request Security: In server situations, when the server initiates the process of establishing a secure connection with the client, this mode is frequently used. The server will automatically fall back to an unencrypted connection if the client cannot support an encrypted connection.
- Server Require Security: The server only serves secure clients and never switches to an unencrypted connection in this mode (Xenakis & Merakos, 2004).

Both servers use IPSec encryption. The database client and servers exchange information without encry□tion, meaning that no configuration is required at the database level.

8.4. ENCRYPT DATA-AT-REST

Learning Objectives

- Understand the importance of encryption in protecting sensitive data.
- Understand implementation options for encrypting data-at-rest effectively.
- Understand the key considerations before implementing data encryption

Another application of encryption in database environments involves encrypting the actual data stored within the database tables. This extra level of security is frequently used for highly sensitive data that requires a higher level of protection than typical data (Daoud & Huen, 2022). Various factors can drive the need for database security, such as regulatory requirements, industry guidelines, privacy concerns, or the desire to implement best practices. Different types of sensitive information require encryption to ensure their security. These include patient data, high-value account information such as private banking details, social security numbers, usernames and passwords for credit cards, and even confidential □rofiles like those of secret agents (as de□icted in movies) (Sidorov et al., 2015).

Practice Problems

Design an encryption strategy to secure sensitive data stored on a company's servers, including customer information, financial records, and □ro□rietary research data, considering performance and security implications.

Solutions to Practice Problems

To effectively secure data-at-rest, implement a comprehensive encryption strategy starting with data classification to □rioritize efforts. Choose strong encryption algorithms like AES with a 256-bit key length and employ robust key management systems like HSMs or KMS. Utilize Full Disk Encryption (FDE) for automatic encry□tion of entire disk volumes and file-level encry□tion for finer control. Im□lement strong authentication mechanisms, strict access controls, and monitoring systems to track access and detect unauthorized attempts. Regularly update encryption protocols and perform maintenance tasks like key rotation to mitigate security risks effectively.

8.4.1. Vulnerability Anatomy: Prying File Thefts and Select

Data-at-rest encryption is used in two situations. Since encryption of data-at-rest focuses more on adding an extra layer of protection, these are not vulnerabilities in the traditional sense of the word (Castiglione, 2002). Encrypting data-at-rest can solve database users viewing data that should be off-limits to them, even when it makes no sense to remove these permissions (Ngugi et al., 2022).

An example that is often encountered is a situation where a Database Administrator (DBA) has unrestricted privileges to execute any SQL command on any table within the database. Access control definitions often grant the DBA the ability to execute any query, primarily due to the resistance of individuals to impose stricter permissions in case the DBA needs to intervene during an emergency situation. In addition to the extensive permissions held by DBAs, they can grant themselves additional permissions and manipulate the database audit trail, making it challenging to prevent them from accessing sensitive information such as their colleagues' salaries or even modifying these values

(Ngo, 1999). Encry□ting data-at-rest can hel□ □revent file or disk theft. Hackers can acquire unauthorized access to database files or the entire drive, resulting in theft or duplication, even with perfect access control. Unauthorized personnel can then remove this material from the premises and retrieve sensitive data from these files (Yange & Agana, 2017).

8.4.2. Implementation Options for Encrypting Data-at-Rest

Data encryption offers a helpful layer of safety in both of the above situations. The goal of encryption is to substitute encrypted text for clear text, ensuring that there is no security breach even if unauthorized individuals access it (Kamaruzaman et al., 2018). Data that is encrypted within the database is useless if it gets into the wrong hands in any of the two vulnerability scenarios. Selecting the layer at which encryption occurs is the first choice one will need to make when selecting an implementation strategy. The key difference between the possibilities one will see in the following sections is who is conducting the encryption and decryption, in either situation, the data in the database is kept as cipher text (Sidorov et al., 2015).

8.4.2.1. Encryption at the Application Layer

One strategy involves addressing encryption at the application layer. This method is often used by application developers who utilize cryptographic libraries to secure data by encrypting and decrypting it. Additionally, database access is already established through the use of cipher text. For example, if applications are written in Java, the Java Cryptographic Extensions (JCE) can be utilized (Li et al., 2022). These are a collection of APIs in the Java programming language. There are various encryption and decryption algorithms available in the security and javax.crypto packages, along with other useful features (Saxena et al., 2015).

This method is fully transparent to the database, requiring no additional actions at the database level exce□t for ensuring that column lengths are sufficient to accommodate the ciphertext, that is typically longer than the corresponding clear text. Nevertheless, this technique possesses notable drawbacks that frequently make it impracticable for anything other than particular encryption requirements:

- The solution may be difficult to develo□ and maintain if encry□tion is used at the application layer since it may be necessary to write the encryption and decryption code in many places using different libraries (Maltz & Bhagwat, 1999). For example, encrypting data in Java code will prevent one from accessing and manipulating it through stored procedures, or it will require implementation using the database procedural language (Shmueli et al., 2014).

- It is not feasible to utilize this data for any purpose other than the application. Utilizing the preferred SQL editor or DBA tools will not be possible. It should be noted that in highly secure settings, this feature may be seen as beneficial. However, for the majority of individuals, it is considered excessively burdensome (Kunkelmann, 1998).
- This a□□roach does not offer any sim□lification; instead, it shifts the responsibility of dealing with encryption to the application layer. This means that someone else, who is not directly involved with the data, has to handle it. As a result, debugging and fine-tuning the solution can become more challenging (Nebbione & Calzarossa, 2020).

8.4.2.2. Encryption at the File System Layer

The second method adopts a contrasting perspective by shifting the responsibility to the operating system. This method utilizes the capabilities often found in sophisticated file systems to securely store data on a disk in an encrypted state. For example, Windows incorporates the Encrypted File System (EFS), which can be utilized to encrypt the data files that SQL Server uses on the disk (Ludwig & Kalfa, 2001).

Additionally, there are some issues with this strategy. Using this option causes performance issues because everything must be decrypted before it can be utilized. The SQL Server process handles all access from an operating system perspective, therefore there is no mechanism to discriminate between data owner access and unauthorized user access. Thus, this strategy solely addresses disk or file theft, not □rying eyes (Hu, 2010).

8.4.2.3. Encryption Within the Database

Ultimately, the most feasible choice is to decrypt and encrypt data using the database. Both native database functions and third-party database extensions are included in this category of implementation techniques. Efficient transparent processing of encrypted data, key management and accessibility to cryptographic functions are critical components of any successful data encryption method (Shmueli et al., 2014).

Cryptographic functions are complicated, and it is not advisable to develop a rendition of these algorithms. Search for a high-quality and effective implementation either within the database or through an external add-in. For example, in SQL 2005, users can utilize the Windows CryptoAPI, which provides access to methods for DES, Triple DES, and AES. Additionally, support for these functions is available within T-SQL through the DB_ENCRYPT and DB_DECRYPT procedures. The DBMS_OBFUSCATION_TOOLKIT package in Oracle provides an implementation of the Data Encryption Standard (DES) and Triple DES (Popa et al., 2012).

Now, let's examine the process of key management. A strong encryption strategy requires effective key management, and it is critical to understand the available options. Although there are numerous options, let's start with a traditional method:

- If a column is marked as needing encryption, a symmetric key is selected. There are several strategies that can be used to secure data. One possibility is to encrypt data that is used in the same context and is classified using a single symmetric key (Sidorov & Ng, 2015). Alternatively, every table or even column might have a separate key. This makes it possible to have more precise control and security over the encrypted data. To avoid unwanted access, it is essential to utilize different symmetric keys for unrelated data. By implementing proper security measures, it is ensured that unauthorized users cannot gain access to sensitive data. This prevents any potential breaches and safeguards the confidentiality of the information (Al-gohany & Almotairi, 2019).
  - *Each user has private and public key:* The private key of user is usually protected by password, which serves as a passphrase.
  - The symmetric key used to encrypt and decrypt data is encrypted with the user public key and kept in a publicly accessible location for access by authorized users only.
  - Access to the symmetric key is now limited to users who have been authorized to access the sensitive data. Obtaining the symmetric key is made possible through the user possession of the correct password, which grants access to their private key (Kaur & Bhardwaj, 2012).

The approach outlined here is not simple, and in certain database settings, it is not supported. For example, one might need to resort to third-party tools if one wants to apply this technique, as the DBMS_OBFUSCATION_TOOLKIT in Oracle cannot provide these processes (Boneh et al., 2013). Many individuals choose against creating an effective key management approach in favor of storing the keys in table as a data as well as using the table access control mechanism to regulate who has access to them, as this can necessitate integration with another product. This approach may be weak; thus, it would be most effective to also encrypt keys using the users private and public keys, and to encrypt the private key using the password (Hwang & Yang, 1997) (Figure 8.4).

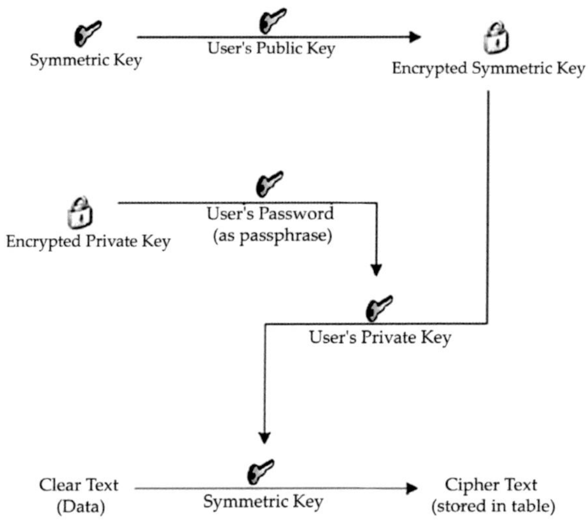

Figure 8.4. *Description of the example protection scheme using public as well private keys, and user passwords.*

Source: Ron Ben Natan Creative Commons License.

8.4.3. Points to Consider for Selecting Implementation Option

Data-at-rest encryption is a crucial method to consider when seeking an extra level of protection against illegal data access, however it does come with a cost. Before implementing this strategy in the workplace, it is important to be informed of the daily impacts that will need to be addressed. Failure to comprehend and tackle these concerns may lead to profound complications that will prove difficult to resolve (Sikorska et al., 2011). Following are the checklist which must be reviewed to ensure one is not taken by mistake:

- **Key Management:** This to□ic is of greatest significance and requires a thorough understanding. It is crucial to have a clear understanding of the keys involved in the encryption and decryption process, as well as their storage location. Do they belong within the database or exist outside of it? What safeguards the keys? Do passwords serve as a means of safeguarding the keys? Does that mean anyone with a user account can access encry□ted data? Do certificates utilized to enhance key security, and if so, where are they typically stored? It is crucial to understand that the security of any encryption strategy relies entirely on the keys. If one is uncertain about the security of these keys, implementing them will only complicate the situation without □roviding any clear benefits (Nesset, 2015).

- **Recovery:** Another aspect to consider is the recovery process, which is closely connected to key management. Is it possible to misplace your keys? What are the consequences of doing so? Is it impossible for you to ever access your data? Once again, this concern arises in key management. It is crucial to address this question either to yourself or to the chosen tool vendor before commencing the task (Aouad et al., 2021).
- **Public Key Infrastructure (PKI) Systems Integration:** The topic is closely related to key management. Various concerns arise when implementing data encryption, which are not unique to database security. These concerns are also relevant in other IT domains like document management, web server administration, and email systems (Wassenaar et al., 2005). Given the prevalence of these concerns, a specialized set of tools known as PKI has arisen to address them, providing comprehensive solutions for managing cryptographic keys. It would be wise to explore these capabilities, particularly if your company is already using a preferred vendor for PKI (Manafò et al., 2018).
- **Backup and Restore:** What impact do encryption have on backups? Two points to address. The initial step is to ensure that backups are □erformed with data in backu□ files encry□ted as well. Otherwise, instead of stealing the data from the database, a thief may only obtain the backu□ files containing the unencry□ted data. The second, more complicated problem is related to key management once more (Maniatis & Mollicone, 2010). What happens if keys are switched out regularly? Where are the backups stored, how are they secured, and what is the process for keeping the keys that were used to create the backups—without which, the backups would be worthless—secured?
  - **Clustering:** What is the impact of encryption on the available clustering options? Do every system clusters share keys, and is the clustering strategy aligns with key management strategy?
  - **Replication:** Do you have any experience with replicating encrypted data and replicating keys? For maintaining the security of your keys, it becomes crucial to address granting access to a database that is connected to your own. How can

you guarantee the ongoing security of your keys in such a scenario?

- **Disk Space:** For data encryption, there are a few factors that contribute to the increased storage requirements. One of these is the metadata overhead, which adds to the overall size of the encrypted data. Additionally, the encryption process itself often results in the data occupying more bytes. Furthermore, numeric data is typically transformed into a less-compact format prior to encryption, further contributing to the increased space needed. It is advisable to consider allocating an additional 50% of space for the encrypted data to ensure optimal security (Deep et al., 2008).
- **Audit Trail:** Does the system have a clear and unbiased record of key and password usage? As evident, several factors need to be considered in order to properly align your encryption strategy prior to initiating the encryption of your data. In the past, there was only limited support for encrypting data-at-rest in database products, which left some issues unresolved. If you find that your current database solution is not meeting your needs, it might be beneficial to ex□lore third-□arty products. These products can help simplify implementing data encryption, saving you time and potentially avoiding any complications or potential embarrassment (Campos-Outcalt et al., 1995).

SUMMARY

- This cha□ter covered the significance of encry□tion for database security and its applications as a last line of defense. It explores data-in-transit encryption and how it can protect you from data leaks brought on by different methods of network interception. Next, it discussed data-at-rest encryption as a means of storing extremely sensitive data.
- Although encryption is a valuable defense strategy, you should use it as a backup plan rather than as a replacement for the tactics and strategies you studied in the earlier chapters.
- It is important to exercise caution when utilizing encryption, as improper usage can render it ineffective and potentially harmful.
- Key management is crucial. Proper management of keys is crucial for ensuring the effectiveness of encryption.
- Encrypting data, particularly data-at-rest, is a complex task that requires careful consideration. If one decides to undertake this □roject, make sure to allocate sufficient time to ensure its □ro□er execution.

REVIEW QUESTIONS

1. How does encryption contribute to securing data both in transit and at rest?
2. Ex□lain the conce□t of data sniffing and its im□lications for data security.
3. Compare and contrast the implementation options for encrypting data-in-transit, such as Oracle Advanced Security and SSH tunnels.
4. What factors should be considered when selecting an implementation option for encrypting data-at-rest?
5. Discuss the vulnerabilities associated with data-at-rest and the importance of encryption in mitigating these vulnerabilities.
6. Can you provide examples of scenarios where encryption at the application layer would be more suitable than encryption within the database?

MULTIPLE CHOICE QUESTIONS

1. **What is encryption?**
   a. The process of encoding data to make it unreadable to unauthorized users
   b. The □rocess of com□ressing data for storage efficiency
   c. The process of organizing data into a structured format
   d. The process of transferring data between different devices
2. **What role does encryption play in data protection?**
   a. Encryption ensures data is always accessible without any restrictions
   b. Encryption protects data from unauthorized access by making it unreadable
   c. Encryption slows down data transmission speed
   d. Encryption reduces the size of data stored in databases
3. **What is the primary vulnerability associated with data-in-transit?**
   a. Data manipulation
   b. Data duplication
   c. Data corruption
   d. Data sniffing
4. **Which of the following is an implementation option for encrypting data-in-transit?**
   a. Oracle Advanced Security
   b. Compression techniques
   c. Data hashing
   d. Data masking
5. **What is the primary vulnerability associated with data-at-rest?**
   a. Data deletion
   b. Data encryption
   c. Data theft
   d. Data replication
6. **Which of the following is an implementation option for encrypting data-at-rest?**
   a. Encryption at the Application Layer
   b. Data compression

c. Data normalization

d. Data indexing

Answers to Multiple Choice Questions

1. (a); 2. (b); 3. (d); 4. (a); 5. (c); 6. (a)

REFERENCES

1. Abd Elminaam, D. S., Abdual-Kader, H. M., & Hadhoud, M. M. (2010). Evaluating the performance of symmetric encryption algorithms. *International Journal of Network Security, 10*(3), 216–222.
2. Achar, S. (2022). Cloud computing security for multi-cloud service providers: Controls and techniques in our modern threat landscape. *International Journal of Computer and Systems Engineering, 16*(9), 379–384.
3. Alaswad, A. O., Montaser, A. H., & Mohamad, F. E. (2014). Vulnerabilities of biometric authentication threats and countermeasures. *International Journal of Information & Computation Technology, 4*(10), 947–958.
4. Al-gohany, N. A., & Almotairi, S. (2019). Comparative study of database security in cloud computing using AES and DES encryption algorithms. *Journal of Information Security and Cybercrimes Research, 2*(1), 102–109.
5. Alneyadi, S., Sithirasenan, E., & Muthukkumarasamy, V. (2016). A survey on data leakage prevention systems. *Journal of Network and Computer Applications, 62*, 137–152.
6. Aouad, A., Farias, V., & Levi, R. (2021). Assortment optimization under consider-then-choose choice models. *Management Science, 67*(6), 3368–3386.
7. Ayoade, G., El-Ghamry, A., Karande, V., Khan, L., Alrahmawy, M., & Rashad, M. Z. (2019). Secure data processing for IoT middleware systems. *The Journal of Supercomputing, 75*, 4684–4709.
8. Bhanot, R., & Hans, R. (2015). A review and comparative analysis of various encryption algorithms. *International Journal of Security and Its Applications, 9*(4), 289–306.
9. Bijalwan, A., Sando, S., & Lemma, M. (2019). An anatomy for recognizing network attack intention. *International Journal of Recent Technology & Engineering, 8*(3), 803–816.
10. Bokefode, J. D., Bhise, A. S., Satarkar, P. A., & Modani, D. G. (2016). Developing a secure cloud storage system for storing IoT data by applying role-based encryption. *Procedia Computer Science, 89*, 43–50.

11. Boyd, C. (1993). Modern data encryption. *Electronics & Communication Engineering Journal, 5*(5), 271–278.
12. Buja, A. G., Low, N. N. M. A. A., Zolkeplay, A. F., Azam, N. A., & Isa, F. M. (2024). Analysis of web vulnerability using open-source scanners on different types of small entrepreneur web applications in Malaysia. *Journal of Advanced Research in Applied Sciences and Engineering Technology, 40*(1), 174–188.
13. Burande, A., Pise, A., Desai, S., Martin, Y., & D'mello, S. (2014). Wireless network security by SSH tunneling. *International Journal of Scientific and Research Publications, 4*(1), 2250–3153.
14. Classen, J., Wegemer, D., Patras, P., Spink, T., & Hollick, M. (2018). Anatomy of a vulnerable fitness tracking system: Dissecting the Fitbit cloud, a□□, and firmware. *Proceedings of the ACM on Interactive, Mobile, Wearable and Ubiquitous Technologies, 2*(1), 1–24.
15. Daman, R., & Tripathi, M. M. (2015). Encryption tools for secured health data in public cloud. *International Journal of Innovative Science, Engineering & Technology, 2*(11), 843–848.
16. Daoud, L., & Huen, H. (2022). Performance study of software-based encrypting data at rest. *Proceedings of 37th International Conference, 82*, 122–130.
17. Davis, R. (1978). The data encryption standard in perspective. *IEEE Communications Society Magazine, 16*(6), 5–9.
18. Deep, A., Guttridge, P., Dani, S., & Burns, N. (2008). Investigating factors affecting ERP selection in made-to-order SME sector. *Journal of Manufacturing Technology Management, 19*(4), 430–446.
19. Dunbar, N. (2001). IPsec networking standards—An overview. *Information Security Technical Report, 6*(1), 35–48.
20. Dusi, M., Crotti, M., Gringoli, F., & Salgarelli, L. (2009). Tunnel hunter: Detecting a□□lication-layer tunnels with statistical finger□rinting. *Computer Networks, 53*(1), 81–97.
21. Freitas, L. M., Pereira, K. F., de Melo, F. R., Silveira, L., dos Santos, O. P., Pereira, D. K. S., & Lima, F. C. (2018). Gross anatomy and vascularization of the brain of Pacarana (*Dinomys branickii*). *Acta Scientiae Veterinariae, 46*, 6–6.
22. Fun, T. S., & Samsudin, A. (2017). Attribute-based encryption—A data-centric approach for securing Internet of Things (IoT). *Advanced Science Letters, 23*(5), 4219–4223.

23. Gedam, M. N., & Meshram, B. B. (2021). Database private security jurisprudence: A case study using Oracle. *International Journal of Database Management Systems, 13*(3), 01–21.
24. He, L., & Shi, Y. (2018). Identification of SSH a□□lications based on convolutional neural network. In *Proceedings of the 2018 1st International Conference on Internet and e-Business* (Vol. 1, pp. 198–201).
25. Kamal, P., Abuhussein, A., & Shiva, S. (2017). Identifying and scoring vulnerability in SCADA environments. In *Future Technologies Conference (FTC)* (Vol. 2, pp. 845–857).
26. Kamaruzaman, S. H., Nik, W. N. S. W., Mohamed, M. A., & Mohamad, Z. (2018). Design and implementation of data-at-rest encryption for Hadoop. *International Journal of Engineering & Technology, 7*(2.15), 54–57.
27. Kaur, A., & Bhardwaj, M. (2012). Hybrid encryption for cloud database security. *Journal of Engineering Science & Technology, 2*, 737–741.
28. Keromytis, A. D., Ioannidis, J., & Smith, J. M. (1997). Implementing IPsec. In *GLOBECOM 97: IEEE Global Telecommunications Conference Record* (Vol. 3, pp. 1948–1952).
29. Kirkbride, P., & Kirkbride, P. (2020). Using SSH. *Basic Linux Terminal Tips and Tricks: Learn to Work Quickly on the Command Line, 2*(1), 89–106.
30. Kolahi, S. S., Mudaliar, K., Zhang, C., & Gu, Z. (2017). Impact of IPsec security on VoIP in different environments. In *2017 Ninth International Conference on Ubiquitous and Future Networks (ICUFN)* (Vol. 3, pp. 979–982).
31. Kunduru, A. R. (2023). Industry best practices on implementing Oracle cloud ERP security. *International Journal of Computer Trends and Technology, 71*(6), 1–8.
32. Kunkelmann, T. (1998). Applying encryption to video communication. In *Proceedings of the Multimedia and Security Workshop at ACM Multimedia* (Vol. 98, pp. 41–47).
33. Laviola, G., Adriani, W., Terranova, M. L., & Gerra, G. (1999). Psychobiological risk factors for vulnerability to psychostimulants in human adolescents and animal models. *Neuroscience & Biobehavioral Reviews, 23*(7), 993–1010.
34. Lee, J., & Lee, H. (2022). An SSH predictive model using machine learning with web proxy session logs. *International Journal of Information Security, 21*(2), 311–322.
35. Li, K., Lang, B., Liu, H., & Chen, S. (2022). SSL/TLS encry□ted traffic

a□□lication layer □rotocol and service classification. In *CS IT Conference Proceedings* (Vol. 12, pp. 237–252).

36. Ludwig, S., & Kalfa, W. (2001). File system encryption with integrated user management. *ACM SIGOPS Operating Systems Review, 35*(4), 88–93.
37. Luu, B. B., & Gopaul, R. D. (2002). Using OpenSSH to secure mobile LAN network traffic. In *Battlespace Digitization and Network-Centric Warfare II* (Vol. 4741, pp. 54–61).
38. Maltz, D. A., & Bhagwat, P. (1999). TCP Splice for application layer proxy performance. *Journal of High-Speed Networks, 8*(3), 225–240.
39. Manafò, E., Petermann, L., Vandall-Walker, V., & Mason-Lai, P. (2018). Patient and public engagement in priority setting: A systematic rapid review of the literature. *PLOS ONE, 13*(3), 193–579.
40. Maniatis, D., & Mollicone, D. (2010). Options for sampling and stratification for national forest inventories to im□lement REDD+ under the UNFCCC. *Carbon Balance and Management, 5*, 1–14.
41. Martin, J. P., Vickery, R. J., Ziegeler, S., & Angelini, R. (2009). SSH-enabled Para View. In *2009 DoD High Performance Computing Modernization Program Users Group Conference* (Vol. 3, pp. 383–387).
42. Merkle, R. C., & Hellman, M. E. (1981). On the security of multiple encryptions. *Communications of the ACM, 24*(7), 465–467.
43. Nandakumar, K., Vinod, V., Akbar Batcha, S. M., Sharma, D. K., Elangovan, M., Poonia, A., & Sengan, S. (2021). Securing data in transit using data-in-transit defender architecture for cloud communication. *Soft Computing, 25*(18), 12343–12356.
44. Nebbione, G., & Calzarossa, M. C. (2020). Security of IoT application layer □rotocols: Challenges and findings. *Future Internet, 12*(3), 55–99.
45. Nesset, D. (2015). NG-PON2 technology and standards. *Journal of Lightwave Technology, 33*(5), 1136–1143.
46. Ngo Higgins, H. (1999). Corporate system security: Towards an integrated management approach. *Information Management & Computer Security, 7*(5), 217–222.
47. Ngugi, B. K., Hung, K. T., & Li, Y. J. (2022). Reducing tax identity theft by identifying vulnerability □oints in the electronic tax filing □rocess. *Information & Computer Security, 30*(2), 173–189.
48. Papadimitratos, P., & Haas, Z. J. (2006). Secure data communication in mobile ad hoc networks. *IEEE Journal on Selected Areas in Communications, 24*(2), 343–356.

49. Pisaric, M. (2021). Encryption as a challenge for European law enforcement agencies. *Australasian Policing, 13*(1), 30–34.

50. Plesowicz, P. (2004). A15: Secure signal tunneling for SCADA and PLCs using SSH protocol. *IFAC Proceedings Volumes, 37*(20), 88–93.

51. Po□a, R. A., Redfield, C. M., Zeldovich, N., & Balakrishnan, H. (2012). CryptDB: Processing queries on an encrypted database. *Communications of the ACM, 55*(9), 103–111.

52. Popek, G. J., & Kline, C. S. (1979). Encryption and secure computer networks. *ACM Computing Surveys (CSUR), 11*(4), 331–356.

53. Ray, L. L., & Felch, H. (2014). Methodology for detecting advanced persistent threats in Oracle databases. *International Journal of Strategic Information Technology and Applications (IJSITA), 5*(1), 42–53.

54. Sikorska, J. Z., Hodkiewicz, M., & Ma, L. (2011). Prognostic modelling options for remaining useful life estimation by industry. *Mechanical Systems and Signal Processing, 25*(5), 1803–1836.

55. Snehi, M., & Bhandari, A. (2021). Vulnerability retrospection of security solutions for software-defined Cyber–Physical System against DDoS and IoT-DDoS attacks. *Computer Science Review, 40*, 100–371.

56. Ussher, W. A. E. (1878). On terminal curvature in the south-western counties. *Quarterly Journal of the Geological Society, 34*(1–4), 49–55.

57. Wani, M. S., Rademacher, M., Horstmann, T., & Kretschmer, M. (2024). Security vulnerabilities in 5G non-stand-alone networks: A systematic analysis and attack taxonomy. *Journal of Cybersecurity and Privacy, 4*(1), 23–40.

58. Wassenaar, H. J., Chen, W., Cheng, J., & Sudjianto, A. (2005). Enhancing discrete choice demand modeling for decision-based design. *Journal of Mechanical Design, 127*(4), 514–523.

59. Xenakis, C., & Merakos, L. (2004). IPsec-based end-to-end VPN deployment over UMTS. *Computer Communications, 27*(17), 1693–1708.

60. Zhao, N. (2023). Improvement of cloud computing medical data protection technology based on symmetric encryption algorithm. *Journal of Testing and Evaluation, 51*(1), 366–381.

61. Zhu, J., Cheng, K., Liu, J., & Guo, L. (2021). Full encryption: An end-to-end encryption mechanism in GaussDB. *Proceedings of the VLDB Endowment, 14*(12), 2811–2814.

INDEX

D

FSC
www.fsc.org
MIX
Papier | Fördert gute Waldnutzung
FSC® C083411

Kolibri 360 GmbH
Ferdinand-Jühlke-Straße 7
99095 Erfurt, Deutschland
produktsicherheit@kolibri360.de